Older Women Who Work

Psychology of Women Book Series

Bringing Cultural Diversity to Feminist Psychology: Theory, Research, and Practice
Edited by Hope Landrine

Featuring Females: Feminist Analyses of Media
Edited by Ellen Cole and Jessica Henderson Daniel

Feminist Family Therapy: Empowerment in Social Context
Edited by Louise B. Silverstein and Thelma Jean Goodrich

The Glass Ceiling in the 21st Century: Understanding Barriers to Gender Equality
Edited by Manuela Barreto, Michelle K. Ryan, and Michael T. Schmitt

Listening to Battered Women: A Survivor-Centered Approach to Advocacy, Mental Health, and Justice
Lisa A. Goodman and Deborah Epstein

The New Civil War: The Psychology, Culture, and Politics of Abortion
Edited by Linda J. Beckman and S. Marie Harvey

Older Women Who Work: Resilience, Choice, and Change
Edited by Ellen Cole and Lisa Hollis-Sawyer

Practicing Feminist Ethics in Psychology
Edited by Mary M. Brabeck

Psychological Practice With Women: Guidelines, Diversity, Empowerment
Edited by Carolyn Zerbe Enns, Joy K. Rice, and Roberta L. Nutt

Psychology and Economic Injustice: Personal, Professional, and Political Intersections
Bernice Lott and Heather E. Bullock

Relationships Among Asian American Women
Edited by Jean Lau Chin

Sexuality, Society, and Feminism
Edited by Cheryl Brown Travis and Jacquelyn W. White

Shaping the Future of Feminist Psychology: Education, Research, and Practice
Edited by Judith Worell and Norine G. Johnson

Talking About Sexual Assault: Society's Response to Survivors
    Sarah E. Ullman

Transnational Psychology of Women: Expanding International and Intersectional Approaches
    Edited by Lynn H. Collins, Sayaka Machizawa, and Joy K. Rice

Womanist and Mujerista *Psychologies: Voices of Fire, Acts of Courage*
    Edited by Thema Bryant-Davis and Lillian Comas-Díaz

Woman's Embodied Self: Feminist Perspectives on Identity and Image
    Joan C. Chrisler and Ingrid Johnston-Robledo

Older Women Who Work

Resilience, Choice, and Change

Edited by Ellen Cole and
Lisa Hollis-Sawyer

AMERICAN PSYCHOLOGICAL ASSOCIATION

Published by
American Psychological Association
750 First Street, NE
Washington, DC 20002
https://www.apa.org

Order Department
https://www.apa.org/pubs/books
order@apa.org

In the U.K., Europe, Africa, and the Middle East, copies may be ordered from Eurospan
https://www.eurospanbookstore.com/apa
info@eurospangroup.com

Typeset in Charter and Interstate by Circle Graphics, Inc., Reisterstown, MD

Printer: Sheridan Books, Chelsea, MI
Cover Designer: Gwen Grafft, Minneapolis, MN

Library of Congress Cataloging-in-Publication Data

Names: Cole, Ellen, editor. | Hollis-Sawyer, Lisa A., 1963- editor.
Title: Older women who work : resilience, choice, and change /
  edited by Ellen Cole and Lisa Hollis-Sawyer.
Description: Washington, DC : American Psychological Association, [2021] |
  Series: Psychology of women series | Includes bibliographical references and index.
Identifiers: LCCN 2020015827 (print) | LCCN 2020015828 (ebook) |
  ISBN 9781433832888 (paperback) | ISBN 9781433833175 (ebook)
Subjects: LCSH: Older women—Employment. | Retirement age. | Career changes. |
  Ageism. | Age and employment.
Classification: LCC HD6056 .O385 2021 (print) | LCC HD6056 (ebook) |
  DDC 331.4084/6—dc23
LC record available at https://lccn.loc.gov/2020015827
LC ebook record available at https://lccn.loc.gov/2020015828

https://doi.org/10.1037/0000212-000

Printed in the United States of America

10 9 8 7 6 5 4 3 2 1

Contents

Contributors	*ix*
Series Foreword—Mary Wyer	*xi*
Foreword—Bonnie R. Strickland	*xiii*
Acknowledgments	*xv*

Introduction   3
Ellen Cole and Lisa Hollis-Sawyer

I. PERSONAL AND CAREER IDENTITIES FOR OLDER WOMEN   13

1. **From Striving to Thriving: How Facing Adversity Across the Lifespan Can Foster Workplace Resilience**   19
Ashley M. Stripling and Jodie Maccarrone

2. **The Aging Woman Worker in a Lifespan Developmental Context**   33
Valory Mitchell

3. **Shifting Values and Late Course Adjustments in the Careers of Older Women**   49
Lorraine Mangione, Kathi A. Borden, and Elizabeth Fuss

4. **Work-Related Choice and Identity in Older Women**   69
Nicky J. Newton and Katherine M. Ottley

5. **Plenty More at the Factory Gate: An Autoethnography of a Precarious Work (Life) in Progress**   87
Jackie Goode

II. SOCIETAL ROLES OF AGING WOMEN WORKERS   103

  6. The Secret Poor Among Us: Older Women Who Work to
Make Ends Meet   109
Mary Gergen and Ellen Cole

  7. Work–Life Balance and the Older Working Woman   133
H. Lorraine Radtke and Janneke van Mens-Verhulst

  8. What, Retire? Not Now—Maybe Not Ever   153
Patricia A. O'Connor

  9. "You're Too Young/Old for This": The Intersection of
Ageism and Sexism in the Workplace   161
Ruth V. Walker and Alexandra I. Zelin

III. DIVERSITY AND PERSONAL GRIT IN THE WORKPLACE
AND BEYOND   189

  10. Appalachian Grit: Women and Work in West Virginia   195
*Julie Hicks Patrick, Abigail M. Nehrkorn-Bailey, Michaela S. Clark,
and Madeline M. Marello*

  11. Missions Continued: Contextualizing Older Women's Work
Pursuits and Passions in Lifelong Journeys   213
Niva Piran

  12. Older Immigrant Women Who Work: Building Resilience,
Changing Perceptions and Policies   227
Jasmin Tahmaseb McConatha and Frauke Schnell

  13. Use It or Lose It: Older Women and Civic Engagement   241
Lisa Hollis-Sawyer

Appendix: Employment Resources for Older Women   259
Index   263
About the Editors   281

Contributors

Kathi A. Borden, PhD, Antioch University New England, Keene, NH, United States

Michaela S. Clark, MS, West Virginia University, Morgantown, WV, United States

Ellen Cole, PhD, Russell Sage College, Troy/Albany, NY, United States

Elizabeth Fuss, MS, Antioch University New England, Keene, NH, United States

Mary Gergen, PhD, Penn State University, Brandywine, Media, PA, United States

Jackie Goode, PhD, Loughborough University, Loughborough, England

Lisa Hollis-Sawyer, PhD, Northeastern Illinois University, Chicago, IL, United States

Jodie Maccarrone, MBA, MS, Nova Southeastern University, Fort Lauderdale, FL, United States

Lorraine Mangione, PhD, Antioch University New England, Keene, NH, United States

Madeline M. Marello, BS, West Virginia University, Morgantown, WV, United States

Jasmin Tahmaseb McConatha, PhD, West Chester University, West Chester, PA, United States

Valory Mitchell, PhD, California School of Professional Psychology at Alliant University (Distinguished Emerita) and Private Practice, Berkeley, CA, United States

Abigail M. Nehrkorn-Bailey, PhD, Colorado State University, Fort Collins, CO, United States

Nicky J. Newton, PhD, Wilfrid Laurier University, Waterloo, ON, Canada

Patricia A. O'Connor, PhD, Russell Sage College, Troy/Albany, NY, United States

Katherine M. Ottley, PhD, University of Saskatchewan, Saskatoon, SK, Canada

Julie Hicks Patrick, PhD, West Virginia University, Morgantown, WV, United States

Niva Piran, PhD, University of Toronto, Toronto, ON, Canada

H. Lorraine Radtke, PhD, University of Calgary, Calgary, AB, Canada

Frauke Schnell, PhD, West Chester University, West Chester, PA, United States

Bonnie R. Strickland, PhD, University of Massachusetts, Amherst, MA, United States

Ashley M. Stripling, PhD, Nova Southeastern University, Fort Lauderdale, FL, United States

Janneke van Mens-Verhulst, PhD, Utrecht University (Emerita), Utrecht, Netherlands

Ruth V. Walker, PhD, Missouri State University, Springfield, MO, United States

Mary Wyer, PhD, Associate Department Head and Director of Graduate Programs, Department of Psychology, NC State University, Raleigh, NC, United States

Alexandra I. Zelin, PhD, University of Tennessee, Chattanooga, TN, United States

Series Foreword

This work represents a collective and community effort by the volume editors and contributors for the Society for the Psychology of Women (Division 35) Book Series of the American Psychological Association (APA). This series is devoted to supporting and disseminating scholarship that provides cutting edge and contemporary perspectives by, for, and about women—in order to recover lost knowledge, re-center current knowledge, and advance new knowledge.

Today, as I write this, it is Mother's Day, May 10, 2020. The world is in the midst of a pandemic health crisis sparked by COVID-19. Billions of people are under "stay-at-home" orders as governments work to mitigate the spread of the disease. Women are the mothers, sisters, daughters, aunts, friends, neighbors, and strangers, who make up 76% of health care providers in the United States and 70% of health care providers worldwide, according to recent figures from the U.S. Census and World Health Organization.[1,2] This means that women are on the front lines in a battle with a pandemic. As a day to celebrate mothers, indeed all women, for our caring and caretaking commitments (paid and unpaid), this particular Mother's Day surely ranks high.

---

[1]Day, J. C., & Cristnacht, C. (2019, August 14). *Your health care is in women's hands*. U.S. Census Bureau. https://www.census.gov/library/stories/2019/08/your-health-care-in-womens-hands.html
[2]Ghebreyesus, T. D. (2019, March 20). *Female health workers drive global health*. World Health Organization. https://www.who.int/news-room/commentaries/detail/female-health-workers-drive-global-health

Yet, women as caregivers, breadwinners, and workers face economically precarious life circumstances. Because women are overrepresented among those who have jobs in the service sector, the economic disruptions of the pandemic have disproportionately affected women, who have shouldered 60% of job losses. Four out of five African American mothers are breadwinners, and the majority (56%) are single mothers. Two out of three Native American mothers (64%) are breadwinners, and 40% are single mothers. The unemployment rate for Hispanic women has increased over 300% from February 2020 to May 2020, and for single mothers of all ethnicities, the unemployment rate tripled between March and May 2020. According to the Institute for Women's Policy Research,[3] women who are classified as "essential workers" as health care workers, for instance, must face a biting choice between their lives and their livelihoods, between risks to the health of their children or losing their jobs. Women who can be and want to be employed, who are sustaining their own and their families' and friends' food, shelter, health care, education, and emotional needs, are the backbone of a recovery from these devastating times. These are women with grit, no matter their age, but especially if they are graying; especially if they could be living a little easier life but have chosen a more difficult path.

I can only hope that by the time you read this, these facts will be out of date, an account of a difficult historical moment that is no longer descriptive. We can hope that times will soon improve and women will return to the workforce newly recognized and embraced for our long-standing and thoroughgoing contributions to human health and well-being. It is unknowable now. What we can, will, and must do is to continue to care for one another—mothers, sisters, daughters, aunts, friends, neighbors, and strangers.

Older Women Who Work: Resilience, Choice, and Change is emblematic of these generous-hearted efforts. The contributors cut a wide swath across genres in academic narratives. From the close-up views in autobiographies, to historical case studies, to sharp critiques of White privilege and ageism in scholarship about women and work, the common thread herein is the authors' shared and resilient commitment to social justice—empowered by and within community.

—*Mary Wyer*

---

[3] Shaw, E., Mason, C. N., Lacarte, V., & Jauregui, E. (2020, May 8). *Holding up half the sky: Mothers as workers, primary caregivers, and breadwinners during COVID-19*. Institute for Women's Policy Research. https://iwpr.org/publications/holding-up-half-the-sky-mothers-as-workers-primary-caregivers-breadwinners-during-covid-19/

Foreword

Statisticians love to design groupings of people that give them more specific information about general characteristics. Political strategists place potential voters in boxes that help them understand voting preferences. Psychologists work to devise various diagnostic categories. We combine the general information we take in to give us easier ways to understand the people and events that surround us. Although every individual is different, this book looks specifically at a group that has been systematically overlooked in the past—namely, older women who are still working after the typical retirement age.

As some readers of this book will have experienced firsthand, women's roles have changed dramatically over the past 80 years. Women who came of age in the 1940s and 1950s were not likely to be working as they became seniors. They continued to remain in a role-related status, such as homemaker. But, increasingly, as the workforce has expanded, women have considered new opportunities and assumed new positions in society. Today, many older women continue to work out of financial necessity. Others work for personal and emotional reasons. Some choose to retire from the workforce. Each woman's story is different, although several themes do emerge in this book that help us identify groupings and trends.

Almost 20 years ago, I was in the enviable position of having the possibility of fully retiring or continuing in my position as a college professor. For a while I tried the new, to me, enticements of part-time retirement. I took up golf, I volunteered, and I engaged in a variety of nonwork activities. However, I flunked traditional retirement and kept returning to my first love, teaching. It took some time and some energy for me to find a balance across work and nonwork. I was lucky. I had the freedom to make choices and define my life according to my interests. Many women of retirement age don't have that luxury.

I am continually striving to balance life and work; I didn't know it would be such a challenge. Most of us would like to live safely and happily in whatever circumstances we find ourselves. Some of us worry too much that we are not making the right choices in our lives. Some have only limited choices and struggle to come to a meaningful understanding of how one can meet adversity. The struggle is always with us. And it may be especially worrisome and tiring for older women who are in the workplace. Sometimes, working older women may have to give up independence and self-sufficiency to please their bosses. They may find themselves always needing to prove their competence. They may realize that they might easily be replaced by a younger worker.

The older woman worker is also faced with the inexorable march of aging. How does one retain health and vigor? What if the frailties of aging lead to lowered work performance?

This book paints a picture of what life can be like for the older woman still in the workplace. The editors and authors have given us scholarly and readable narratives that provide new insights into the phenomenon of older women in the workplace. With contributions ranging from societal statistics to individual memoirs, the book takes a unique place in our understanding of this fascinating population.

—*Bonnie R. Strickland*

Acknowledgments

Ellen Cole

I am 79 at the time of this writing, already calling myself 80 in preparation for what seems like a big year to come. I started a phased retirement plan in September 2019 and will officially retire in June 2022 at the age of 81. The topic of older, or old women, like myself and not like myself, who continue to work beyond the traditional retirement age of 65 is a gripping one for me, certainly personally but also because we constitute an invisible, diverse, and powerful segment of society. My hope is that this book will bring us and this topic into the light.

Lisa Hollis-Sawyer

My own dedication to creating this book comes from my lifelong commitment and passion to support older women's quality of life in the workplace and beyond. I am guided in my professional life through my teaching, research, and community service to be an advocate for diverse aging women and older workers' rights.

We, Ellen and Lisa, cannot fully express our deep gratitude to everyone involved in this labor of love, from wonderful guidance to emotional support throughout every step in this book's development process. More than any other publication, we both feel that *Older Women Who Work: Resilience, Choice, and Change* is closest to our hearts and identity. Coediting this book and authoring or coauthoring one chapter each has brought us both joy and self-reflection, allowing us to examine our own lives and futures and inspiring us to think of older women who work in new and complex ways.

As we both like to say, "it takes a village" to accomplish any worthwhile activity, and we would like to thank the many contributors to the edited book, from Bonnie Strickland for her wonderful foreword to the talented and very patient chapter authors. Thank you, Bonnie, Ashley, Jodie, Valory, Lorraine M., Kathi, Elizabeth, Nicky, Katherine, Jackie, Mary G., Lorraine R., Janneke, Pat, Ruthie, Alex, Julie, Abigail, Michaela, Madeline, Niva, Jasmin, and Frauke!

This book could not have happened if we did not have a great coediting partnership. We, Ellen and Lisa, met in 2014 through the Women and Aging Committee of the American Psychological Association's (APA) Division 35 (Society for the Psychology of Women), and our professional relationship has grown into one of mutual admiration and affection. We quickly became equal partners on this book, although Ellen wants to be clear that the original concept was 100% Lisa's. We cannot think of a single way, from that time on, that our collaboration could have been better.

We would both like to acknowledge the wonderful support of our family members during this book's development. Thank you, Doug, Tom, Josh, and May!

We want to thank Angelique (Angel) Parks, a graduate student and graduate assistant at Sage Graduate School, where Ellen teaches. When we began to conceptualize the book, we needed first to know what was already written about working women over 65. Angel prepared a 27-page annotated bibliography that we referred to throughout the book's development. Thank you, Angel!

And in some ways, we have saved the best for last: our editor at APA's Division 35 (Society for the Psychology of Women), Mary Wyer; our acquisitions editor at APA Books, Christopher Kelaher; and our APA development editor, Susan Herman. Each of you believed in this project and supported us at every step, not always making it easy for us, but always making it better. Thank you, thank you, Mary, Chris, and Susan!

Older Women Who Work

INTRODUCTION

ELLEN COLE AND LISA HOLLIS-SAWYER

Please note: The economic and social trends presented in this volume do not incorporate data from the COVID-19 pandemic, due to the timing of the research itself, the publication process, and the sudden onset of the pandemic. However, we believe that each of the chapters remains relevant in many ways—in regard to older women who continue to work, now online or still on-site; older women who have been furloughed or fired; and older women who have made the decision, given the state of things, to retire. We encourage readers who are interested to consult sources on women who work that do get frequently updated, in order to track new developments that may then augment the insights provided in the following chapters. For example, two sites that we have been following are http://www.fairygodboss.com, where you can find up to date research on women and work, and Our World in Data (http://www.ourworldindata.org/female-labor-supply; Ortiz-Ospina et al., 2018), which has shown that "the global expansion of the female labor supply has gone together with an increase in the average age of women in the labor force." This book is intended to educate a variety of audiences about state-of-the-art research on women age 65 and older

https://doi.org/10.1037/0000212-001
Older Women Who Work: Resilience, Choice, and Change, E. Cole and L. Hollis-Sawyer (Editors)

who work, to offer suggestions for the application of this research, and to provide helpful support resources for older women seeking employment or currently active in the workforce as well as professionals who work with this population. It is a project of the Committee on Women and Aging of the American Psychological Association's Division 35 (Society for the Psychology of Women). We, the coeditors, as well as the authors have been deeply committed to this project from its inception, recognizing its importance, even urgency, at a time when a majority of the baby boom generation plans to work into their 70s and beyond. Because women tend to outlive their male counterparts, aging in the workplace becomes increasingly a women's issue.

We have learned from the book's chapters that there are many reasons that women are continuing to work longer than ever before. Reasons range from identification with one's career to finding meaning, purpose, and social connectivity through work to the need for financial stability and paying bills, particularly, our authors tell us, those related to healthcare. Many older women workers continue to help family members. Some work because they choose to. Some work because they must.

Many countries have already begun to see rapid growth in the number of older workers staying in or attempting to reenter the workforce. The U.S. Bureau of Labor Statistics (2013), for example, reported that the 65- to 74-year-old population of men and women at that time participated in the workforce at a rate of 26%, but that participation is expected to increase to 31% by 2022. In 1992, the participation rate of women age 62 to 64 was 30.5%, but it is anticipated that by 2022, their participation rate will be 47.4%. Among women age 65 to 74, their participation rate is predicted to grow from having been 12.5% in 1992 to 28.3% by 2022. In contrast, the labor force participation rates of men are declining.

We anticipate and hope that many will benefit from this book. Workplace practitioners, such as human resource managers, industrial and organizational psychologists, and consultants with health care centers or senior living facilities, will benefit from a greater understanding of older women employees and their associated workplace support needs, such as skills training in new technologies. We expect and hope that readers will be better prepared to advise policymakers around issues related to poverty, precarious work environments, and health care needs of older workers. For academic audiences, we believe this will be a beneficial reading source for any course examining women's development, the workplace, or broader issues of societal roles and public policies. Mental health professionals from a variety of disciplines as well as media and consumer psychologists will benefit from a greater understanding of the fastest growing demographic in the United States and beyond.

Our range of topics, genres, writing styles, and research methodologies is intentionally broad, presenting diverse perspectives about older women's later-life work-role experiences through a feminist lens by authors from different but related fields and areas of expertise. We have attempted to achieve a balance between scholarship and advocacy while addressing a diversity of populations that include Appalachian women, immigrant women, poor women, women who choose to continue to work, and women in precarious work situations. We believe the various chapters compellingly demonstrate the impact of crosscutting factors such as sexism and poverty along with an exploration of boots-on-the-ground issues such as retirement, work–life balance, and civic engagement, as well as broad conceptual issues such as changing values and lifespan contexts.

Each contribution highlights strengths that older women bring not only to the workplace but also to the broader society. As with any essay collection, we expect the reader will benefit from a gateway perspective that allows each separate piece to complement the whole. To that end, we have divided the book into the following three parts, each with its own introduction: Part I—Personal and Career Identities for Older Women, Part II—Societal Roles of Aging Women Workers, and Part III—Diversity and Personal Grit in the Workplace and Beyond.

We believe the book provides one of the first in-depth examinations of older women delaying retirement and working past traditional retirement age. Because the topic is exceedingly current and there are currently no clear guidelines regarding the factors to consider or the resources needed to succeed in this extended career trajectory, our book is intended to break new ground on topics of interest to clinicians, educators, researchers, workplace practitioners, and anyone who is or knows a woman who is aging—mother, sister, friend, daughter, or spouse.

A GLIMPSE INTO OUR JOURNEY

To our surprise, we, the coeditors, experienced something familiar yet unexpected when we began this project. It reminded us of when we were pregnant as younger women and started noticing other pregnant women everywhere. This time we began noticing older women who work. Here is one example:

At a lunch counter not long ago, Susan (age 68) and Tanya (age 83)— these are their real ages but not their real names—began to talk about their busy practices as real estate agents. Ellen asked them (politely, and with their permission) why they were still working. Susan said, "for the bacon." She needed the money to pay the taxes:

> We got ourselves into a conundrum. We bought a house so our daughter could live with us, and she doesn't pay rent in spite of our repeatedly asking her to. It's very awkward. But I enjoy real estate. It's a good business when you still want to travel. The trouble is, people expect you to be at their beck and call.

Tanya, with her husband, runs a popular bed and breakfast (B&B) in addition to her real estate business. She said, "Frankly, the real estate business is for the income. The B&B gets harder and harder. You assume your pension and Social Security will cover everything, but expenses and taxes go up." Both women agreed on another reason they work, expressed first by Susan: "If I didn't work, my husband and I would kill each other. We spend too much time together, as is." Tanya agreed: "He has to go everywhere with me. But he can't come to my women's lunches or go out on real estate calls."

Please look around, and you, too, are likely to see what had previously not been on your radar screen: older women who work.

And another thing happened. Friends and colleagues, one after another, made suggestions for topics. One woman, who is celebrating her 50th year as a Catholic nun, asked, "Do you know that nuns never retire?" Here is an excerpt from an email she (Mary Lou Liptak, Sister of Mercy) sent the next day:

> Another example of older women who work that could warrant examination as a model of endurance beyond traditional retirement age would be the thousands of women religious who literally built up the American Catholic Church throughout the 18th, 19th, and 20th centuries and continue into the 21st. Impelled by following the mandates of their baptismal vows to serve, and strengthened by their religious vows of poverty, chastity, and obedience, they are inclined to meet the needs of the downtrodden, wherever that may lead them. Women Religious are the fore runners in the feminist movement and innovators in ministry. They rolled up their sleeves to provide solutions to present day problems.
>
> The whole concept of belonging to a religious community suggests that women religious never retire from that lifestyle but rather continue to fulfill their duties as long as they are able. When a Sister feels she no longer can serve in her present role, often times she will agree to a ministry of less intensity such as part-time worker, or serve in a volunteer role in hospitals, nursing homes, prisons, or the many outreach ministries such as soup kitchens, food pantries, and other agencies that serve the poor. Sisters are often seen still ministering to the people of God well into their 70s, 80s and even 90s, beyond the age that society sets for retirement. Sisters who are physically unable to continue to serve in even a small role in active ministry, continue to provide a network of prayer for the Sisters who are still ministering, furthering their work and fulfilling their vows until death.

Another suggestion came from Leona Brandwene, associate director of education at the University of Pennsylvania's Positive Psychology Center. "What about athletes who later become coaches?" she asked, following up, too, with an explanatory email:

> The sports arena is literally and figuratively an environment which stretches women to excellence and thriving through a passion for sport. With the passing of Title IX in 1972, the doors to sport opened for many women in the United States, and today's 65+ year old collegiate coaches who lead NCAA [National Collegiate Athletic Association] programs across the country often blazed the trail as athletes themselves for new NCAA and scholastic programs that were launched in the 70s, 80s, and 90s. Their pioneering spirit, first as athletes, and now as coaches, is the very expression of a life-long passion.

WHAT THIS BOOK COVERS

We ended up not including chapters about women in religious orders or women in athletics careers, even though these topics piqued our interest. As our thoughts developed on the book project, our focus veered away from specific career paths and toward broader themes, such as resilience, lifespan development, meaning-making, economics, how societies value older women who work and the work itself, and systems-level change to make work a healthier experience for older women.

The chapters in Part I are related to older women's perceptions of self in their evolving later-life career trajectories. Chapter 1, by Ashley M. Stripling and Jodie Maccarrone, illustrates how challenges for older working women such as ageism, lookism, and caregiving intersect with previously experienced hurdles (i.e., sexism, wage gaps) and how these may be more pronounced for women who already experience discrimination based on race, ethnicity, country of origin, religion, disability, or sexual orientation. This chapter outlines pathways through which these challenges can facilitate growth and proposes a model of resiliency factors to inform gerodiverse women, professionals, and organizations about how to promote psychological well-being among our diverse and flourishing late-life female workforce.

Chapter 2, by Valory Mitchell, focuses on how developmental theory might regard the aging working woman. For example, the final two stages of the Eriksons' lifespan theory—generativity and integrity—offer a sharp contrast. Generativity has an outward focus, generating and nurturing one's contributions to society, whereas integrity looks inward, asking who one is and has been. Does a purposive work life keep the aging woman from her "appropriate" inner task? Or should developmental theories be flexed and ultimately revised to better capture a woman's journey toward transcendence and end of life, when these transitions play out in the context of her work life?

Chapter 3, by Lorraine Mangione, Kathi A. Borden, and Elizabeth Fuss, addresses the meaning of work for the current cohort of professional women age 60 and older. How does this group make meaning out of their work and their decision to keep working? How connected is work to their values and sense of identity? What do they consider when they decide to keep working? These questions are explored within an existential, feminist, and lifespan development framework through personal and professional commentaries by the authors and themes and comments coming from women invited to write narratives about the meaning of work in their lives.

Chapter 4, by Nicky J. Newton and Katherine M. Ottley, presents original research examining the relationship to personal identity of voluntary versus involuntary retirement or continued work participation among older women. Associations with health, age, household income, and type of occupation are also examined. The authors note that women who chose to either continue working or retire exhibited higher levels of identity certainty than did women forced to do either, although findings differed by occupation type. They also demonstrate how qualitative data provides a broader picture of work-related identity, highlighting the importance of contextualizing retirement-linked research within the individual's life course.

Chapter 5, by Jackie Goode, is an autoethnographic account of the meanings of work for an older White Englishwoman. It traces her winding path into and out of different kinds of part- and full-time professional work alongside raising a family and her journey after retirement undertaking both paid and unpaid work. In doing so, it problematizes both the traditional notion of career as a linear unidirectional trajectory and the idea that work holds either instrumental or intrinsic value.

Part II presents a series of chapters related to women's roles in the workplace and in their communities in later life. Chapter 6, by Mary Gergen and Ellen Cole, examines through interviews and content analysis the topic of older women needing to work past traditional retirement age because of economic need, such as personal and/or family support. Issues discussed include declining health and other aging-related changes that affect continued employment for older women who are working, some of whom would prefer not to. The heart of the chapter consists of descriptions of how life goes for women who must work at low-income jobs in their older years. How do they manage? What are the positive aspects of their lives? What social and governmental assistance might make their lives better?

Chapter 7, by H. Lorraine Radtke and Janneke van Mens-Verhulst, explores the meaning of work–life balance/integration for older women, including those who work beyond "normal" retirement age. This collaborative effort integrates insights from two cultural contexts, the Netherlands and Canada. Although both share the status of being developed countries in the global north, there are some distinctive cultural norms of interest for considering older women, work, and work–life balance. Through critical analysis, the chapter addresses gaps created by research and theory development that has focused mainly on women below the age of 65 (the traditional retirement age in many countries).

Chapter 8, by Patricia O'Connor, describes a qualitative study of women 70 years of age and older who are working by choice. Rather than focusing solely on reasons for continuing to work that are related to self-identity, the study also highlights the effect of their working on their relationships with family and friends.

Chapter 9, by Ruth V. Walker and Alexandra I. Zelin, addresses women's and men's experiences with ageism in the workplace, using results from a phenomenological study of 70 participants, 22 to 87 years old, who participated in either story circles or in-depth interviews. Their results demonstrate that experiences with ageism are not a phenomenon reserved for older adulthood and that gender intersects with age to create opportunities for both oppression and resistance across the lifespan.

Part III includes chapters related to individual-difference factors affecting older women's workforce participation. Chapter 10, by Julie Hicks Patrick, Abigail M. Nehrkorn-Bailey, Michaela S. Clark, and Madeline M. Marello, explores some of the factors that influence employment trends among older Appalachian women. Appalachia includes all of West Virginia and portions of 12 other states, encompassing 25 million residents. Appalachians live with lower annual incomes, higher poverty, higher unemployment, and higher morbidity and mortality rates than are seen in other regions in the United States.

Chapter 11, by Niva Piran, describes a study with 31 women of diverse social locations, age 50 to 70, about their embodied journeys. The findings suggest that work at an older age, although a discrete experience in women's lives, reflects needs, wishes, and pursuits that derive their meanings from women's unique life histories. Examples from the study include stories about overcoming physical and geographic constraints as well as constraints related to social power, relational connections, and cultural discourses.

Chapter 12, by Jasmin Tahmaseb McConatha and Frauke Schnell, focuses on the resilience and challenges faced by older immigrant working women in the United States. Many of these women toil at low-income, dead-end jobs; discriminatory treatment often blocks their upward mobility. The authors present a case study of an older immigrant who arrived in the United States as a young woman. Through her story they identify resources that build resilience and explore ideas for policies, programs, and media culture that can change social perceptions and improve how these women fare.

Chapter 13, by Lisa Hollis-Sawyer, applies the "use it or lose it" principle to volunteerism and other outlets for physical, mental, and social engagement for older women. The chapter reviews positive personal and social outcomes of civic engagement and identifies factors that support women who wish to stay active in such networks and become "womentors" to others.

Overarching themes are explored at greater length in each of the part introductions, but here we'd like to offer a sampler of the types of questions we hope readers will consider while interacting with this text:

- What strengths do older women bring to the workforce?

- What must human resources professionals, managers, and executive leaders do or understand in order to capitalize on older women's strengths?

- What needs to change in workplace cultures and other systems to make work a safe, healthy place where older women can thrive?

- What role do counselors and clinicians play in providing resources and advice for older women who want or need to pursue work opportunities?

- What roles can researchers play in shaping the workplace for older women's needs? For example, how can they influence policy and other systems change?

There are many other topics and authors we would have liked to incorporate in this book. We received several excellent proposals that because of time and page limits and other factors we were unable to include, and we hope to see them published elsewhere, soon. One in particular was a chapter by Maria Alexandra d'Araújo and Jaime R. S. Fonseca regarding the importance of leisure in the lives of older working women in Portugal. Another was based on interviews of older Brazilian women conducted by Monica Teixiera, demonstrating that women who officially retire can find new and meaningful purpose.

We imagine that some readers will be shouting at our pages, "How could you not include [insert important topic here]?" This would warm our hearts because we know this work is important.

AND FINALLY

The U.S. Census Bureau (see Vespa, 2018) has targeted 2035 as the year the United States will pass an important population milestone: Older adults will outnumber children for the first time in U.S. history. Estimates expect 78 million Americans 65 and older that year versus 76.7 million Americans younger than 18.

Laura Carstensen (2009), from the Stanford Center on Longevity, coined the term "the longevity revolution," with the bottom-line premise that more and more people are living to be centenarians—more than 1 million are expected in the United States by 2050. It then stands to reason that more and more of us will be in the workforce.

The takeaway for us, the coeditors of this volume, is the recognition that (a) the time is now for this topic and (b) we have been unable to cover it all. Please consider this book an invitation for you and others to follow.

REFERENCES

Carstensen, L. L. (2009). *A long bright future: An action plan for a lifetime of happiness, health, and financial security*. Broadway Books.

Ortiz-Ospina, E., Tzvetkova, S., & Roser, M. (2018, March). *Women's employment*. https://ourworldindata.org/female-labor-supply

U.S. Bureau of Labor Statistics. (2013, December). Labor force projections to 2022: The labor force participation rate continues to fall. *Monthly Labor Review*. http://www.bls.gov/opub/mlr/2013/article/labor-force-projections-to-2022-the-labor-force-participation-rate-continues-to-fall.htm

Vespa, J. (2018, September 6). *The U.S. joins other countries with large aging populations*. https://www.census.gov/library/stories/2018/03/graying-america.html

PART **I** PERSONAL AND
CAREER IDENTITIES
FOR OLDER WOMEN

INTRODUCTION

Personal and Career Identities for Older Women

Chapters 1 through 5 are devoted to older women's perceptions of self in their evolving later-life career trajectories. For a majority of working women, workforce participation is a defining or highly influential aspect of the self for most of their lifespan (e.g., having a "well-lived" life; Kashdan & McKnight, 2009). In today's society, across many industrialized nations, more older women will be working longer than ever before and well past traditional retirement age (Hayes, 2017). In the United States, it is projected that women age 65 and older will comprise approximately one quarter of the entire workforce of women by 2024 (Hayes, 2017). This new employment trend will be, by necessity, a universal experience across diverse groups of older women by age, race/ethnicity, socioeconomic status, education level, and cultural background (Cook et al., 2005; Elder & George, 2016). For example, there will be a dramatic increase in the number of Hispanic labor force participants among all age groups in the coming decades, and this is critical to understand within this aging workforce trend (Toossi & Torpey, 2017). Diversity acknowledgment is essential to supporting a growing number of aging women of color needing support for positive aging outcomes (e.g., see Baker et al., 2015, for needs of the successful aging of Black women).

From the positive aging perspective, it is critical to understand the issues of career work–life extension for growing numbers of older women who are dealing with evolving personal identities, life roles, and social networks impacted by aging changes (Elder & Johnson, 2003; Moen & Spencer, 2006). One might argue that the continuation of women's work roles in later life facilitates a feeling of self-esteem and life purpose that may not be experienced to the same extent in retirement (Hedberg et al., 2009; Irving et al., 2017; Ko et al., 2019). This feeling of life purpose and positive self-esteem through later-life workforce engagement can meaningfully enhance older women's feelings of positive mental and physical health over the later-life course of their development (e.g., feeling "generative"; Jones & McAdams, 2013; Pinquart, 2002). A feeling of life purpose can facilitate positive psychosocial adjustment for diverse women as they age (Reker & Wong, 2012). The challenges of remaining or reentering the workforce can be daunting because of potential obstacles of encountering a "glass ceiling" within a profession (Pompper, 2011) or age discrimination, sometimes with the double-jeopardy issue of being denied workplace training opportunities because of being both older and a woman of color (Manzi et al., 2019).

Understanding and confronting these issues of workplace bias, particularly as they intersect with older women's need for a feeling of life purpose, is needed to ensure fairness and opportunities for ongoing career development for all women in later life who wish or need to work for many different reasons past traditional retirement age (Zhu et al., 2017).

Across the chapters in Part I, emerging themes include the following:

- positive aging (Chapter 2),
- career and self-identity (Chapters 3, 4, and 5),
- autonomy and self-identity (Chapter 4),
- nonlinear career paths (Chapter 5), and
- precarious employment (Chapter 5).

REFERENCES

Baker, T. A., Buchanan, N. T., Mingo, C. A., Roker, R., & Brown, C. S. (2015). Reconceptualizing successful aging among Black women and the relevance of the strong Black woman archetype. *The Gerontologist, 55*(1), 51–57. https://doi.org/10.1093/geront/gnu105

Cook, E. P., Heppner, M. J., & O'Brien, K. M. (2005). Multicultural and gender influences in women's career development: An ecological perspective. *Journal of Multicultural Counseling and Development, 33*(3), 165–179. https://doi.org/10.1002/j.2161-1912.2005.tb00014.x

Elder, G. H., & George, L. K. (2016). Age, cohorts, and the life course. In M. Shanahan, J. Mortimer, & J. M. Kirkpatrick (Eds.), *Handbook of the life course* (pp. 59–85). Springer. https://doi.org/10.1007/978-3-319-20880-0_3

Elder, G. H., & Johnson, M. K. (2003). The life course and aging: Challenges, lessons, and new directions. In R. A. Settersten, Jr. (Ed.), *Invitation to the life course: Toward new understandings of later life* (pp. 49–81). Baywood Publishing.

Hayes, K. (2017, August 8). *More older women in the workforce.* American Association of Retired Persons. https://www.aarp.org/work/on-the-job/info-2017/older-women-workforce-fd.html

Hedberg, P., Brulin, C., & Aléx, L. (2009). Experiences of purpose in life when becoming and being a very old woman. *Journal of Women & Aging, 21*(2), 125–137. https://doi.org/10.1080/08952840902837145

Irving, J., Davis, S., & Collier, A. (2017). Aging with purpose: Systematic search and review of literature pertaining to older adults and purpose. *International Journal of Aging & Human Development, 85*(4), 403–437. https://doi.org/10.1177/0091415017702908

Jones, B. K., & McAdams, D. P. (2013). Becoming generative: Socializing influences recalled in life stories in late midlife. *Journal of Adult Development, 20,* 158–172. https://doi.org/10.1007/s10804-013-9168-4

Kashdan, T. B., & McKnight, P. E. (2009). Origins of purpose in life: Refining our understanding of a life well lived. *Psihologijske Teme, 18*(2), 303–316.

Ko, H. J., Hooker, K., Manoogian, M. M., & McAdams, D. P. (2019). Transitions to older adulthood: Exploring midlife women's narratives regarding purpose in life. *Journal of Positive Psychology and Wellbeing, 3*(2), 137–152. http://journalppw.com/index.php/JPPW/article/view/pdf

Manzi, C., Paderi, F., Benet-Martínez, V., & Coen, S. (2019). Age-based stereotype threat and negative outcomes in the workplace: Exploring the role of identity integration. *European Journal of Social Psychology, 49*(4), 705–716. https://doi.org/10.1002/ejsp.2533

Moen, P., & Spencer, D. (2006). Converging divergences in age, gender, health, and well-being: Strategic selection in the third age. In R. H. Binstock, L. K. George, S. J. Cutler, J. Hendricks, & J. H. Schulz (Eds.), *Handbook of aging and the social sciences* (6th ed., pp. 127–144). Academic Press. https://doi.org/10.1016/B978-012088388-2/50011-0

Pinquart, M. (2002). Creating and maintaining purpose in life in old age: A meta-analysis. *Ageing International, 27,* 90–114. https://doi.org/10.1007/s12126-002-1004-2

Pompper, D. (2011). Fifty years later: Mid-career women of color against the glass ceiling in communications organizations. *Journal of Organizational Change Management, 24*(4), 464–486. https://doi.org/10.1108/09534811111144629

Reker, G. T., & Wong, P. T. P. (2012). Personal meaning in life and psychosocial adaptation in the later years. In P. T. P. Wong (Ed.), *The human quest for meaning: Theories, research and application* (2nd ed., pp. 433–456). Routledge.

Toossi, M., & Torpey, E. (2017, May). *Older workers: Labor force trends and career options.* Career Outlook. U.S. Bureau of Labor Statistics. https://www.bls.gov/careeroutlook/2017/article/pdf/older-workers.pdf

Zhu, J. J., Lomas, T., Burke, J., & Ivtzan, I. (2017). Exploring the role of purpose in the lives of career changers: A qualitative inquiry. *Journal of Positive Psychology and Wellbeing, 1*(2), 109–128.

1

FROM STRIVING TO THRIVING

How Facing Adversity Across the Lifespan Can
Foster Workplace Resilience

ASHLEY M. STRIPLING AND JODIE MACCARRONE

My mission in life is not merely to survive, but to thrive; and to do so with
some passion, some compassion, some humor, and some style.

—Maya Angelou (2011)

As women in the workforce age, they face a number of new challenges that intersect with previously experienced hurdles. These challenges are more pronounced in the case of older women, who may already experience discrimination based on other identities such as ethnic background or sexual minority status. This chapter outlines pathways through which these challenges facilitate growth and proposes a model outlining factors that promote well-being and flourishing within the late-life diverse female workforce.

AGEISM AND OLDER WOMEN IN THE WORKFORCE

As women age and remain in the workplace longer, the risk and duration of exposure to discrimination increase, as do the continuous challenges to self-esteem, identity, and psychological and physical well-being. In other

https://doi.org/10.1037/0000212-002
Older Women Who Work: Resilience, Choice, and Change, E. Cole and L. Hollis-Sawyer (Editors)

words, older women in the workplace face a set of obstacles that may include a seemingly daunting array of isms. For example, sexism materializes under both hostile and benevolent intentions in the workforce, resulting in discrepancies in wages and leadership roles as well as sexual harassment, perceived incompetence, and being passed over for important assignments (Gramlich, 2017; U.S. Bureau of Labor Statistics, 2017; Zarya, 2018). Furthermore, women of color, who experience sexism in addition to racism, report higher incidences of discrimination and even less representation in leadership roles (American Association of University Women, 2018; Gramlich, 2017), which have been linked to reduced well-being, health, job satisfaction, and self-esteem (Fraser et al., 2015; Pascoe & Richman, 2009).

Additionally, as women age, they can encounter ageism, defined as "prejudice toward, stereotyping of, and/or discrimination against any person or persons directly and solely as a function of their having attained a chronological age which the social group defines as 'old'" (American Psychological Association Committee on Aging, 2009, p. 12), which has been associated with lower quality of life, body esteem, health status, and psychological well-being (Bodner & Cohen-Fridel, 2010). These ill effects are likely due in part to lookism (Sims, 2017), which has been documented in corporate and academic settings as limiting women's wages and advancement (French, 2002; Granleese & Sayer, 2006; Jones et al., 2017). Taken together, these and other isms can combine, leaving women to "never [feel] the right age" for the workplace and, along with other workplace stressors, result in low organizational commitment and job satisfaction and increased turnover and burnout (Ayalon & Tesch-Römer, 2017; Duncan & Loretto, 2004; Velez et al., 2018).

RESILIENCE IN LATER LIFE

The collective impact of prejudice and discrimination on women in the workplace is cumulative. Therefore, as women age, the risk of negative outcomes resulting from both hostile and subtle acts and missed opportunities can be devastating. However, repeated exposure to societal discrimination often necessitates adoption of more effective coping styles, including the ability to reframe negative experiences positively and build higher self-esteem and other skills acquired from gradual but constant exposure to adversity (Kumpfer, 1999). Thus, despite these hurdles, research indicates that as women age, they often thrive, living happy, healthy, and satisfying lives. This resilience, or the "dynamic process encompassing positive adaption within the context of significant adversity" (Luthar et al., 2000), is considered an important component of adaptive aging (Chow et al., 2007). As such, it should come as no surprise that over time many terms have been coined to document this resiliency in later life, including "successful aging" (Rowe & Kahn, 1987), "healthy aging" (Guralnik & Kaplan, 1989), "productive aging" (Gleason & Butler, 1985), "optimal aging" (Aldwin & Gilmer, 2004), and "aging well" (George & Clipp, 1991). Taken together, this body of literature provides key insights into resilience and the mechanisms by which adversity can promote late-life psychological well-being. Specifically, resilience among older women has been associated with overall adjustment to aging and specific late-life challenges such as widowhood, chronic pain, dementia, and preparing for one's own death (Harris, 2008; Karoly & Ruehlman, 2006; Nelson-Becker, 2006; Ong et al., 2006; Rossi et al., 2007).

The mechanism of action for this coping appears to be multifaceted, including the interaction of external environmental factors (i.e., strong social, family support) and intrapersonal factors (i.e., identity affirmation, high self-esteem, autonomy, a positive outlook; Fredriksen-Goldsen et al., 2013, 2017; Mcdonald et al., 2016; Ott et al., 2007; van Heugten, 2013; Van Wagenen et al., 2013; Wells, 2012). The results are successful adaptation, higher physical and psychological well-being, and an improved ability to handle stressors (Ong et al., 2006; Wells, 2012).

PROPOSED RESILIENCY MODEL FOR OLDER FEMALE WORKERS

In application to older female workers, Kumpfer's (1999) and King and Rothstein's (2010) resilience frameworks combined with Zacher's (2015) and Kooij's (2015a, 2015b) successful aging at work paradigms provide solid scaffolding on which resiliency in this population can be understood. Specifically, as outlined in Figure 1.1, workplace resiliency for older women is a dynamic process that is put in motion by personal or occupational stressors.

Stressors or Challenges

Occupational stressors reported by working women are varied and far reaching, including, but not limited to, work–family conflict, workplace bullying, interpersonal conflict, work overload, repetitive tasks, emotional labor, and exposures to hazardous chemicals, such as disinfectants, hair dyes, and textile dust (Bhave & Glomb, 2016; Eng et al., 2011; Lutgen-Sandvik et al., 2007; Scott et al., 2015). Unfortunately, these workplace stressors often co-occur with gender-based stressors such as having to prove competency

FIGURE 1.1. Proposed Model for Resiliency in Later-Life Female Workforce

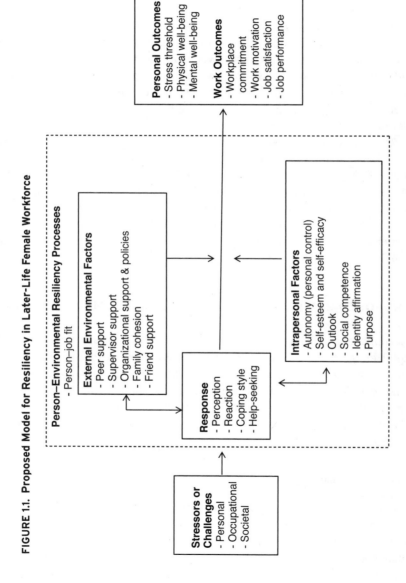

and commitment, competition with other women for limited opportunities, overcoming gender and racial stereotypes, and, for women with one or more minority statuses, isolation due to differences (Fidas et al., 2015; Williams et al., 2016). Moreover, as workers age, these existing occupational stressors often combine with ageist perceptions such as education obsolescence and reduced cognitive and occupational capacity, which results in fewer opportunities for continued training and development (Hansson et al., 2001). Beyond these occupational stressors, older women may face a number of personal life stressors brought on by declines in either their own or their loved ones' health, physical, and/or sensory functioning, which may lead to job change, informal caregiving, or financial stress (Aldwin, 1990). Yet despite these complex stressors and challenges, older women workers cope effectively in the workplace with little or no reduction in productivity and less reported stress than do their younger counterparts (Hansson et al., 2001). In fact, resiliency research demonstrates that these stressors and challenges are instrumental to the growth process, without which adaptation and strengthening would not be possible (Kumpfer, 1999).

Personal-Environmental Resiliency Process

The complex process by which resiliency is built and then maintained in the late-life female workforce relies not only on isolated individual and environmental factors but also in the interactional process between these factors.

To illustrate this dynamic process, let us take a close look at nurses, the largest occupational group in the health care workforce (Cope et al., 2016), which is dominated by women and considered to be at the highest risk for job stress, burnout, and turnover (Gascon et al., 2013). The workplace adversity faced by nurses, including everything from leadership instability with hospital mergers to workplace violence and coping with difficult emotions when a patient dies, is well-documented (Hsieh et al., 2016; Payne, 2001; Russo et al., 2018). However, resiliency factors that improve coping are also well-documented among this group. Specifically, research has identified that environmental factors (i.e., suppression of competing activities, instrumental and emotional social support from peers, physicians, family, and friends) and personal factors (i.e., occupational satisfaction, pride, high self-efficacy, positivity, altruism, humor, acceptance, reflection, and awareness of impact; Cope et al., 2016; Draper-Lowe, 2016; Gabriel et al., 2011; Guo et al., 2017; Hsieh et al., 2016; McDermid et al., 2016; Russo et al., 2018) appear to combine in various ways to result in resiliency. For example, resilient nurses with high levels of extraversion and self-efficacy are more likely to treat difficulties as opportunities for growth by utilizing positive coping styles, peer support, and healthy lifestyle strategies, such as exercising and not smoking (Guo et al., 2017; Hsieh et al., 2016). This then results in better patient care, career longevity, and higher well-being, which in turn results in increased personal resiliency factors such as occupational satisfaction (Draper-Lowe, 2016; Gabriel et al., 2011) and, therefore, reinforces this resiliency cycle.

Impressively, this dialectical cycle appears to be strengthened with continued productive reactions to stressors and age. In fact, one study of older, senior female nurses and midwives found that those with a longer work history were able to utilize collegial support, self-care, self-motivation, positive self-talk, autonomy, and enjoyment at work to reduce the impact of workplace adversity and thrive in the workplace (Mcdonald et al., 2016). These senior nurses are not alone. Among diverse groups of women workers, factors such as social and organizational support along with autonomy have been shown to increase resilience to workplace bullying resulting in increased workplace commitment, higher well-being, and lower levels of depressive symptoms (Cooper-Thomas et al., 2013; Gattis, 2017; Maidaniuc-Chirilă, 2015; van Heugten, 2013). Women who experience minority stressors and marginalization on top of challenging occupational factors appear to thrive in the workplace utilizing a similar resiliency cycle, albeit with their own unique challenges and stressors. Specifically, despite the sexual and gender minority stress and marginalization both within and outside of the lesbian, gay, bisexual, and transgender community, older adults in that community show extraordinary resilience in coping with challenges in physical health and mental health through a strong social network, identity affirmation, and positive workplace climate (Bilimoria & Stewart, 2009; Fredriksen-Goldsen et al., 2013, 2017; Van Wagenen et al., 2013). In fact, in line with the proposed model, identity affirmation and social resources appear to combine to promote mental health, which in turn leads to increased health-promoting behaviors and reduced health risk behaviors, which in turn improves physical health, resulting in a buffer against marginalization (Fredriksen-Goldsen et al., 2017).

The same dynamic interplay of personal and environmental resiliency factors (i.e., social skills, motivation, confidence, tolerance of risk, positive thinking, self-initiated mentoring) has also been identified in older women with multiple minority statuses (i.e., Indonesian Muslim entrepreneurial women and older African American women) as increasing occupational success despite discrimination, business failures, limited capital, and social and cultural barriers (Ayalon & Gum, 2011; Loh & Dahesihsari, 2013; Lugo & Shelton, 2017). In fact, despite older African American women reporting the greatest number of discrimination events, they have the lowest rate of associated negative mental health outcomes and, among entrepreneurs, the highest levels of resiliency (Ayalon & Gum, 2011; Lugo & Shelton, 2017). These personal factors are likely enhanced in part by social support as evidenced by findings that resilient African American women entrepreneurs have more social resources than does any other group (Lugo & Shelton, 2017); likewise, resiliency accounted for 15% of the willingness to seek mental health care in older African Americans (Smith, 2009). In summary, there appears to be ample support for a resiliency cycle that strengthens with the continued challenges and stressors faced by aging diverse women in the workforce.

IMPLICATIONS AND APPLICATIONS

To help optimize flourishing in this late-life female workforce, the following section provides key takeaways and applications for women, professionals, and organizations.

Tools for Older Women Workers, Researchers, and Clinicians: What Works

In light of the large number of intrapersonal factors inherent in the resiliency model, it stands to reason that older women who are struggling in the workforce may benefit from resiliency training. Resiliency training has been found to enhance employees' mental health, ability to cope with stress, and subjective well-being as well as improve psychosocial functioning and workplace performance (Leppin et al., 2014; Robertson et al., 2015). Despite the consensus that resiliency is a dynamic trainable process, methodological limitations and design variations prevent tangible recommendations about specific interventions (Chmitorz et al., 2018). Thus, in lieu of direct intervention recommendations, we encourage working older women to "lift the mask" of invincibility and leverage their social support networks to optimize resiliency when they find themselves facing life and occupational stressors by seeking help from their peers, families, supervisors, and trained mental health professionals. Furthermore, we recommend clinicians treating older women to integrate increased awareness of occupational stressors and resiliency into assessment and treatment, either informally or formally with measures such as the Workplace Resiliency Inventory (McLarnon & Rothstein, 2013) or the Resilience at Work Scale (Winwood et al., 2013). Finally, we echo the call of Chmitorz and colleagues (2018) to improve the quality and quantity of resilience intervention research to guide clinicians and improve the quality of care for older women workers.

Tools for Organizational Resiliency: Fostering Growth and Diversity

From an organizational perspective, the workplace continues to be a complex and unbalanced environment for women and minorities despite considerable efforts to foster inclusiveness and diversify the workforce. As such, Table 1.1 provides recommendations for organizations interested in increased resiliency among employees through fostering diversity. These recommendations are in line with research showing that organizational climate factors (e.g., womanist attitudes, person–organization fit, organizational support, self-esteem) can mediate the impact of discrimination and reduce burnout,

TABLE 1.1. Fostering Diversity: Organizational Opportunities

Opportunity	Rationale	Advantage
Educate leadership	Organizations must empower human resource departments to recognize all forms of bias (Burrell, 2016).	Educated leadership fosters trust and a culture that supports the growth, safety, and inclusiveness of all employees.
Change diversity communication	Diverse groups place distinct values on the importance of individual differences and equality (Apfelbaum, 2016).	Addressing employees' values in organizational communication fosters a supportive environment and perceived organization fit. Inclusive language encourages a more inclusive environment and reduces feelings of alienation.
Implement innovative diversity strategies	Common approaches to fostering diversity are ineffective (Dobbin & Kalev, 2016).	Recruiting programs, diversity task forces, and mentoring programs have been proven to more effectively engage employees and integrate the workforce.
Increase leadership access opportunities	Individuals with minority status do not often occupy leadership positions (Marshall & Wingfield, 2016).	Equal access to leadership will allow for increased participation in merit-based evaluations and networking opportunities.
Offer training and incentives to support work-life balance	Women in environments supportive of work–family balance have more favorable work outcomes (Clark et al., 2017).	Working women with supportive supervisors report lower levels of work-family spillover and intent to quit as well as higher job satisfaction.

turnover intentions, depression, and anxiety (Velez et al., 2018). By establishing and retaining a more diverse workforce, it is our hope that more organizations and workers will experience the well-documented benefits (Harvard Business Review, 2016).

CONCLUSION

In summation, as women in the workforce age, intersections of identity coalesce with environmental factors to create unique experiences, not all of which are positive. Women who have prior experience with discrimination, isolation, or microaggressions—whether at work or in other settings—often have previously mastered the intrapersonal factors needed to meet these challenges through prior resiliency processes. As a result, ingrained pathways can be activated to meet these challenges and facilitate future flourishing, particularly when buffered by external workforce factors. We thus hope that the proposed model and recommendations will inform managers, clinicians, human resources professionals, and others who are in a position to help women activate these resiliency pathways, ultimately improving the lives of older working women and promoting thriving organizations.

REFERENCES

Aldwin, C. M. (1990). The Elders Life Stress Inventory (ELSI): Research and clinical applications. In M. A. Stephens, J. H. Crowther, S. E. Hobfoll, & D. L. Tennenbaum (Eds.), *Stress and coping in later-life families* (pp. 49–69). Hemisphere Publishing.

Aldwin, C. M., & Gilmer, D. F. (2004). *Health, illness, and optimal aging: Biological and psychosocial perspectives*. Sage.

American Association of University Women. (2018). *Barriers and bias: The status of women in leadership*. https://www.aauw.org/resources/research/barrier-bias

American Psychological Association Committee on Aging. (2009). *Multicultural competency in geropsychology*. https://www.apa.org/pi/aging/programs/pipeline/multicultural-competency.pdf

Angelou, M. (2011, July 5). *My mission in life is not merely to survive, but to thrive; and to do so with some passion, some compassion, some humor, and some style* [Status update]. Facebook. https://m.facebook.com/MayaAngelou/posts/10150251846629796

Apfelbaum, E. (2016, August 8). Why your diversity program may be helping women but not minorities (or vice versa). *Harvard Business Review*. https://hbr.org/2016/08/why-your-diversity-program-may-be-helping-women-but-not-minorities-or-vice-versa

Ayalon, L., & Gum, A. M. (2011). The relationships between major lifetime discrimination, everyday discrimination, and mental health in three racial and ethnic groups of older adults. *Aging & Mental Health*, *15*(5), 587–594. https://doi.org/10.1080/13607863.2010.543664

Ayalon, L., & Tesch-Römer, C. (2017). Taking a closer look at ageism: Self and other-directed ageist attitudes and discrimination. *European Journal of Ageing, 14*, 1–4. https://doi.org/10.1007/s10433-016-0409-9

Bhave, D. P., & Glomb, T. M. (2016). The role of occupational emotional labor requirements on the surface acting–job satisfaction relationship. *Journal of Management, 42*(3), 722–741. https://doi.org/10.1177/0149206313498900

Bilimoria, D., & Stewart, A. (2009). "Don't ask, don't tell": The academic climate for lesbian, gay, bisexual, and transgender faculty in science and engineering. *NWSA Journal, 21*(2), 85–103. http://www.jstor.org/stable/20628175

Bodner, E., & Cohen-Fridel, S. (2010). Relations between attachment styles, ageism and quality of life in late life. *International Psychogeriatrics, 22*(8), 1353–1361. https://doi.org/10.1017/S1041610210001249

Burrell, L. (2016, July–August). We just can't handle diversity. *Harvard Business Review*, 70–74. https://hbr.org/2016/07/we-just-cant-handle-diversity

Chmitorz, A., Kunzler, A., Helmreich, I., Tüscher, O., Kalisch, R., Kubiak, T., Wessa, M., Lieb, K. (2018). Intervention studies to foster resilience—A systematic review and proposal for a resilience framework in future intervention studies. *Clinical Psychology Review, 59*, 78–100.

Chow, S. M., Hamagani, F., & Nesselroade, J. R. (2007). Age differences in dynamical emotion–cognition linkages. *Psychology and Aging, 22*(4), 765–780. https://doi.org/10.1037/0882-7974.22.4.765

Clark, M. A., Rudolph, C. W., Zhdanova, L., Michel, J. S., & Baltes, B. B. (2017). Organizational support factors and work-family outcomes: Exploring gender differences. *Journal of Family Issues, 38*(11), 1520–1545. https://doi.org/10.1177/0192513X15585809

Cooper-Thomas, H., Gardner, D., O'Driscoll, M., Catley, B., Bentley, T., & Trenberth, L. (2013). Neutralizing workplace bullying: The buffering effects of contextual factors. *Journal of Managerial Psychology, 28*(4), 384–407. https://doi.org/10.1108/JMP-12-2012-0399

Cope, V., Jones, B., & Hendricks, J. (2016). Why nurses chose to remain in the workforce: Portraits of resilience. *Collegian, 23*(1), 87–95. https://doi.org/10.1016/j.colegn.2014.12.001

Dobbin, F., & Kalev, A. (2016, July–August). Why diversity programs fail. *Harvard Business Review*, 52–60. https://hbr.org/2016/07/why-diversity-programs-fail

Draper-Lowe, L. (2016). *Exploring the lived experience and meaning of resilience for nurses: A descriptive phenomenological inquiry* [Doctoral dissertation, University of Northern Colorado]. Scholarship & Creative Works @ Digital UNC. https://digscholarship.unco.edu/dissertations/353

Duncan, C., & Loretto, W. (2004). Never the right age? Gender and age-based discrimination in employment. *Gender, Work and Organization, 11*(1), 95–115. https://doi.org/10.1111/j.1468-0432.2004.00222.x

Eng, A., Mannetje, A. T., McLean, D., Ellison-Loschmann, L., Cheng, S., & Pearce, N. (2011). Gender differences in occupational exposure patterns. *Occupational and Environmental Medicine, 68*(12), 888–894. https://doi.org/10.1136/oem.2010.064097

Fidas, D., Cooper, L., & Raspanti, J. (2015). *The cost of the closet and the rewards of inclusion: Why the workplace environment for LGBT people matters to employees.* Human Rights Campaign. https://assets2.hrc.org/files/assets/resources/Cost_

of_the_Closet_May2014.pdf?_ga=2.43807717.1190904875.1535993655-116271374.1535993655

Fraser, G., Osborne, D., & Sibley, C. G. (2015). "We want you in the workplace, but only in a skirt!" Social dominance orientation, gender-based affirmative action and the moderating role of benevolent sexism. *Sex Roles*, *73*, 231–244. https://doi.org/10.1007/s11199-015-0515-8

Fredriksen-Goldsen, K. I., Emlet, C. A., Kim, H. J., Muraco, A., Erosheva, E. A., Goldsen, J., & Hoy-Ellis, C. P. (2013). The physical and mental health of lesbian, gay male, and bisexual (LGB) older adults: The role of key health indicators and risk and protective factors. *The Gerontologist*, *53*(4), 664–675. https://doi.org/10.1093/geront/gns123

Fredriksen-Goldsen, K. I., Kim, H. J., Bryan, A. E., Shiu, C., & Emlet, C. A. (2017). The cascading effects of marginalization and pathways of resilience in attaining good health among LGBT older adults. *The Gerontologist*, *57*(Suppl. 1), S72–S83. https://doi.org/10.1093/geront/gnw170

French, M. T. (2002). Physical appearance and earnings: Further evidence. *Applied Economics*, *34*(5), 569–572. https://doi.org/10.1080/00036840010027568

Gabriel, A. S., Diefendorff, J. M., & Erickson, R. J. (2011). The relations of daily task accomplishment satisfaction with changes in affect: A multilevel study in nurses. *Journal of Applied Psychology*, *96*(5), 1095–1104. https://doi.org/10.1037/a0023937

Gascon, S., Leiter, M. P., Andrés, E., Santed, M. A., Pereira, J. P., Cunha, M. J., Albesa, A., Montero-Marín, J., García-Campayo, J., & Martínez-Jarreta, B. (2013). The role of aggressions suffered by healthcare workers as predictors of burnout. *Journal of Clinical Nursing*, *22*(21–22), 3120–3129. https://doi.org/10.1111/j.1365-2702.2012.04255.x

Gattis, V. M. (2017). *A case study of workplace bullying, resilience, and professional women* [Unpublished doctoral dissertation]. Grand Canyon University.

George, L. K., & Clipp, E. C. (1991). Subjective components of aging well. *Generations: Journal of the American Society on Aging*, *15*(1), 57–60.

Gleason, H. P., & Butler, R. N. (1985). *Productive aging: Enhancing vitality in later life*. Springer Publishing.

Gramlich, J. (2017, December 28). *10 things we learned about gender issues in the U.S. in 2017*. Pew Research Center. http://pewrsr.ch/2BMUUyF

Granleese, J., & Sayer, G. (2006). Gendered ageism and "lookism": A triple jeopardy for academics. *Women in Management Review*, *21*(6), 500–517. https://doi.org/10.1108/09649420610683480

Guo, Y. F., Cross, W., Plummer, V., Lam, L., Luo, Y. H., & Zhang, J. P. (2017). Exploring resilience in Chinese nurses: A cross-sectional study. *Journal of Nursing Management*, *25*(3), 223–230. https://doi.org/10.1111/jonm.12457

Guralnik, J. M., & Kaplan, G. A. (1989). Predictors of healthy aging: Prospective evidence from the Alameda County study. *American Journal of Public Health*, *79*(6), 703–708. https://doi.org/10.2105/AJPH.79.6.703

Hansson, R. O., Robson, S. M., & Limas, M. J. (2001). Stress and coping among older workers. *Work (Reading, Mass.)*, *17*(3), 247–256.

Harris, P. B. (2008). Another wrinkle in the debate about successful aging: The under-valued concept of resilience and the lived experience of dementia. *International Journal of Aging & Human Development*, *67*(1), 43–61. https://doi.org/10.2190/AG.67.1.c

Harvard Business Review. (2016). *The latest research: Diversity.* https://hbr.org/product/the-latest-research-diversity/DIVRES-PDF-ENG

Hsieh, H. F., Hung, Y. T., Wang, H. H., Ma, S. C., & Chang, S. C. (2016). Factors of resilience in emergency department nurses who have experienced workplace violence in Taiwan. *Journal of Nursing Scholarship, 48*(1), 23–30. https://doi.org/10.1111/jnu.12177

Jones, K. P., Sabat, I. E., King, E. B., Ahmad, A., Mccausland, T. C., & Chen, T. (2017). Isms and schisms: A meta-analysis of the prejudice-discrimination relationship across racism, sexism, and ageism. *Journal of Organizational Behavior, 38*(7), 1076–1110. https://doi.org/10.1002/job.2187

Karoly, P., & Ruehlman, L. S. (2006). Psychological "resilience" and its correlates in chronic pain: Findings from a national community sample. *Pain, 123*(1–2), 90–97. https://doi.org/10.1016/j.pain.2006.02.014

King, G. A., & Rothstein, M. G. (2010). Resilience and leadership: The self-management of failure. In M. G. Rothstein & R. J. Burke (Eds.), *Self-management and leadership development* (pp. 361–394). Edward Elgar Publishing. https://doi.org/10.4337/9781849805551.00021

Kooij, D. T. A. M. (2015a). Clarifying and discussing successful aging at work and the active role of employees. *Work, Aging and Retirement, 1*(4), 334–339. https://doi.org/10.1093/workar/wav024

Kooij, D. T. A. M. (2015b). Successful aging at work: The active role of employees. *Work, Aging and Retirement, 1*(4), 309–319. https://doi.org/10.1093/workar/wav018

Kumpfer, K. L. (1999). Factors and processes contributing to resilience: The resilience framework. In M. D. Glantz & J. L. Johnson (Eds.), *Resilience and development: Positive life adaptations* (pp. 179–224). Kluwer Academic Publishers.

Leppin, A. L., Bora, P. R., Tilburt, J. C., Gionfriddo, M. R., Zeballos-Palacios, C., Dulohery, M. M., Sood, A., Erwin, P. J., Brito, J. P., Boehmer, K. R., & Montori, V. M. (2014). The efficacy of resiliency training programs: A systematic review and meta-analysis of randomized trials. *PLOS ONE, 9*(10), e111420. https://doi.org/10.1371/journal.pone.0111420

Loh, J. M., & Dahesihsari, R. (2013). Resilience and economic empowerment: A qualitative investigation of entrepreneurial Indonesian women. *Journal of Enterprising Culture, 21*(1), 107–121. https://doi.org/10.1142/S0218495813500052

Lugo, M. V., & Shelton, L. (2017). The interface of ethnicity and gender in the resilience of minority and women entrepreneurs. *Academy of Management Proceedings, 2017*(1). https://doi.org/10.5465/AMBPP.2017.280

Lutgen-Sandvik, P., Tracy, S. J., & Alberts, J. K. (2007). Burned by bullying in the American workplace: Prevalence, perception, degree and impact. *Journal of Management Studies, 44*(6), 837–862. https://doi.org/10.1111/j.1467-6486.2007.00715.x

Luthar, S. S., Cicchetti, D., & Becker, B. (2000). The construct of resilience: A critical evaluation and guidelines for future work. *Child Development, 71*(3), 543–562. https://doi.org/10.1111/1467-8624.00164

Maidaniuc-Chirilă, T. (2015). A multi-mediation model of the relationship between workplace bullying, psychological resilience, coping strategies and employee's strain: Insights for a training program's efficiency. *Romanian Journal of Human Resources Psychology, 13*, 63–82.

Marshall, M., & Wingfield, T. (2016, July 1). Getting more Black women into the C-suite. *Harvard Business Review.* https://hbr.org/2016/07/getting-more-black-women-into-the-c-suite

McDermid, F., Peters, K., Daly, J., & Jackson, D. (2016). Developing resilience: Stories from novice nurse academics. *Nurse Education Today, 38,* 29–35. https://doi.org/10.1016/j.nedt.2016.01.002

Mcdonald, G., Jackson, D., Vickers, M. H., & Wilkes, L. (2016). Surviving workplace adversity: A qualitative study of nurses and midwives and their strategies to increase personal resilience. *Journal of Nursing Management, 24*(1), 123–131. https://doi.org/10.1111/jonm.12293

McLarnon, M. J., & Rothstein, M. G. (2013). Development and initial validation of the Workplace Resilience Inventory. *Journal of Personnel Psychology, 12,* 63–73. https://doi.org/10.1027/1866-5888/a000084

Nelson-Becker, H. B. (2006). Voices of resilience: Older adults in hospice care. *Journal of Social Work in End-of-Life & Palliative Care, 2*(3), 87–106. https://doi.org/10.1300/J457v02n03_07

Ong, A. D., Bergeman, C. S., Bisconti, T. L., & Wallace, K. A. (2006). Psychological resilience, positive emotions, and successful adaptation to stress in later life. *Journal of Personality and Social Psychology, 91*(4), 730–749. https://doi.org/10.1037/0022-3514.91.4.730

Ott, C. H., Lueger, R. J., Kelber, S. T., & Prigerson, H. G. (2007). Spousal bereavement in older adults: Common, resilient, and chronic grief with defining characteristics. *Journal of Nervous and Mental Disease, 195*(4), 332–341. https://doi.org/10.1097/01.nmd.0000243890.93992.1e

Pascoe, E. A., & Richman, L. S. (2009). Perceived discrimination and health: A meta-analytic review. *Psychological Bulletin, 135*(4), 531–554. https://doi.org/10.1037/a0016059

Payne, N. (2001). Occupational stressors and coping as determinants of burnout in female hospice nurses. *Journal of Advanced Nursing, 33*(3), 396–405. https://doi.org/10.1046/j.1365-2648.2001.01677.x

Robertson, I. T., Cooper, C. L., Sarkar, M., & Curran, T. (2015). Resilience training in the workplace from 2003 to 2014: A systematic review. *Journal of Occupational and Organizational Psychology, 88*(3), 533–562. https://doi.org/10.1111/joop.12120

Rossi, N. E., Bisconti, T. L., & Bergeman, C. S. (2007). The role of dispositional resilience in regaining life satisfaction after the loss of a spouse. *Death Studies, 31*(10), 863–883. https://doi.org/10.1080/07481180701603246

Rowe, J. W., & Kahn, R. L. (1987). Human aging: Usual and successful. *Science, 237*(4811), 143–149. https://doi.org/10.1126/science.3299702

Russo, C., Calo, O., Harrison, G., Mahoney, K., & Zavotsky, K. E. (2018). Resilience and coping after hospital mergers. *Clinical Nurse Specialist, 32*(2), 97–102. https://doi.org/10.1097/NUR.0000000000000358

Scott, K. L., Ingram, A., Zagenczyk, T. J., & Shoss, M. K. (2015). Work–family conflict and social undermining behaviour: An examination of PO fit and gender differences. *Journal of Occupational and Organizational Psychology, 88*(1), 203–218. https://doi.org/10.1111/joop.12091

Sims, C. H. (2017). Genderized workplace lookism in the U.S. and abroad: Implications for organization and career development professionals. In *Discrimination* and diversity: Concepts, methodologies, tools, and applications (pp. 61–85). IGI Global. https://doi.org/10.4018/978-1-5225-1933-1.ch005

Smith, P. R. (2009). Resilience: Resistance factor for depressive symptom. *Journal of Psychiatric and Mental Health Nursing, 16*(9), 829–837. https://doi.org/10.1111/j.1365-2850.2009.01463.x

U.S. Bureau of Labor Statistics. (2017, November). *Women in the labor force: A databook.* https://www.bls.gov/opub/reports/womens-databook/2017/home.htm

van Heugten, K. (2013). Resilience as an underexplored outcome of workplace bullying. *Qualitative Health Research, 23*(3), 291–301. https://doi.org/10.1177/1049732312468251

Van Wagenen, A., Driskell, J., & Bradford, J. (2013). "I'm still raring to go": Successful aging among lesbian, gay, bisexual, and transgender older adults. *Journal of Aging Studies, 27*(1), 1–14. https://doi.org/10.1016/j.jaging.2012.09.001

Velez, B. L., Cox, R., Jr., Polihronakis, C. J., & Moradi, B. (2018). Discrimination, work outcomes, and mental health among women of color: The protective role of womanist attitudes. *Journal of Counseling Psychology, 65*(2), 178–193. https://doi.org/10.1037/cou0000274

Wells, M. (2012). Resilience in older adults living in rural, suburban, and urban areas. *Online Journal of Rural Nursing and Health Care, 10*(2), 45–54.

Williams, J. C., Phillips, K. W., & Hall, E. V. (2016). Tools for change: Boosting the retention of women in the STEM pipeline. *Journal of Research in Gender Studies, 6*(1), 11–75. https://doi.org/10.22381/JRGS6120161

Winwood, P. C., Colon, R., & McEwen, K. (2013). A practical measure of workplace resilience: Developing the resilience at work scale. *Journal of Occupational and Environmental Medicine, 55*(10), 1205–1212. https://doi.org/10.1097/JOM.0b013e3182a2a60a

Zacher, H. (2015). Successful aging at work. *Work, Aging and Retirement, 1*(1), 4–25. https://doi.org/10.1093/workar/wau006

Zarya, V. (2018, May 21). The share of female CEOs in the Fortune 500 dropped by 25% in 2018. *Fortune.* http://fortune.com/2018/05/21/women-fortune-500-2018

2 THE AGING WOMAN WORKER IN A LIFESPAN DEVELOPMENTAL CONTEXT

VALORY MITCHELL

In the long run, we shape our lives and we shape ourselves. The process never ends until we die. And the choices we make are ultimately our own responsibility.

—Eleanor Roosevelt

Eleanor Roosevelt, who worked far into her 70s, laid the groundwork for lifespan development in her quotation above. The premise of this chapter is that lifespan developmental theories, concepts, and findings provide structure, language, and information that can help us grasp the meaning of work for women in late adulthood.

Having access to lifespan theories may be especially valuable in late adulthood because the culture provides next to nothing in guidance or expectations for what women of this age "should" do. Instead, it presents contradictory images: Is this going to be "the Third Age, the Crown of Life" (James & Wink, 2006), or is it a meandering slough without a sense of direction? No longer middle-aged, but also not the oldest of the old, women between 65 and 80-plus are in largely uncharted territory.

https://doi.org/10.1037/0000212-003
Older Women Who Work: Resilience, Choice, and Change, E. Cole and L. Hollis-Sawyer (Editors)

Why is this? The 20th century brought a spectacular increase in the number of disability-free years that people live. A hundred years ago, women in the United States were expected to live, on average, to age 52; today they are expected to live, on average, to 82 (Henry J. Kaiser Family Foundation, n.d.). In the 1930s, enshrined and institutionalized by Social Security, age 65 became the normative retirement age. But retirement, the only cultural milestone designated for this period of life, had very different meanings back then, when most people did not live to 65 and when those who did were truly elderly and near death. Perhaps our society has not had time to catch up and consider what this new gift of time between 65 and 80-plus can or should be about. Alternatively, we live in an ageist culture, where *old* is synonymous with *unimportant*. Perhaps the period over 65 has been left unmapped because it has been cast as trivial, not worth considering.

In 2015, more than one third of women aged 65 to 69 were working full-time, and nearly one fourth of women aged 70 to 74 were doing so. This is a 25% to 50% increase, occurring mainly since 2000—and it is an increase in full-time, year-round work (Goldin & Katz, 2018). The women who continue to work differ from previous generations of women: They have more education, more continuity in their careers, and greater enjoyment of their job. These women also differ among themselves on most dimensions of intersecting identity (e.g., race, religion, geography, ethnicity, sexual orientation, ability/disability). Importantly, the increase in older working women is not found among women who work because they need to earn a living; the same percentage of working-class women remain in the workforce today as they did 40 years ago. Rather, the increase is found among women who enjoy their work; who gain challenge as well as status, flexibility as well as structure; and who often are self-employed.

WHITE PRIVILEGE, SEXISM, AND DEVELOPMENTAL THEORIES: A CAVEAT

Just like all of us, developmental theories, too, are products of their time and place and of the intersecting identities of their authors. That is to say that they have been created, largely, by affluent middle-aged White men living in the 20th century. As such, they are vulnerable to the ageism, sexism, classism, racism, and general egocentrism of White privilege that has plagued many endeavors, including psychological theorizing and academic research. Most theory has little to say about lives in which developmental opportunities are squelched by financial constraints or class limitations. Presumptions about the meaning and functioning of family, based on unacknowledged

White cultural premises, overlook the sense of extended identity that shapes life decisions for many members of non-White cultural groups.

In addition, until very recently, no theorists had lived into old age, so their views of it were likely distorted by stereotypes, fears, and ignorance; the Eriksons, writing when in their 90s, said this had been true of them in younger years (Erikson & Erikson, 1997).

Less than 90 years ago, Freud (1931/1973) theorized that women experience a creeping psychological rigidity at about age 30 that foretold a limitation of their scope as persons! Perhaps as a result, much developmental theory and longitudinal research have not included women (Borrero & Kruger, 2015). In recent decades, outstanding women researchers have produced critiques, knowledge about women's lives, and new concepts and theory. Ravenna Helson and Valory Mitchell (in press), Abigail Stewart (Stewart et al., 2001), and Ruthellen Josselson (2017) have all published longitudinal studies of adult women; following the same women over time allows us to see their growth. Carol Franz and Kathleen White (1985) and Sheila Greene (2014) offered critiques that altered our ways of looking at dimensions of development. Jane Loevinger (1976) and Carol Gilligan (1982) provided new theory. New concepts have been studied and their relevance established by Carol Ryff (2008) in positive psychology, Gisela Labouvie-Vief (Labouvie-Vief & Medler, 2002) in emotions, and Laura Carstensen (2006) in aging.

Today, developmental theory, constructs, and research have much to offer us women. Lifespan developmental theories state, as their premise, that there is potential for development—that is, growth—at every phase of life. Each phase is a distinct and valuable part of the life journey. Lifespan theories outline trajectories of development and describe their course; they identify key issues or normative crises that most people encounter at particular zones of the lifespan. They name and describe the strengths and skills we gain as we age. Perhaps, unbeknownst to us, developmental pressures and perspectives have already informed our choices. From a lifespan perspective, this chapter examines the psychological meaning and purpose of women's work after 65, in relation to the developmental tasks and opportunities that are in the spotlight during this phase of life.

THE ERIKSONS' EIGHT STAGES OF LIFE

Perhaps the best-known lifespan theory, authored by Erik Erikson and his wife, Joan, holds that eight (or nine) issues enter the psychological spotlight as we traverse our lives. Each is always present, but theory holds that they move to center stage one at a time, in a set sequence. In childhood, for example, we grapple with trust versus mistrust, autonomy versus shame and doubt, initiative versus guilt, and industry versus inferiority. In adolescence and early adulthood we are occupied with establishing an identity, our sense of who we are and where we fit in the adult world. Next, we strive for intimacy versus isolation, hoping to make close connections in a couple and/ or friendship network and community. Three additional issues (generativity, integrity, and gerotranscendence), engaged in middle and late adulthood, complete our trajectory of psychological development as seen by the Eriksons' theory.

DEVELOPMENTAL SHIFTS ACROSS OUR GENERATIVE YEARS

The issue that follows intimacy will remain in focus for most of our adulthood: generativity versus stagnation. Generativity is about care—caring about, taking care of, caring for, leaving a legacy of contribution. Most of us manifest our generativity by caring for our children and helping our community and society through our work, although these are not the only ways generativity becomes apparent. A substantial minority of women do not have children, and some do not have careers—and these women express their generativity in an array of other ways. We may also take care to maintain and preserve what is valued; we may create new and useful, interesting, or beautiful things, ideas, or experiences that add to what has existed before; we may nurture the young (young people, young plants and animals, young products, young aspirations) and help them to grow until they can stand on their own. Generativity directs our attention outward, toward others and society, and is the focus of development for several decades.

Much takes place during those decades to transform the way we see ourselves and our work. During the second half of adulthood, we start developing a different set of values, strategies, and concerns. Jungian theory (Jung, 1969) suggests that the purpose of life shifts from the achievement of societal (collective) goals to a striving for personal wholeness through the cultivation of qualities that were neglected in young adulthood. In midlife, traditionally masculine and feminine traits and concerns are now equally present in, and important to, women (Harker & Solomon, 1996). Our goals and values are less constrained, contain more agentic elements, and are more individual. In mature middle age, we are adding self-care and self-interest to the more collective values of family and work that we had emphasized in younger years.

As we get older, women develop new strategies for managing their emotional lives, such as *affect optimization* (Labouvie-Vief & Medler, 2002), in which they become able to focus on positive emotion and decrease their focus on the negative, and *selective optimization* (Baltes & Baltes, 1990), in which they select areas that are especially important to them and optimize them by engaging in behavior that cultivates continued growth. A third midlife accomplishment is the integration of our ideals with what is possible and realistic. We all have *possible selves* (Ryff, 2008), which are images we hold of ourselves, blueprints for development. Middle age seems to be an optimal time for reining in possible selves so they are more realistic compared with the loftier, perhaps unattainable possible selves of youth. Having selected a realistic possible self, we feel there is time in middle age to improve and move toward that self.

Ascendant Phase

Most of us launch our family and work projects, our generativity, in early adulthood. We start families. We seek education and training, become interns and apprentices, acquire entry-level positions. This ascendant phase is all about expansion, upward mobility, and commitment to multiple roles and social schedules as children are growing and careers building. In early adulthood, women are keenly aware of the timing norms of our culture and moment in history, and we monitor ourselves in relation to them: Are we on time with our projects? Did we begin our family too early? Choose a career too late so that we need to catch up? (Helson et al., 1984).

Maintenance Phase

As we move toward the middle of middle age, we are likely to have reached the peak of our powers in areas such as status, skill, and responsibilities. We move from an ascending expansion phase to one in which we are maintaining our high productivity and its rewards. Research on women's personality change (Helson et al., 2006) has shown that between ages 21 and 52, women have become increasingly confident, competent, and decisive. We have experience and are more able now to be selective and self-aware and to have strategies for regulating our emotions and working with our environments. Certainty about our identity increases steadily across the decades of middle age, as do confident power and motivation to make a lasting contribution to society and the next generation (Stewart et al., 2001).

From a generative perspective, this means that our work can make a more effective, vivid, enduring, or powerful contribution to that which we care about and care for in our work life—a sort of pinnacle of generative usefulness. We have already proved our ability, and this creates an opening for new ways of being in relationship with others in our field and even in relationship to the field itself. A woman experiencing mature generativity may come to recognize the human landscape of the work-world as a place to increasingly bring her care, using her power and knowledge to further the people and endeavors she cares about.

But other change is also afoot. We are able to see where we have been but are now newly aware of the path ahead. This may bring a sense of urgency about realizing hopes and ambitions. As our time perspective begins to change and life is structured less in terms of time since birth and more in terms of time left to live, we may find ourselves with greater reflectiveness and empathy and perhaps with a desire to revise our life narrative. Women's views of the future as a time of opportunities do not change between ages 40 and 60 (Cate & John, 2007). However, awareness of aging, low but steadily increasing between the late 20s and the early 50s, increases sharply by age 60. Accompanying that awareness comes a reorganization of values, as women emphasize "time left" more than long-range goals (Stewart et al., 2001). This complex outlook, looking ahead to a future of opportunities but with an increasingly visible end point, brings depth to our perspective on work.

Acceptant Phase

Toward the end of middle age, our phase of maintenance begins to blend with an acceptant phase. Here, a woman begins relaxing the effort to achieve future goals and higher status, becoming content with the present or beginning to lessen commitment to the public sphere and increase attention to private pursuits. The 50s have been characterized as a "decade of reminders" (Karp, 1988), when we are repeatedly shown that we are aging—we are in the middle between our aging parents and our adult children, and some of us become grandparents. We deal with body changes, recognize that we are the oldest cohort in our workplace, and experience deaths and illnesses of friends and family. Whereas the emphasis in early adulthood had been on the time-normed social-clock projects of family and work, these timing norms fall away and the emphasis in later middle age is on facilitation of others and the responsible use of power. These marked changes in personality and priorities are often accompanied by a loss of social centrality.

THREE LIFESPAN DEVELOPMENTAL THEORIES

Overlaid on these changes are the progressions outlined by three theories: Loevinger's theory of the development of the ego, Gilligan's theory of the development of care, and Levinson's theory of the life structure.

Loevinger's Theory of Ego Development

When Loevinger said that the ego develops, she was saying that there are systemic changes in style of life, method of acting on problems, opinions about self and others, character, cognitive style, interpersonal relations, impulse control, conscious preoccupations, and moral judgment. All these are affected because the ego is the synthetic function. Ego development is the development of the self.

Ego development is not linked to any particular age, and some women may not develop very far. On the basis of thousands of tests, Loevinger (1976) concluded that the average adult in the United States has reached the self-aware level, just past the conformist stage, the second of six stages. For those who reach higher stages, there is considerable development of personality, change in the course and texture of lives, and shifts in concerns, with consequences for our approach to our work life (Helson et al., 1985).

Here is a brief description of Loevinger's stages. A desire to belong, to be "normal" and "happy," and to fill one's role and a preoccupation with acceptability are keynotes of the conformist ego stage. Whereas the conformist feels there is one way of life, the self-aware phase brings a dawning sense of alternatives. Perhaps as a result, we become preoccupied with the self as separate from the group, furthered by our renewed introspection and self-consciousness. In the next, conscientious stage, a sense of choice emerges, and the self is seen as the origin of a person's destiny. We live more by self-evaluated standards yet are also our brother's keeper. Our interpersonal style is now more intensive, with great concern for communication. Inwardly, a person at the conscientious stage steps away from cliché and stereotype toward an awareness of patterning and motive and a concern for ideals and self-respect. Interpersonally, the superficial is replaced by a desire for authentic mutuality. A hallmark of the autonomous stage is a willingness, almost a desire, to articulate and grapple with conflicting needs and duties. This desire forms a motivational nexus in a larger concern for growth and personal development. Self-fulfillment emerges as a salient goal. An intra- and interpersonal atmosphere of autonomy, tolerance for ambiguity, and the cherishing of individuality and personal ties give this stage a flavor of lively maturity. Loevinger found it difficult to describe the final, integrated stage but believed it has all the qualities of the autonomous stage, but more so, and brought together with greater clarity.

Loevinger said that we go along at the same level until we encounter information or experiences that we just can't make sense of within the system of meanings and associations we are currently using. When this happens, we must build new ego structure, and thus we move to a new ego level. Some of the shifts described in middle age, such as thinking less about our age since birth and more about how many years we still have or being perceived to be older than one feels, may not fit into our old ways of thinking. If so, we will build new ego structures to make a place for our new understandings.

One challenge we all face, and which may cause us to build new psychological structure, is coming to terms with an ageist culture in which we are the target; we are "othered." What are the psychological consequences of this challenge? Does it require an alteration in self-concept? New coping strategies? A different understanding of the boundary between self and other? As women and members of other marginalized groups, we have a long history of being othered—objectified, diminished, condescended to— as we reckoned with the sexism in the culture. Now, with ageism, we are differently othered. If reckoning with these experiences leads to ego development, our lives are enhanced with an expanded capacity to think, to feel, to appreciate ourselves and those who matter to us, to handle complexity and ambiguity, to feel at home in whole new ways. These changes affect every facet of our lives, including our late-life approach to our work.

Gilligan's Theory of the Development of Care

Gilligan's (1982) intention was to contrast an ethic of care with an ethic of rights as two potential cornerstones for moral development. Her work was specifically intended to be a theory of women's development. She had found that, in addressing moral dilemmas, women were more likely than men to resolve a moral quandary in the direction of care than in the direction of a universal rule or principle, perhaps an instance of women's prioritizing connection over separateness. She stated that "the elusive mystery of women's development lies in the recognition of the continuing importance of attachment in the human life cycle" (p. 23) and posited a sequence of development where "the major transitions . . . involve changes in the understanding and activities of care" (p. 171).

Gilligan theorized that all of us begin with an egocentric survival-like focus on caring for oneself. Empathy and an appreciation of the separate existence and needs and desires of others are developmental accomplishments. We gradually become able to recognize that failure to consider others is selfish, and we shift our focus toward responsibility. During this second phase we are drawn to take care of other people and things that are placed in our care—partners, children, family members, friends, clients, patients, students, work—and are at risk of confusing care for others with self-sacrifice. However, the third level of development is marked by a recognition of "the illogic of the inequality between the other and the self" (p. 74). At this point, women begin to include themselves inside their circle of care. Responsible care now takes into account both the possibilities and limitations of one's actions in the lives of others as well as one's responsibility for self-development.

How is work, as well as the place of work, changed in the life of the older working woman who has achieved the perspective of Gilligan's third stage? She may feel less of a need to fix situations or others. Recognizing that she bears responsibility for herself, she may act with regard for her own needs, including her need to become more whole, more differentiated, more conscious. By including herself within her circle of care, she can maintain her stamina, be less vulnerable to burnout, and in these ways is able to be a more active participant in a wider human community.

Levinson's Theory of the Structure of the Life Course

Lives are not just a continuous flow of days. They have structure, and this structure can inform us about the meaning of each phase of life. Structure helps us locate where we are, where we have been, where we are headed. For example, many older women workers recognize that we want to modify the structure we erected to maximize the height of our careers and that we need a structure that will work effectively as we head toward times that are not focused on building.

Levinson's (1978) theory is based on the symbol of seasons of life, each with distinct features and purpose. In this theory, the life course is divided into 20-year eras: childhood (birth–20), early adulthood (20–40), middle adulthood (40–60), late adulthood (60–80), and old age (80-plus). For each era, we build a life structure suited to the needs of that era. A first question, one not addressed by Levinson, is this: What is the array of life structures created by contemporary women for their age 60 to 80 late-adulthood era?

Structuring the Late-Adulthood Era
For women who continue to work, how is work important as they create the structure for their fourth era of life? And for women who do not continue to

work, how does work become unimportant? Working women will likely build a structure where work is centered, and they are available for it at times when they can be most effective. Women who want work to become progressively less important will increasingly relegate it toward the periphery of their structure, adding to the time they work remotely and incorporating structure that supports a decline in additional work.

The woman who intends (or suspects, or discovers) that she will continue working through the late-adulthood era (age 60–80) will design and live within a life structure that is markedly and pervasively different from that of the majority of women (those who are unemployed or retired). The experience of retirement from paid work is monumental and requires drastic and thorough revision of the life structure that has existed before.

It could be argued that women who continue to work simply maintain the life structure they had established during their middle adult era. However, there are limits to the extent that we can rely on momentum to offer a design for the fourth era. The same aspects of life, whether marriage, parenting, community engagement, or work, become important in different ways in different eras and may take different places within that era's structure. In our 60s, if we have children, we are transitioning the last of them into their own more independent young adulthood; in this we are learning to let go. Relationships with our children work best when we recognize that we have already taught them what we believe in and now is not the time for our guidance and advice (unless we're asked). Instead, we step back, still offering connection, recognition, and support.

If we have a partner, we can likely anticipate 15 years of living with them, with no one else living in the home. At 65, just over 50% of women are married (though more are coupled). This number decreases with age for women in heterosexual couples, as women live longer than do male spouses (Wang, 2018). Living only with a partner who may no longer be in a workplace is likely an experience that we have never had before. Just as we approach parenting and couple relationships differently now, we are likely to approach work differently as well.

Revising the Life Structure

Once a structure is built, we maintain it and live within it. Because it is a structure with interdependence of parts, it resists change. However, between each era, Levinson described a transition period in which the individual evaluates the structure she has been living in and asks which parts of it should be retained or changed, modified or discarded, as she builds a life structure for the era she is entering. Conditions have changed.

As with the transition to midlife, when we transition to late adulthood, we may find ourselves reevaluating our life in terms of our dream. In our efforts to succeed, certain aspects of the personality have been developed at the cost of others, and these neglected aspects may now press for attention. We know very well that life is finite and that we can anticipate declining powers, so we seek to retain our vitality through whatever means make sense to each of us. Some women realize that, to be the person they want to be, it is urgent to develop a particular aspect of self. This becomes their purpose and is a central theme organizing the life structure they create (Mitchell & Helson, 2016).

Working women also have valued engagements—in the couple, family, friendships, community, special interests (artistic, political, spiritual, athletic, learning), or other endeavors—that require them to distribute their time and energies and create distinct and credible places for them in the life structure. In addition, with the developments we have described in personality, ego functions, coping, care, regulation of emotion, and selectivity of purpose, we can now be more fully aware of aspects of our lives that are unsatisfactory or outmoded, be more able to envision alternatives, and have the energy, courage, and coping ability to persevere and/or make changes. These changes will be reflected in our life structure.

The Midera Correction
Midway through each era, Levinson posited a smaller transition that allows evaluation and modification within that era's structure. What, if any, modifications in our structures take place at the midpoint of the late-adulthood era (at age 70), and why? Perhaps there will be none, if we feel the structure accurately reflects our priorities for the coming decade. However, we may want to reduce the centrality of work now, working fewer hours or limiting the projects for which we are responsible. If so, we may incorporate these modifications into our structure. One woman established a weekly beach day to replace what had been a work day. We are older now, and we know it, as minor physical and energy or stamina changes (or more) emerge. Friends and colleagues have retired. Children have their own separate lives and may have children of their own, making some of us grandparents now. We all think about retirement, whether we move toward it or not. Retirees are no longer tied to a workplace and may relocate or travel extensively, make significant investment of time and energy in new pursuits, or rediscover the long-absent experience of unstructured free time. To what extent do these endeavors call out to the working woman in her 8th decade and become reflected in the modifications to her life structure?

We may choose (or need) to modify our work lives, or not. We are likely to have begun wondering what life will hold for us in the coming 10 to 20 years. Can we count on abundant energy and physical and cognitive health? I was recently talking about retirement over lunch with a psychotherapist friend, and she said, "Well, I don't plan to retire soon, but I sure will not allow my clients to have to deal with me losing my marbles, or deal with me dropping dead in my therapy chair!" At 70, people in our social network may have suddenly become ill or disabled or may have died. What will our story be? This unanswerable question, I believe, becomes part of the backdrop of life for people in their 70s and brings a puzzling, precious, and adventurous quality to even ordinary days.

FORESHADOWING FUTURE DEVELOPMENT: INTEGRITY AND GEROTRANSCENDENCE

As mentioned above, in the Eriksons' theory of the stages of life, two stages follow generativity: integrity versus despair and gerotranscendence versus struggle. As we focus on developing a sense of integrity, we enter an inwardly focused period when we look back on our life and look ahead to the end of life. Life review creates integrity when we are able to see and accept our life entirely, as it has been, and to cherish it. This radical acceptance, the Eriksons stated, allows us to approach death as a natural ending.

As we become involved in this developmental task, we enter a time of reflection and a sort of "disengaged engagement" that can bring wisdom. Integrity involves a growing experience of one's place in the panorama of human experience: We feel keenly the boundaries of the small slice of historical time in which we've lived our lives. Yet, at the same time, we sense a growing awareness and sharing in universals—plants and animals, the seasons of the year, births and deaths, and growing up and older—experiences shared by all humans across the entirety of existence. Thus, the Eriksons claim, our identity expands, and we come to identify ourselves more with humanity as a whole, perhaps with others who, centuries ago, did the same kind of work.

The final phase, gerotranscendence versus struggle, is focused on dealing with physical limitations and decline. The Eriksons did not describe it as fully as they had the earlier stages but wrote about the profound challenge of meeting daily life with limited capacity and the goal of gerotranscendence, that is, a shift in metaperspective from a materialistic and rational vision to a more cosmic and transcendent one, accompanied by a profound peace of mind. Gerotranscendence includes a redefinition of time, space, life and death, and the self.

Integrity in a Generative Context

Is the pursuit of integrity anathema to the generativity-focused woman worker? For the woman immersed in her work and her generativity, retirement and the engaging of integrity as a developmental task may indeed be anathema for a variety of psychological reasons. Generativity has an outward focus toward others and involves tangible and visible results; integrity involves a turn inward to the self, where results have more to do with intangibles such as gratitude, self-reflection, and peace of mind. The generative woman may not want to give up her treasured roles and her career identity, especially if she has not conceptualized new roles and a modified identity, risking that roles are just lost and not replaced. The woman enjoying her generativity may not intend to retire and may regard it as (for her) an experience of becoming irrelevant, useless, and without purpose (Burdick, 2006). On the other hand, the woman drawn to the process of attaining integrity may long for unscheduled time and an exploration of her own rhythms and inner life and therefore may look forward to retirement from work.

Is it possible to address the developmental task of attaining integrity within the outward-looking generative context of work? I suggest it is. The older working woman lives with the recognition that there will, at some time, be an end to her active contribution to her field, to her business, to those whom she serves. This recognition echoes the larger recognition that one's life, too, will end. Continuing in our work, we may nonetheless embark on the tasks necessary to achieving integrity. We may find ourselves recalling the history of our career and key moments from our personal past. Looking at our career in its completeness, including mishaps and roads not taken, we have the opportunity to accept it in its entirety as having led us to where, and who, we are today. In the workplace, too, we reckon with our growing awareness that we will have been present for only a slice of the undertaking to which we have devoted so much time, energy, and care. And yet, these thoughts may awaken a fresh sense of comradeship with those who came before us and those who will come after, creating the expanded identity that, the Eriksons say, creates integrity and prepares us for our final life transition.

We may not only experience our work as a location to engage the concerns of the integrity stage; we may also find that those integrity concerns inform and enhance the kind of generativity that we manifest during the third age.

A part of generativity is about leaving the world a better place than we found it and contributing to a future that will outlive us. These themes connect strongly with the stock-taking and big-picture perspective that characterize the integrity stage. Just as the parent of a young child spends daily hours in addressing immediate needs, so the young worker spends hours addressing the urgent deadlines of the workplace. Perhaps this comparison between parent and worker can inform the difference between the roles of the younger and older worker, too. The parent of a young adult child is rarely engaged with their daily needs; rather, at best, they become a supportive presence, able to hold the big picture of their adult child's larger goals and hopes. Similarly, even while continuing the daily practice of her work, the older woman may find herself thinking more about the larger mission that each small effort is intended to serve.

The Changing Face of Women's Generativity and Integrity

In the year that the Eriksons proposed their stages, the average American woman could expect to live about 20 fewer years than she does today. Vastly fewer women worked for pay outside the home, and most people died by their 60s. When active parenting ended and all the children had moved from the family home, the average woman had 1.6 years to live with her partner before her partner died (Glick, 1977). Generativity for women was mainly understood as the birthing and raising of children. In that context, the Eriksons hoped that, once the paid and parenting work was done, the woman (and her partner) would have a few years to shift from an endlessly outward working focus to look within, reflect on the lives they'd had, and make peace with them, leading to a solid sense of personal integrity.

In contrast, many of today's women have the gift of those 20 active years in a relational context as well as the achievement of choice in the kind of work they do and how long they want to do it. Their sense of generativity is vastly enriched by the availability of meaningful work in addition to parenting. The extent that they control the amount, content, and quality of that work also allows them to choose the extent that generativity will remain a focal developmental achievement as they move toward old age.

CONCLUSION

I have argued that both the practice and the psychological meaning of work change for women across the 40-plus years when work is our focus. Generativity, as a stage that now characterizes nearly 50 years of adult life, should itself evolve into a more differentiated sequence of stages, informed by the developmental changes of midlife. Similarly, we need to be able to talk about the meaning of work in a developmentally informed, more differentiated way. What we do at work, how we do it, and what it means to us have evolved tremendously over the arc of our careers.

As the opportunities have exploded for women to have work in which they feel they are making a valued contribution to society and helping others move forward and in a context of challenge, flexibility, and autonomy that make work engaging and fulfilling, the psychological meaning of work is not limited to generativity. Work also addresses the vital developmental tasks of identity, intimacy, and integrity, which make up all of the tasks that the Eriksons viewed as central to adulthood. Our sense of identity—of who we are and where we fit in the adult world—is continuously established in the daily practice of our career. In enduring relationships with colleagues, clients, and students, we participate in the community and connection that affirm our sense of intimacy over isolation. Our growing capacity to see ourselves and our work within a long view encourages our sense of integrity, with its appreciation and gratitude for the life and the work that we've had and a comfortable anticipation of letting go within an ending that is natural, expected, and right.

REFERENCES

Baltes, P., & Baltes, M. (1990). Psychological perspectives on successful aging. In P. Baltes & M. Baltes (Eds.), *Successful aging: Perspectives from the behavioral sciences* (pp. 1–34). Cambridge University Press. https://doi.org/10.1017/CBO9780511665684.003

Borrero, L., & Kruger, T. M. (2015). The nature and meaning of identity in retired professional women. *Journal of Women & Aging, 27*(4), 309–329. https://doi.org/10.1080/08952841.2014.950141

Burdick, C. (2006). Retirement—The final question mark? In N. Bauer-Maglin & A. Radosh (Eds.), *Women confronting retirement: A non-traditional guide* (pp. 319–325). Rutgers University Press.

Carstensen, L. L. (2006). The influence of a sense of time on human development. *Science, 312*(5782), 1913–1915. https://doi.org/10.1126/science.1127488

Cate, R. A., & John, O. P. (2007). Testing models of the structure and development of future time perspective: Maintaining a focus on opportunities in middle age. *Psychology and Aging, 22*(1), 186–201. https://doi.org/10.1037/0882-7974.22.1.186

Erikson, E., & Erikson, J. (1997). *The life cycle completed.* W. W. Norton.

Franz, C., & White, K. (1985). Individuation and attachment in personality development: Extending Erikson's theory. *Journal of Personality, 53*(2), 224–256. https://doi.org/10.1111/j.1467-6494.1985.tb00365.x

Freud, S. (1973). Femininity. In J. Strachey (Ed. & Trans.), *The standard edition of the complete psychological works of Sigmund Freud* (Vol. 22, pp. 139–167). Penguin. (Original work published 1931)

Gilligan, C. (1982). *In a different voice.* Harvard University Press.

Glick, P. (1977). Updating the life cycle of the family. *Journal of Marriage and Family*, *39*(1), 5–13.

Goldin, C., & Katz, L. F. (2018). Women working longer: Facts and some explanations. In C. Goldin & L. F. Katz (Eds.), *Women working longer: Increased employment at older ages* (pp. 11–53). University of Chicago Press.

Greene, S. (2014). *The psychological development of girls and women: Rethinking change in time*. Routledge.

Harker, L., & Solomon, M. (1996). Change in goals and values of men and women from early to mature adulthood. *Journal of Adult Development, 3*, 133–143. https://doi.org/10.1007/BF02285774

Helson, R., & Mitchell, V. (in press). *Women on the river of life: A fifty-year study of adult development*. University of California Press.

Helson, R., Mitchell, V., & Hart, B. (1985). Lives of women who became autonomous. *Journal of Personality, 53*(2), 257–285. https://doi.org/10.1111/j.1467-6494.1985.tb00366.x

Helson, R., Mitchell, V., & Moane, G. (1984). Personality and patterns of adherence and non-adherence to the social clock. *Journal of Personality and Social Psychology, 46*(5), 1079–1096. https://doi.org/10.1037/0022-3514.46.5.1079

Helson, R., Soto, C. J., & Cate, R. A. (2006). From young adulthood through the middle ages. In D. Mroczek & T. Little (Eds.), *Handbook of personality development* (pp. 337–352). Lawrence Erlbaum.

Henry J. Kaiser Family Foundation. (n.d.). *Life expectancy at birth (in years): 2010–2015*. https://www.kff.org/state-category/health-status/life-expectancy

James, J., & Wink, P. (2006). The crown of life: Dynamics of the early post-retirement period. *Annual Review of Gerontology and Geriatrics*. Springer Publishing.

Josselson, R. (2017). *Paths to fulfillment: Women's search for meaning and identity*. Oxford University Press.

Jung, C. G. (1969). The stages of life. In J. Campbell (Ed.), *The portable Jung* (pp. 3–22). Penguin Books.

Karp, D. A. (1988). A decade of reminders: Changing age consciousness between fifty and sixty years old. *The Gerontologist, 28*(6), 727–738. https://doi.org/10.1093/geront/28.6.727

Labouvie-Vief, G., & Medler, M. (2002). Affect optimization and affect complexity: Modes and styles of regulation in adulthood. *Psychology and Aging, 17*(4), 571–588. https://doi.org/10.1037/0882-7974.17.4.571

Levinson, D. (1978). *The seasons of a man's life*. Knopf.

Loevinger, J. (1976). *Ego development*. Jossey Bass.

Mitchell, V., & Helson, R. (2016). The place of purpose in life in women's positive aging. *Women & Therapy, 39*(1–2), 213–234. https://doi.org/10.1080/02703149.2016.1116856

Ryff, C. (2008). Know thyself and become what you are: A eudaimonic approach to psychological well-being. *Journal of Happiness Studies, 9*, 13–39.

Stewart, A., Ostrove, J., & Helson, R. (2001). Middle aging in women: Patterns of personality change from the 30s to the 50s. *Journal of Adult Development, 8*, 23–37. https://doi.org/10.1023/A:1026445704288

Wang, W. (2018). *The state of our unions*. Institute for Family Studies.

3

SHIFTING VALUES AND LATE COURSE ADJUSTMENTS IN THE CAREERS OF OLDER WOMEN

LORRAINE MANGIONE, KATHI A. BORDEN, AND ELIZABETH FUSS

I'll walk where my own nature would be leading:
It vexes me to choose another guide:
Where the grey flocks in ferny glens are feeding;
Where the wild wind blows on the mountain side.

—Emily Brontë, "Stanzas"

Identity, meaning, being, and becoming—these are important aspects of who we are and what we do. What gives life meaning? How do we define and describe ourselves? What is important for us? How do we feel about who we have become and what we do? All of these questions animate our lives and our sense of self. In this chapter, we look at such fundamental and significant issues of existence as we consider the role of work in women's lives as they reach their 60s and beyond. Many writers have focused on meaning,

A small portion of this material was included in a workshop at the National Council of Schools and Programs of Professional Psychology's annual meeting in January 2019 and in a conversation hour for the American Psychological Association's Division 35 at the annual convention in August 2019.

https://doi.org/10.1037/0000212-004
Older Women Who Work: Resilience, Choice, and Change, E. Cole and L. Hollis-Sawyer (Editors)

values, existence, and development across various contexts such as psychotherapy, social psychology, or loss (Bruner, 1993; Frankl, 1946/1984;
Markman et al., 2013; Neimeyer et al., 2014; Overholser, 2005; Yalom,
1980). Their work forms the basis for our interest in looking at experiences
of women working beyond 60 years old. We also situated this research in
an adult development framework, particularly Erikson's (1993) generativity
versus stagnation, which we revisit in the conclusion along with other adult
developmental concepts.

Although women in the United States entered the workforce temporarily
during World War II, women entered the workforce en masse and stayed
in it for the first time with the baby boom generation. Now those women
are at or close to retirement age. What has work meant to this large cohort
of women? What does it still mean to them? How does work connect to
their sense of identity, meaning, and values? Researchers have examined
why women choose to work and what it means to be an aging woman in
the workforce from a sociological perspective. A survey in 2007 found that
around 70% of baby boomers planned to work past retirement age for reasons
other than financial need (Fideler, 2012). In this chapter, we explore the
experience of working and the range of reasons that women choose to work
after the age of 60 through a psychological lens. Although we rely heavily
on our own narrative study, we also incorporate some existing literature and
our thinking from other experiences as psychologists and our own lives to
better understand women's relationship to work at this stage of life.

A study by Fideler (2012) alluded to reasons why women continue to
work after 60, noting that for some women, work was related to their self-
esteem and sense of well-being. In the same study, women noted that
continuing to work was satisfying and meaningful and put their skills to
good use. In a study on predictors of late retirement, researchers found
that women who felt their work positively affected others or who worked
in a male-dominated field planned for late retirement (Frieze et al., 2011).
Frieze et al. (2011) also noted that women who planned for late retirement
had less traditional views of gender roles than did those who planned to
retire earlier. In a qualitative study of 53 older working women, 45 participants cited independence from men as a reason for continuing work
(Altschuler, 2004).

The encore stage, as described by Birkett et al. (2017), is when professionals engage in meaningful activities during the retirement period. These
authors found that whereas some women choose to volunteer during this
time and are excited for retirement, others see this period as a time for late
career development. Those who entered their career later in life or received
promotions later in life worried about a loss of professional identity if they

chose to retire. Research shows that higher education level also is associated with higher likelihood of working past typical retirement age (Fideler, 2012). Mor-Barak (1995) discovered four primary reasons why older adults choose to stay in the workplace: the Social Contact factor (respect, power, prestige, socialization), the Personal factor (self-esteem, satisfaction, pride), the Financial factor (income), and the Generativity factor (teaching, training, passing on knowledge to the younger generation).

OUR NARRATIVE STUDY

Two of the authors of this chapter (Mangione and Borden) are part of the near-retirement population. We wanted to look closely at issues of identity and meaning, which we see as the significant psychological aspects of work. One of us has been running groups for women beyond midlife and before retirement (Mangione & Forti, 2018), and another of us (Borden) has taken on a major new role in her work, so we are definitely part of the conversation, too. The third author (Fuss) is a member of the millennial generation who joined us as a research assistant and eventually as third author. The three of us invited women over 60 to write a narrative using a series of prompts. Participants were able to respond to as many or as few prompts as they wished. Suggested topics for the narratives are presented in Exhibit 3.1. We asked them to comment on reasons for working other than finances, although we recognized that is often an important and sometimes compelling reason to continue working.

To find participants over 60 years old working at least half-time in jobs requiring at least a bachelor's degree, in late July 2018, we contacted colleagues who had access to women in the target demographic, asking them

---

EXHIBIT 3.1. Narrative Prompts

Participants were asked to write about the meaning of work in their lives. We provided this instruction: "We would like to explore why some women stay in their jobs other than, or in addition to, financial security (which we recognize is a significant need!)." The prompts listed below were provided as suggested topics, and participants were instructed that they could respond to any or none of the prompts.

- Changes in the workplace, work relationships, and type of work
- The role of work and the decision to keep working
- Identities, values, and mission-driven aspects of work
- Self-esteem in relation to work
- Thoughts on aging and remaining healthy
- Goals for work and retirement plans
- The meaning of work and workplace relationships
- The changing roles of women in the workplace

---

to forward our project announcement. Women who sent an email expressing their interest in participating received a return email with the narrative prompts. In total we received 14 narratives. All names have been changed in the excerpts below to protect the confidentiality of the participants.

Our 14 participants ranged in age from 61 to 75 years, with a median age of 65 and a mean of 66 years. All identified as White, most were of Eastern or Western European background, and all of them lived in the United States. All but one were married. Job titles and settings are presented in Table 3.1. Participants were highly educated; all had bachelor's degrees, six held master's degrees, and five held doctorates. Although we realize the limitations of a racially homogeneous and professional or highly educated group of participants, we believe they offered us a great deal of rich material.

In the following pages, we outline the major themes that seem to best describe the women's responses, taking into consideration important psychological factors such as sense of self, sense of purpose, development, and relationships. We look at these areas in depth: First, why do we continue to work? Responses highlighted an emphasis on mission, identity, legacy, and love of work. Second, given the emphasis often placed on relationships in women's development and identity, we also look specifically at workplace relationships. We hope we have woven a rich narrative, just as our participants have done in generously responding to our prompts, to communicate the intensity of some women's relationships to their work and the nuance of their reflections on their place in the life cycle. In the final pages, we bring everything together, emphasize our theoretical frames, and give voice to our

TABLE 3.1. Participant Jobs and Work Settings

Number	Name	Age	Title	Job setting
1	Barbara	62	Professor	University
2	Carol	62	Senior vice president	Corporate
3	Cindy	63	Assistant professor	University
4	Debbie	70	Assistant director	Community services
5	Donna	65	Director, women's health	Health plan
6	Alice	75	Artist and writer	Self-employed
7	Janet	62	Research editor	Nonprofit organization
8	Karen	63	Dyslexia tutor	K-12 school
9	Kathleen	75	Salesperson	Work from home
10	Linda	65	Appellate justice	State government
11	Susan	65	Family nurse practitioner	Community health
12	Sharon	61	Psychologist	Private practice
13	Martha	68	Writer	Self-employed
14	Anne	67	Associate provost	University

own stories and reflections, so our conclusions might be of help to women as they approach that magical age when everyone starts asking, "When are you going to retire?"

WHY DO OLDER WOMEN CONTINUE TO WORK?

A life and career that are filled with meaning and purpose, however those are defined for each person, seem to lie at the heart of the work enterprise for many people. Although most jobs are likely to have their share of the tedious and mundane, those enterprises that hold out the possibilities for meaningful work, such as work that helps the community, inspires growth and change in the person working, creates something of value for a profession, or fits with an internal sense of purpose and identity, are ones to which women feel more committed. In a recent article, Deangelis (2018) focused on the search for meaning and noted that prior research has shown that the most common sources of meaning "tend to fall into two main categories: meaningful relationships and meaningful occupation, whether that's a career, hobby or other pursuit" (p. 40). Our participants' responses reflected these two categories. Most notably, the passion and intensity with which women feel the mission-driven aspect of their work were palpable in our participants. Although not all women can work in some area or field in which they feel so inspired and that gives them such a purpose in life, for many women this may be the primary reason to work in the first place and to continue working as an older adult.

In addition to an overall or specific sense of purpose of mission, some women also just loved their work, how it has grown and changed, and how they have grown and changed with it. Others felt that there was something very particular about this time of their work lives, such as that they needed to leave something to their field or to future generations. They spoke of a sense of generativity and legacy. Still others felt that work was an intertwined part of their identity, something so deep and rooted that it was hard to separate out from who they are. Finally, relationships play a role, albeit a changing and maybe unexpected one, in continuing to work. These five areas—meaning and purpose, loving one's work, generativity and legacy, identity, and relationships—constitute a richly textured response to the question of why our respondents continue to work.

Mission and Meaning in Life

Almost all the women were able to articulate a sense of meaning in their work, a purpose, and even a feeling of being mission-driven. An assistant professor in a business department in her early 60s, Cindy (#3) expressed this in some detail:

> Having a purpose is important. Teaching is enjoyable; research is equally enjoyable. I am able to think and reflect. The paycheck is a fraction of what I earned in the corporate world. Work is less about the money and more about contributing to society. The contribution is helping students progress through their learning journey. In my case, helping them learn how to think innovatively and entrepreneurially. . . . The mission is helping students learn how to solve problems and think critically. This is so important as I witness those who follow our current President. Thinking critically and learning how to take in information is a skill that I view as my mission with students.

She summed up her work in this way: "My mission is to change the culture at the University to be innovative and entrepreneurial. This is bold." And she saw her career trajectory as encompassing this mission: "Past—the career journey. Reaching for the 'brass ring'—always. Present—contributing to the betterment of the University and students. Future—concluding the vision."

A 70-year-old assistant director at a community services agency, Debbie (#4) responded in this way, making mission central:

> 1) I am a community organizer by training and experience so being mission-driven is part of my DNA; 2) social justice is the driving force behind the choices I have made about where to focus my professional talents; 3) as a secular humanist I am not influenced whatsoever by religions [sic] values or culture.

An artist and writer whose work has encompassed many different areas over her career, 75-year-old Alice (#6) wrote about the purpose of her art on a very broad level: "The deep concern for humanity, on helping people find their voice, on sharing those experiences, is a key motivation." When discussing her writing about artists' work, she commented,

> The satisfaction comes from seeing a major piece, with color photographs, presented in an egalitarian newspaper that reaches a large number of people. For me, it is a way to share the message that creativity is accessible, and that artists are able to give voice to many feelings and issues. My hope is that by giving artists the opportunity to talk about their work, the stereotype of the elitist artist will be broken down, and art will be seen as more approachable.

A research editor in her early 60s, Janet (#7) described her work in this way: "My current work is focused on human rights. I do not make a lot of money. My contribution to saving the world is tiny." So, although she saw the enormity of the endeavor of saving the world, she saw purpose and meaning in her small role in this endeavor and was deeply motivated in her human rights work.

A dyslexia tutor in her early 60s, Karen (#8) saw her contribution in palpable, individualized ways but was no less mission-driven: "All children deserve to learn to read and literacy in our country is in crisis. I am glad in a small way, I can help." Her family's trajectory contributed to that mission:

> I came to [current location, far from where the family had lived] kicking and screaming. It was not a move that I wanted at the time. However, as I look back over the 17 years I have been here, I believe that God (or the universe or however you want to characterize the force that is beyond us as individuals) placed me here to do this work. I am thankful.

Linda (#10), a state court judge in her mid-60s, commented briefly on purpose and mission: "I also feel that I have a role to play in shaping my state's law, which is important to me as a lawyer and as a citizen." Finally, Susan (#11), a family nurse practitioner (NP) in her mid-60s, spoke to the long view of her career and its meaning:

> I have been at my job for 30 years. I am committed to the work I do with [an] underserved population from spiritual and social justice bases. I believe health care is a right, and I believe in the dignity and worth of all people, and I try to live that out in my work, treating each patient with love and care (although there are some days, I am less loving and caring).
>
> I have given a lot of time to my profession—not always through the job, but through the professional organization—and have helped mentor many new NP's. That has given me a lot of satisfaction. I've also gotten satisfaction from working with a special population through the years, migrant & seasonal agricultural workers, and have started to hand that off as a "first step" towards retirement, since it required evening hours in addition to full-time work in the clinic. Part of what has energized me is knowing the good I provide my patients, even when the workplace does not necessarily recognize my contributions.

Associate Provost Anne (#14) summed up many of the salient issues: "Work provides stimulation, social connection, identity, and a sense of accomplishment and importance that will be hard to let go of. I have been fortunate to have been in career paths that involve meaningful work."

Legacy and Generativity

An assistant professor in business, Cindy (#3) spoke of generativity, a sense of giving to others, as she commented: "It is important to be a role model for young women (and men). The virtues of kindness, fairness, and being thoughtful are hopefully helping some integrate into their own values." This idea of creating something for younger people came up for Carol (#2), a senior vice president, in this way: "I have created a series of 'tips' for my students that I originally intended to be business focused. But I see many are for all parts of your life." The role of encouraging other women in leadership positions as part of what she hoped to pass along was significant to the director of a women's health center in her mid-60s, Donna (#5):

> I've had the pleasure of meeting many strong and effective women leaders and I am heartened to see more women in leadership roles, but we need many more. I hope that I have shown younger generations the importance of speaking up, stepping up, not being afraid to make mistakes and to take a wide view.

Donna also saw the continuation of a specific part of her work as something she hoped she would pass on after retirement:

> I am doing something important in my work and it feels like the least I can do before I retire is to finish what I started in such a way that it will continue when I do retire which I plan to be in about 3 years. I am developing a program in my organization that is unique and impactful and that can and should be replicated in order to improve maternal child health outcomes for poor and disabled women. As far as I know, no one else is doing what I am right now, and I have the opportunity to create this program and share the information with others. My work "bucket list" is to get this program fully operational and integrated into the fabric of the organization, collect data to show its impact and document the steps for implementation so others can do it too. Most importantly, I want to be sure it continues without me.

Not everyone, however, thought about or valued the idea of legacy. Debbie (#4), a community services assistant director, said, "I place little value on a legacy beyond the fact that I hope that I have done enough good things to leave some good memories for those who knew me for a reasonable period of time. Beyond that I am unconcerned." A psychologist in practice in her early 60s, Sharon (#12), when writing about an effect on generations behind her, stated, "I am focused on teaching my children, but I do not really think about an effect on others. Maybe after I retire." And Janet (#7), a research editor focused on human rights, recognized that the work may not ever get done: "Most of my work is very long term. I do not expect to live until its completion. My expectation is that the work will have positive impact over time. That's enough."

Love of the Work

The enthusiasm some of the women felt about their work was unmistakable. A college professor in her early 60s, Barbara (#1) described this at length:

> There are also so many great things about the content of my job. For example, I truly love my field of clinical psychology, and I get to talk about it every day! I get to present interesting information to students who are interested in psychology, and I get to see them excited about it. I love the rapport I am able to

develop with my students, and I enjoy helping them gain a better understanding of mental health and psychotherapy. I want to dispel their assumptions about people who have psychological problems, and I think I do. Most psychology majors who have my classes go on to graduate school in a counseling-related field or go directly into human services work. I am gratified to know that my classes have helped in these pursuits. I love getting emails from students who say that they are using things we talked about in class.

Donna (#5), the women's health director, spoke of her love for her job:

> What I love about my current work is it's a phenomenal organization doing good work with a healthy work culture, I am well paid with great benefits, and I have a very supportive boss who gives me freedom and flexibility in my work.

A 75-year-old salesperson, Kathleen (#9), described her work and what she has done for it, as well as what it has done for her, in glowing terms:

> I love my job. It keeps me involved in many neat projects and it keeps me problem solving constantly. Order can be done wrong and UPS & FedEx can mess up. It is up to me to be the problem solver and straighten things out between factories, delivery services, and the client. I have maintained my relationship with the county for 36 years, and it gives me a sense of pride when I can walk into a building, see a plaque that I had done, or a project that I worked on that is written up in the newspaper. I do not tell others about it, but I know.
>
> It has been 36 years since I began in this career, and it has been interesting, exciting, fun and lucrative. When I started this job I stepped out of the house in suburbia, with the station wagon in the carport, the 2.2 kids and the dog, and it has been great.

Identity

Questions of identity resonated with many of the participants, as described straightforwardly in these sentences by Debbie (#4), an assistant director of community services:

> Work is what I do as a vocation and as an avocation. Work is central to my self-identity; my work is what has, in my mind, given my life value. Work is what I am good at. . . . I place a work ethic as among my highest values. . . . [My self-worth/self-esteem] is almost entirely tied to my accomplishments as a worker. [And the meaning of work over time is] all important. Work has defined my identity for most of my adult life.

Certainly, the idea of a vocation casts work in a very dedicated light.

Artist and writer Alice (#6) also saw work as a major part of her identity, reaching far into her childhood:

> I always knew that I would work. I was proud of my mother and grandmother. I loved the fact that my mother wore trousers, when all the other women wore

skirts. I minded her being away at the Institute but relished her difference from other mothers at the same time. The women in my family were strong-minded and independent. I think that I always felt that work was a part of this identity. Even as a very young girl, seven or eight, I was not sure that I wanted to be married. I thought seriously about being a nun, like the teachers in my school. I saw them as independent-minded individuals as well. I was grateful that I went to an all-girls Catholic high school, where I had some intelligent and dedicated women teachers as role models.

She elaborated that

Work has always been a major way that I've defined myself. Work has always provided constant challenges that I've relished, as well as interactions with colleagues and clients. As a developing artist, I learned to spend much more time alone in my studio—likening it to being a monk in a monastery in the early days.

Yet identification comes in many forms. The salesperson, Kathleen (#9), who loved her job, offered this conclusion: "I will say, that this job has definitely identified me and has made me happy." The research editor, Karen (#8), described the sense of identity a bit more ambivalently:

I have always been political. A young me always thought I would work to change the world. Some part of me has always been disappointed in myself for not making that my life's work. . . . It has been surprising to me—without work, my sense of self-worth/self-esteem disappears. Not working is embarrassing.

A sense of identity that is not so completely entwined with work was offered by the practicing psychologist, Sharon (#12):

I would be very bored if I did not work, but its primary role is to provide income for the family. . . . I value providing service to others and I accomplish that through work. My identity includes many things—professional person is the one that intersects with work. The others are for things outside of work.

A writer and novelist in her late 60s, Martha (#13), who put off her writing career as her husband got started in his practice and her children were young, shared about how that felt in terms of who she was and her potential:

However, I did not always do this [put off her career] gracefully: while I enjoyed domestic life—the time it afforded me to put my creative energies into making a comfortable and safe environment for my family—and taking a very active role in my three children's lives both in and out of school, I would be remiss if I did not admit to a daily undercurrent that I was not living up to my personal and professional fulfillment. In addition to writing, I took on various jobs such as: running after-school language programs, teaching at a local language institute, and even trying my hand at selling health and beauty products!

Relationships at Work

Work relationships change over time, often contributing to continuing in one's career and keeping one engaged with people. However, the importance and value of work relationships seemed to take variable paths at this point in the women's careers. Probably the most unabashedly positive experience was discussed by the college professor, Barbara (#1):

> Another integral part of why I love my job is that my friends are there! When I started my current job, there were two women in my department—me and another woman who was also just starting. Now there are 7 women out of the 13 department members. One of those women has separated herself from the department, but the other 6 are all friends! We have traveled together, we get together for birthdays, and we really enjoy each other's company. They are there if I feel like bitching, if I have any kind of problem in my work or personal life, and they are FUN! The woman I started with, 28 years ago, is my best friend and, though she is younger than me by a couple years, we have talked about retiring at the same time. It would be hard to imagine teaching there without her.

Associate Provost Anne (#14) commented that work has helped her develop and maintain social connections:

> Work has been a cornerstone of my identity and my social world. . . . Being somewhat introverted by nature and living with an internal sense of social awkwardness, as the time for retirement draws nearer, I find myself worried about the loss of structure and meaning that work holds for me and the loss of an easy social network.

The assistant director of community services, Debbie (#4), noted: "I regret that I have found it easier to bond with work, social justice projects, and clients of those projects than with people in my personal life including friends and family." She saw relationships at work as

> 1) somewhat important but not as important as constituents who receive benefit from my work efforts; 2) I have made some good, long term friends over the course of my career but, as with family, I have a harder time with personal intimacy so have not developed the depth of friendships that would be a healthier outcome.

The senior vice president, Carol (#2), noticed a lot of changes with her coworkers as younger cohorts were hired, and she saw work relationships as staying at work:

> Since changing jobs last year, the thing I am noticing most is how young our staff is. I knew we were focused on hiring young people right out of school, but I was not paying attention to the number of older people who were leaving. I realized one day I am sitting in a pool of Millennials. They are young, and

smart, with clothes too tight or too low/short who say "like" at least 3 times per sentence, which itself begins with the word, "SOOO. . . ." They talk to me as one of the "guys" and tell me to "have a good one" though what I am supposed to have is unsaid. And yet, they work hard, are very collaborative and seem to be enjoying themselves while getting work done. It's fun to watch. Of course, this highlights my age versus theirs, but I realize I am not too bad for an old gal and, mostly, it makes me laugh (inside, of course!).

I like many of the people I work with. I noticed the other day I am connected to nearly 1,000 people on LinkedIn and most of them I know. I've worked with them, traveled with them, relied on them, won with them, lost with them. I also notice I do very little with them outside of the work environment. And that's fine with me. I fully expect when I retire not to look back.

The assistant professor of business, Cindy (#3), had a new perspective on several work themes, including her colleagues:

I do not identify with work as much as I did in the early years. A PhD is actually less meaningful to me now than having a VP title was in my earlier years. I remain friendly to those at work, but do not want to socialize with them even though many of them are close to my age (most are in their 50s). I find the combination of my past corporate life and this new academic life provides a perspective on work that helps compartmentalize the segments of work, family, etc. Work and the people there are less hierarchical and less important to me. I am respectful, but do not view a Chair, Dean, Provost, President as a superior.

The artist and writer Alice (#6) offered a different slant on relationships with coworkers, in that they are critical to the work and her motivation but not necessarily colleagues or friends:

I am presently working on a public art project, comprised of two large metal panels that will be installed at an affordable housing complex in the section of Boston where I grew up. Several community people who were aware of two other public art sculptures of mine called me to invite me to salvage some of the artifacts from the old ironworks site, and turn them into art. We went through a lengthy process and did manage to get funding for two of the four proposals that were presented. The project is an arduous one, but very satisfying, as my own personal artwork utilizes found objects and gloves, so this is "right up my alley," as we say. It's especially meaningful because of my connection to the community. In another public art piece, I spent months interviewing residents, and culling quotes from them that are inscribed on the 29 granite stones that comprise the 50-foot-long sculpture of a boat. Many of my projects are like a marriage of my former social work life and art.

Art is the essence of my creative practice, and gives me a deep inner peace, as well as meaning to others when I share the work in exhibits. The art is all about our interconnectedness, our common humanity, and that is a message that is universal and absolutely essential in the age in which we live.

In a sense, the dyslexia tutor, Karen (#8), was conveying something similar about the importance of her coworkers: "Ironically, my work is as analytical and challenging as was my work in finance, but it is much more satisfying since the beneficiaries are young people instead of shareholders." The judge, Linda (#10), also commented on the young people involved in her work:

> My work is extremely rewarding to me. It keeps my mind sharp and shapes my day. It is challenging, and I feel it is important. I work with three law clerks and so I have regular interaction with younger people.

The family nurse practitioner, Susan (#11), described a situation that is perhaps quite common and does not feel so warm or welcoming:

> Over time there has been a lot of colleague turnover, so now most of my peers are quite a bit younger than me. That has made a difference in socialization, especially given increased workload, with less time to get to know coworkers, less satisfaction.

And sometimes having one's own business can really change the atmosphere and the work relationships, as the practicing psychologist, Sharon (#12), wrote,

> Going from a corporate setting to private practice means significantly fewer colleagues and more work required to keep them. One nice thing is that I can paint my nails any color I choose☺. I used to feel like I was limited to neutrals. . . . I have a staff of 4 in my office. They are all good people, but not my friends. They are my employees. It's important to me to treat them fairly and appreciate their contributions.

CONCLUDING THOUGHTS AND MOVING FORWARD: THE SELF AND THE WORK

Hearing about this project from the editors, talking together about it and quickly jotting down what the idea stirred in us, dreaming up the study, inventing our format and formulating the narrative prompts, and imagining who would participate were all vividly evocative experiences, tapping into areas that mattered deeply for the two of us (Mangione and Borden) as well as many women we know. Both of us have had conversations on these themes with friends, family, and colleagues ever since we reached the age at which our own inner clocks murmured to us that the hands were speeding up and the external clocks of other people started asking, "So when are you retiring?"

Even with all the anticipatory excitement and commitment that we had, we could not have imagined how the actual material we gathered would increase that excitement and commitment and add nuance, creativity, and dimensions we had not considered. All three of us are grateful for the women who took the time, energy, and thought to respond to our call for participants and the ways in which their responses will help to further the conversation.

Here we highlight and comment on several themes; connect them to our original framework of existential, lifespan developmental, and feminist thinking; and note a few surprises. We include musings from our lives that reverberate with this work. Finally, although we recognize the lack of racial diversity among our participants, who were all well-educated, professional, and White, we believe they offer priorities and lessons learned that will be helpful to women of a certain age across a wide variety of work situations as well as to researchers, clinicians, and teachers.

Existential Reality: Meaning in Life, Movement of Time, Creating the Self

What is significant in life is not necessarily what we do or the choices we make, but what that activity or choice means to us. For most of the women, their work was personally meaningful and important; it brought great satisfaction because their endeavors, whether teaching a child to read or working for human rights, were of great value to the women.

The self is not a given in existential thinking; rather, it must be created and lived out in the world. It is not that we are blank slates but rather that not all of who we are is predetermined or set, especially in a changing society such as the one in which these women live. As they go through their lives and make choices, taking on some challenges and saying goodbye to others, the self of each woman almost visibly grows and evolves. Identity is central, but it is not foreclosed.

Finally, existential psychology is concerned with time and its finite nature, and we saw this in almost all the participants in their awareness of limits. Although some were making plans and others not, most were awakening to the fact of the finitude of their lives and considering what that meant.

Lifespan Development: Who Am I Now and What Does That Mean?

Both change and constancy seem to intertwine in people's lives. Although some people may appear to radically change at points in their adulthood, many others experience a slower kind of evolutionary change, one that responds both to the environment and to one's internal physical or psychological cues about one's place in the life cycle. Most women in our study fit into the more gradual changes, but a few took major risks and redid their whole work life within the same profession or in a new one, leaving comfort behind for something more meaningful. The idea of shifting one's work to better accommodate one's point in life and one's changing interests and capacities seems central.

One of the few women in the beginning of the field of adult development was Bernice Neugarten, who in the 1960s began looking at aging and its intersection with personality, gender, social cohorts, social policy, and meaning (Neugarten, 1996). She contributed the concept of interiority, or a shifting to a more internal focus at midlife, which may be operational here, too, in the changes seen as the women in our study started to reflect and refocus before age 60. Although wisdom is not guaranteed just as a result of aging (Karelitz et al., 2010; Sternberg, 2005), many of these narratives brimmed with wisdom and great observations and commentaries. At age 60 and above, women in the work world have seen a lot and reflected on it, which can often lead to a sense of wisdom or greater understanding.

The concept of generativity, highlighted in Erikson's (1993; Erikson & Erikson, 1997) generativity versus stagnation stage, especially acts of giving to the next generation, seemed key to many women as they sought to pass something of value on to those behind them and, sometimes, enjoyed getting to know the young people. Although Erikson's last stage of ego integrity versus despair was perhaps waiting around a bend for many of these women, their awareness of themselves and their work should be helpful in coming out on the ego integrity side.

More currently, one of the inspiring works for the beyond-midlife group described by Mangione and Forti (2018) is Shapiro's (2012) work on aging baby boomers that uses the metaphor of autumn for this time of life, a time to rethink and reset oneself and enjoy the burst of colors prior to winter, as well as the seventh-inning stretch in a baseball game, a time to stand up and reposition, maybe get a snack to refuel, prior to the grand ending. These metaphors speak to what many of the women have been doing or have done to redirect and sometimes repurpose their lives and themselves.

Feminism: Empowerment and Sense of Self

The group in our study consisted of professional women making choices and living out lives of meaning and purpose. Although we do not know all their backgrounds and the struggles they may have had, it is likely that they encountered obstacles as women moving into and up in the work world in this first wave of women staying in the workplace. They might be considered embodiments of feminist ethics and values as they work in a range of fields with some freedom to define themselves and their work lives and to influence others and the larger organization.

Echoes From Our Lives: Profession as Who I Am (Lorraine)

A few years ago, two of my closest guy friends from junior high, one of whom I had not seen in decades, joined me for a radiant October walk by an old swimming hole in our hometown. I asked them if they were surprised that I had become a psychologist, and one gave me a funny look, saying, "Lorraine, you told us you were going to be a psychologist when we were in 10th grade. Why should I have doubted you?" We all laughed, knowing he was right; my career path unfolded when we had barely heard of psychologists in 1970. When my mother attended my internship "graduation" celebration, the internship director asked if she was surprised that her daughter was a psychologist. My mother answered matter-of-factly, "No, this is just who she is; she's always been like this." As a child I pretended to be a priest, celebrating Mass and caring for those in need, thinking deep thoughts about God. But after learning that the Catholic priesthood was not in the stars for me, reading Viktor Frankl's *Man's Search for Meaning* and an introduction to Freud nurtured psychology within me as a secular priesthood. My work is such a deep and ongoing part of my identity that it is hard to imagine myself without this work or way of approaching the world and also hard to imagine this identity without my mother's influence. She had the heart, soul, and intellect of a psychologist, philosopher, or spiritual guide but not the opportunities to transform those attributes into a career, and she always encouraged my achievements.

Loss and time have also precociously internalized in me, perhaps because of my mysterious childhood illnesses and the death of my adored Italian grandmother when I was 12. As I approached middle age alongside classmate Lisa McCann, a pioneer in vicarious traumatization work (McCann & Pearlman, 1990), we were hyperaware of time (maybe even rushed it a bit!) and created workshops on "Midlife and Beyond," which included asking participants "What three things do you need to do before you die?" years before "bucket lists" dominated the airwaves. Those groups and Lisa's early death reminded me about vigilance about time and that meaning in life is foundational.

My mid-50s saw a purposeful shift toward a multiyear personally and professionally compelling research project on Italian American daughters and dads addressing relationship and loss that culminated in a book (DiCello & Mangione, 2015), articles, and presentations partly defining the past decade of my life. In light of all this, the resonance I felt with this current project hit many internal and external notes for me.

Echoes From Our Lives: Changing Choices Along the Path (Kathi)

My early childhood was unremarkable for the times: Two parents and two children living in one apartment: father working, mother staying home with the children. But a few years later, my mother took a few graduate courses that evolved into master's and doctoral degrees in psychology. Suddenly, we were the family in the neighborhood with a working mom. My father supported my mother's pursuits, as did his immigrant parents who watched us when my mother was in class.

My first job aspiration, to be the first female major league baseball player, was not to be. Girls were excluded from Little League in the 1960s, and it became clear that I would not make the majors, so I pivoted. I liked children and thought teaching would be a good choice. In high school, I sought volunteer opportunities with children and people with disabilities. When volunteering in a Head Start classroom, I observed the effects of the difficult circumstances of many children, such as the child who played being drunk in preschool. Helping children individually was beyond the capabilities of classroom teachers. By then, my mother was a psychology professor and therapist; she invited me to her classroom to watch a movie about autism. I was hooked.

In college, I quickly got involved with psychological research and became a "big sister" in a prevention program for youth at risk for criminal behavior. I loved it all and knew I had found my future professional home.

I have held faculty positions for most of my career and spent 30 of those years in middle management positions that I loved. I had opportunities for further advancement but realized in my 50s that I did not want to rely on a title to feel good about myself. In addition, fiscal concerns and frequent administrative changes at work made innovation difficult, and managing rather than leading became tedious. I stepped down to return to the faculty.

I now know that I need to incorporate more of what I first loved about psychology into my life. I choose projects that are of interest to me rather than those that will advance my career. I value my relationships with mentees. I am a journal editor, reading material I would not otherwise read, mentoring authors, and influencing what gets published. I am active in legislative advocacy. I volunteer as much as time allows. I do not say "yes" to an opportunity unless it feeds my need for contributing to social change, writing about interesting ideas, or enhancing my relationships. Having had an undiagnosed reading disability as a child, I spent much of my early career feeling "less than." I compensated by pushing myself to gain career success and status in an effort to prove to myself and others that I was "good enough." I now fall into that pattern less often, and instead of trying to prove myself, I focus more on the positive impact I can have on people and the world, aspirations with which I truly identify.

Echoes From Our Lives: This is Just the Beginning (Elizabeth)

I was raised in a traditional household with a stay-at-home mother and a working father. Neither of my parents had pursued higher education, but I had no doubt that I wanted to go to college. I am just beginning my career as a psychologist. After collaborating on this project, I have a newfound appreciation of the meaning of work and the importance of being a woman in the workplace. I feel lucky to have been encouraged to pursue the career of my dreams. I chose clinical psychology for several reasons but primarily because I would like to help others. However, I also look forward to finding work's meaning for me.

Our Suggestions for Staying, Leaving, or Changing

Reflecting, glancing around, making changes, reconsidering values and choices, creatively reassessing what they do and how they do it, checking in with family and friends around priorities, assessing how meaning and identity may have morphed over the years, catching up with themselves—these are the vital processes that engage some women as they move past 60. It is as though that teenage question of "Who am I?" resurfaces.

As we were reminded in the course of this study, development does not stop at 60. Instead, it becomes richer as women focus on their priorities. We have much to learn from women approaching retirement age. They have taught us the value of concentrating on what is important, our self-defined purpose, meaning, legacy, happiness, identity, and relationships. These are the lessons we have taken from considering our own lives and trajectories and those of our participants. We hope these speak to others.

REFERENCES

Altschuler, J. (2004). Beyond money and survival: The meaning of paid work among older women. *International Journal of Aging & Human Development, 58*(3), 223–239. https://doi.org/10.2190/HNQH-BM29-KFB3-E461

Birkett, H., Carmichael, F., & Duberley, J. (2017). Activity in the third age: Examining the relationship between careers and retirement experiences. *Journal of Vocational Behavior, 103*(B), 52–65. https://doi.org/10.1016/J.JVB.2017.08.002

Bruner, J. (1993). *Acts of meaning.* Harvard University Press.

Deangelis, T. (2018). In search of meaning. *Monitor on Psychology, 49*(9), 38–44. http://www.apamonitor-digital.org/apamonitor/201810/MobilePagedReplica. action?pm=2&folio=40#pg43r

DiCello, D., & Mangione, L. (2015). *Daughters, dads, and the path through grief: Tales from Italian America*. Impact Publishers/New Harbinger.

Erikson, E. H. (1993). *Childhood and society*. W. W. Norton.

Erikson, E. H., & Erikson, J. M. (1997). *The life cycle complete*. W. W. Norton.

Fideler, E. S. (2012). *Women still at work: Professionals over sixty and on the job*. Rowman & Littlefield.

Frankl, V. (1984). *Man's search for meaning* (3rd ed.). Simon & Schuster. (Original work published 1946)

Frieze, I. H., Olson, J. E., & Murrell, A. J. (2011). Working beyond 65: Predictors of late retirement for women and men MBAs. *Journal of Women & Aging, 23*(1), 40–57. https://doi.org/10.1080/08952841.2011.540485

Karelitz, T. M., Jarvin, L., & Sternberg, R. J. (2010). The meaning of wisdom and its development throughout life. In W. Overton (Ed.), *Handbook of lifespan human development* (pp. 837–881). Wiley. https://doi.org/10.1002/9780470880166. hlsd001023

Mangione, L., & Forti, R. (2018). Beyond midlife and before retirement: A short-term women's group. *International Journal of Group Psychotherapy, 68*(3), 314–336. https://doi.org/10.1080/00207284.2018.1429927

Markman, K. D., Proulx, T., & Lindberg, M. J. (Eds.). (2013). *The psychology of meaning*. American Psychological Association. https://doi.org/10.1037/14040-000

McCann, I. L., & Pearlman, L. A. (1990). Vicarious traumatization: A framework for understanding the psychological effects of working with victims. *Journal of Traumatic Stress, 3*(1), 131–149. https://doi.org/10.1007/BF00975140

Mor-Barak, M. E. (1995). The meaning of work for older adults seeking employment: The generativity factor. *International Journal of Aging & Human Development, 41*(4), 325–344. https://doi.org/10.2190/VGTG-EPK6-Q4BH-Q67Q

Neimeyer, R. A., Klass, D., & Dennis, M. R. (2014). A social constructionist account of grief: Loss and the narration of meaning. *Death Studies, 38*(8), 485–498. https://doi.org/10.1080/07481187.2014.913454

Neugarten, D. A. (Ed.). (1996). *The meanings of age: Selected papers of Bernice L. Neugarten*. University of Chicago Press.

Overholser, J. C. (2005). Group psychotherapy and existential concerns: An interview with Irvin Yalom. *Journal of Contemporary Psychotherapy, 35*(2), 185–197. https://doi.org/10.1007/s10879-005-2699-7

Shapiro, J. L. (2012). *Finding meaning facing fears in the autumn of your years*. Impact Publishers.

Sternberg, R. J. (2005). Older but not wiser? The relationship between age and wisdom. *Ageing International, 30*(1), 5–26. https://doi.org/10.1007/BF02681005

Yalom, I. D. (1980). *Existential psychotherapy*. Basic Books.

4 WORK-RELATED CHOICE AND IDENTITY IN OLDER WOMEN

NICKY J. NEWTON AND KATHERINE M. OTTLEY

I grew up, I mean, I was at the tail of the traditional women but not really at the forefront of the women's movement. I spent my married life as a good wife; I had some part-time work and then when my husband and I divorced I suddenly thought holy shit! (Excuse my language.) I've got to support myself! And finding that I could was very empowering.

—Retired successful businesswoman, age 75

According to the life-course perspective (Elder, 1995; Settersten, 2003), major life transitions such as retirement are embedded in the contexts defined by personal history and social circumstances. The wide variety of contextual factors affecting life transitions can include family situations, socioeconomic status, organizational work contexts and policies, one's own and/or one's partner's health, the nature of one's work, income, and the perception of being pressured to retire (Gibaldi, 2013; Ní Léime, 2017; Shultz & Wang, 2011; Wang et al., 2011). For example, two comparatively recent major policy changes that may affect work-related transitions are the

https://doi.org/10.1037/0000212-005
Older Women Who Work: Resilience, Choice, and Change, E. Cole and L. Hollis-Sawyer (Editors)

elimination of compulsory retirement in 1986 and the raising of Social Security–defined normal retirement age to 67. Additionally, the global financial crisis of 2008 created an environment in which the future of retirement has subsequently been questioned (Hartmann & English, 2009).

Another major factor that influences one's sociohistorical context is one's generation. Baby boomers—those born between 1946 and 1964—grew up during the relatively affluent post–WWII period and were exposed to the social and political movements of the 1960s and 1970s, such as the civil rights movement and the Equal Pay Act (Coon & Feuerherm, 2017). Many baby boomers had and continue to have different expectations of their working lives than had earlier generations, and they are redefining existing patterns of work and retirement (Kojola & Moen, 2016). Whether they are continuing to work or entering retirement, often boomers' focus is on engaging in activities that provide order and purpose.

Yet another major contextual factor is gender (Kim & Moen, 2002), and generation and gender come together in women of the baby boom. In addition to movements highlighting civil rights and equal pay, leading-edge boomer women experienced the introduction of the birth control pill, no-fault divorce, and women's ability to have their own credit cards (Coon & Feuerherm, 2017). Younger women who found the women's movement meaningful often incorporated its principles into their ideas of identity; older women influenced by the movement often took advantage of increased later-life opportunities to return to work after raising a family or getting divorced (Stewart & Healy, 1989), as evidenced by this chapter's opening quotation. In one study, baby boomer women detailed their firsts, often in the work arena: the first woman to drive a mail truck in her town, the first pregnant medical resident at her particular hospital, and so on (Coon & Feuerherm, 2017). As a group, women of this generation have shown greater labor force participation, gained higher levels of education, and have greater financial independence than any previous generation of American women (Hartmann & English, 2009; Skaff, 2006).

For older women, work-related decisions can be central to their identities. There is evidence that labor force participation by older women increased in the second half of the 20th century, particularly since 1985 (Clark & Quinn, 2002). In fact, older women's labor force participation is driving rates of overall work participation in the 65-plus age group (Gibaldi, 2013; Hartmann & English, 2009; James et al., 2016; Kojola & Moen, 2016). Women's reasons for continuing to work vary greatly; some postpone retirement because they love their jobs and find them meaningful. Others, however, forgo retirement and leisure because of financial issues, and for others in poorer health or with few job skills, continuing to work is not an option (Hartmann & English, 2009).

This chapter examines how the degree of choice in decisions to continue working or retire is associated with personal identity. The role of choice in this group was pivotal to their identity certainty—or "a relatively secure and affirmed sense of a place in the social world resulting from a process of searching and self-definition" (Stewart et al., 2001, pp. 27–28)—although the relationship between choice and identity differed by type of occupation. We highlight the importance of context when examining women's work-related decisions and provide an example of our own research. In the next sections, we review theories, conceptualizations, and research concerning later-life work-related decisions, the role of choice, and the relevant importance of identity as it relates to the experiences of continuing to work as older women.

WORK-RELATED DECISIONS IN LATER LIFE

The fact that there are many definitions of retirement and what it means to be retired speaks to retirement's often highly individualized nature and the need to contextualize it within an individual's life course (Borrero & Kruger, 2015; Settersten, 2003). Whereas Atchley (1982) defined retirement in economic terms as "the withdrawal of an individual from employment, along with entitlement to income that is based on having been employed over a period of years" (p. 121), Wang and Shi (2014) characterized retirement from a more psychological perspective: "an individual's exit from the workforce, which accompanies decreased psychological commitment to and behavioral withdrawal from work" (p. 211). There is little doubt, however, that retirement can take many forms. Individuals can phase their retirement (stay in the same job part-time while gradually phasing out of it), engage in bridge employment (move to another company, often part-time or short-term, prior to retirement), or fully retire more than once (Calvo, 2006; Shultz & Wang, 2011). Much of the dynamic and individualized nature of retirement is predicated by changes in the environments surrounding work, career, and family (Shultz & Wang, 2011): Career paths tend to be more disjointed for current generations than they were previously, jobs are less secure, and ostensibly prowork policies encourage older adults to continue working.

Scholars have developed different frameworks to better understand the antecedents of work-related decisions, including stage or temporal models, resource-based dynamic models, and multilevel models. Multilevel models incorporate macro (e.g., economic and social policies, culture), meso (workplaces, institutions), and micro or individual attribute (health, education, gender, work identity) factors (Kojola & Moen, 2016; Wang & Shi, 2014). Recently, Moen (2016) coined the term "encore adulthood," which she defined as the time between a traditional career and old age—a time when age-related frailties have not yet surfaced. She identified four pathways through this time of life, two of which are pertinent to the current study: unanticipated time shifting, which involves retiring unexpectedly or unwillingly, often due to family care responsibilities, and time shifting for the long game, involving working well past conventional retirement age, whether perceived as a chosen continuation of work (such as when a person continues to work because they enjoy their job) or as a forced continuation of work (perhaps for financial reasons).

Fisher et al. (2015) recently applied the push/pull model of retirement (Shultz et al., 1998) to remaining in the workforce in later life. Push factors are generally perceived as negative, whereas pull factors are positive. In terms of retirement, a push factor could be care-taking responsibilities, and a pull factor might be wanting to spend time on something else; in terms of remaining in the workforce, job lock—that is, wanting to retire but being unable to do so due to financial needs—is a push factor, whereas finding work meaningful and satisfying is a pull factor. Usually, a high level of job involvement is associated with continuing to work (Fisher et al., 2015), and different levels of choice are evident in both decisions to retire and decisions to continue working. Additionally, there is little data to support commonly held beliefs that older adults who continue to work are less productive, are less motivated, or do not like learning new things (Czaja, 2006). Furthermore, there is evidence that late-life paid work can help to maintain a sense of purpose and meaning in life, that it is a source of social support, and that it can contribute to better physical health, quality of life, and self-sufficiency (Calvo, 2006; Di Gessa et al., 2018; Hammerman-Rozenberg et al., 2005).

WOMEN'S WORK-RELATED DECISIONS

Most theories and frameworks for retirement are based on models more relevant for men. Researchers have acknowledged the dearth of theory concerning women's retirement experiences, and a few have attempted to redress the imbalance (Calasanti, 1996, 2010; Kim & Moen, 2002). The life-course approach is one framework that may work particularly well for theorizing and contextualizing women's work decisions, given that, compared with men, women are more likely to have noncontinuous work histories, earn less and have less power, have longer life expectancies yet also more chronic diseases, and are more likely to be caregivers by a 1:5 ratio (Altschuler, 2004; Holstein, 2015; Payne & Doyal, 2010). One study suggesting a different approach to women's retirement (Everingham et al., 2007) proposed three models for women that grew from qualitative interviews and focus groups: gateway (end of the working life), transitional (slowing down, testing the waters, easing out), and transforming the nature of work (another working life with greater control). Although earlier research found that women often follow a transitional model, moving from careers to part-time or bridge work before full-time retirement (Clark & Quinn, 2002), Everingham and colleagues favored the transformative model: They found that regaining autonomy and control over working time, while continuing to receive an income, was especially important for women who had less financial reserves put aside for their retirement (Everingham et al., 2007). Additional issues for women when it comes to making decisions concerning work cessation or continuation include feeling of value to society, engagement in social support networks, and having some control over their own vocational future (Calvo, 2006; Payne & Doyal, 2010; Whiston et al., 2015).

A sense of control is related to better physical and mental health across the lifespan (Heckhausen & Schulz, 1995; Lachman & Burack, 1993) but perhaps especially in work-related decisions. Whiston et al. (2015) described control as "denot[ing] a significant influence over one's own vocational future" (p. 107). In their qualitative study of older professional women's work views, six of the 13 women interviewed mentioned themes of control. However, how control is manifested or develops over time can vary from woman to woman. For example, whereas May Cooper (1999), founder of Growing Old Disgracefully—a network of older women who organize workshops and activities in the United Kingdom—wanted new roles, interests, structure, and commitment in her life when she voluntarily retired from academia, Elaine Hutton (1999), who described her retirement as forced, believed that in her case, retirement was really about a redefinition of work. Both women came to the same conclusion that the cessation of full-time, paid work was not the end of their productive lives, but they did so through different paths. Perhaps this was because their identities were associated with their work in different ways: For Cooper (1999), her work "had been my life and my life, my work" (p. 19); for Hutton (1999), work had never been the definer of her identity.

CONNECTING IDENTITY AND WORK

Erikson (1959) posited that a sense of who one is and where one fits into society is the main developmental preoccupation during adolescence and young adulthood; however, he also felt that identity development is a life-long preoccupation. Among other things, identity involves a commitment to a vocation, occupational self-representation, and a level of inner sameness that allows individuals to navigate changes as they move through adulthood (Kroger, 2016; Newton & Stewart, 2012; Whitbourne & Skultety, 2006). Kroger (2002) drew a comparison between late adulthood and adolescence in terms of focusing on identity; she found that adults aged 65 to 75 were engaged in identity reintegration and reevaluation. Other researchers have focused on the social milieu during which identity begins to develop for young adults, suggesting that experiencing social movements during young adulthood may be particularly important for identity formation (Stewart & Healy, 1989; Stewart & Ostrove, 1998). Baby boomers enjoyed a plethora of potentially important identity-forming events during the 1960s and 1970s, with the women's movement perhaps the most noteworthy for women. For instance, Duncan and Agronick (1995) found that women who experienced the women's movement as meaningful in young adulthood scored high in midlife on identity statuses indicating questioning and commitment in midlife. There is also evidence that women's sense of identity certainty increases with age (Stewart et al., 2001; Zucker et al., 2002) and that identity is more salient for women who are more career-focused than family-focused (Newton & Stewart, 2010).

Work participation provides a fundamental source of identity for many people (Calvo, 2006), with a requisite high level of job involvement indicating a strong work identity (Fisher et al., 2015). Most studies examine work identity for older women within the context of retirement, with few studies examining women who remain in the workforce; however, some qualitative studies have examined the meaning of work for older women. For instance, participants in Altschuler's (2004) interview study consistently reported working beyond the minimum requirements of a job, seeing that as part of their work identity, and Price (2000) found that in a small group of retired women, many mentioned the theme of sacrificing their professional identity. This retirement-related shift in previous commitments that had been used to define identity can lead to identity revisions or consolidation (Lodi-Smith & Roberts, 2010; Osborne, 2009). Preretirement identities are often linked to postretirement identities (Reitzes & Mutran, 2006) and can provide a scaffolding for the types of postretirement activities in which professional women engage, such as volunteering or using skills from their professional lives in some way (Borrero & Kruger, 2015).

In sum, having a sense of identity that includes their work lives remains important into older adulthood for many women. For leading-edge baby boomer women, perhaps especially those for whom the women's movement afforded them more opportunities for higher education, work status, and increased decision-making power over their lives, having a sense of control or choice may also be related to greater identity certainty (Coon & Feuerherm, 2017; Lodi-Smith & Roberts, 2010). In the remainder of this chapter, we present findings from our own study of the relationship between level of choice in decisions to retire or continue working and personal identity among older women, many of whom were baby boomers. Consistent with contextualizing work-related decisions within a life-course perspective, we include age, health, income, and type of occupation in our analyses.

METHOD

In this study, women ($N = 221$) were drawn from two studies of women who were born in or who grew up during the period of the post–WWII baby boom (1946–1964): (a) the Radcliffe class of 1964 and (b) the Women's Life Paths Study (WLPS). Women from the Radcliffe class of 1964 (Stewart & Vandewater, 1993) have been followed for approximately 40 years, with follow-up data collection at ages 31, 33, 37, 43, 53, 62, and, most recently, 72 in 2014. As students at the coordinate school to Harvard University, they experienced both its advanced scholarship and the relative novelty of being a female student there in the 1960s; Radcliffe was not officially merged into Harvard until 1999. WLPS women are slightly younger than are those from Radcliffe, having graduated between 1967 and 1973 from the University of Michigan (Tangri & Jenkins, 1986). Many of the WLPS women surveyed were part of activist groups on campus, as per their alumni records. WLPS women have also been followed over time (but at comparatively different intervals to the Radcliffe women) between 1970 and (most recently) 2014, when they were age 67, on average. Both groups of women have been asked similar questions at each follow-up; however, in 2014 they received the same survey that included questions about their health and well-being, personality, work and family lives, activities, values, and beliefs. At the time of data collection in 2014, the combined group of women had an average age of 69.

Retired or Working, Chosen or Forced

To ascertain work status, we used participants' yes/no responses to the question "Are you retired?" If women had responded that they were retired, they were presented with four possible reasons for retiring and asked to rate the importance of each from 1 (*not at all important*) to 4 (*very important*). These reasons were (a) poor health, (b) wanted to do other things, (c) did not like the work, and (d) wanted to spend more time with the family. Participants were also asked to specify other factors influencing their retirement in an open-ended response. If still working, participants were asked: "Right now, would you like to leave work or retire but plan to keep working because: You need the money? (yes/no); You need health insurance? (yes/no); Other reasons? Please tell us." From the quantitative and qualitative responses to these questions, participants were first deemed to either have retired or have remained in work and then further divided by level of choice (forced or not), which resulted in four classification groups: (a) those who chose to retire, (b) those who were forced to retire, (c) those who chose to continue working, or (d) those who were forced to continue working (i.e., were job-locked).

For example, retired women who chose to retire rated as moderate to very important three of the four reasons we provided for retiring—doing other things, not liking the work, and wanting to spend more time with family—or had also rated their own reasons as important (e.g., "lost interest in career," "wanted to travel"). Those who felt forced to retire rated having poor health as moderately to very important and/or also rated their own reasons as important (e.g., "health of another family member," "job got eliminated"). Those who chose to work indicated that they were currently working with no need to do so for money or insurance; their open-ended responses also indicated volition (e.g., "working is a choice for me—I like working"; "I like the work and my identity as an attorney"). Finally, women who were still working because they needed money or their own insurance or whose self-identified reasons indicated other needs (e.g., "working for insurance for my partner") were classified as forced to work or job-locked. In our sample, 51% indicated having chosen to retire, 16% were forced to retire, 22% chose to remain working, and 11% indicated that they were forced to remain working. For examples of each of the four classifications, please see Table 4.1.

Type of Occupation: Professional or Nonprofessional

We adapted Hollingshead and Redlich's (1958) classification of occupations to represent participants' current (or previous) occupation dichotomously as either professional (70% of the sample) or nonprofessional (30% of the sample). All of the women in the sample had received at least a college

TABLE 4.1. Examples of Levels of Choice in Work-Related Decisions

Type of decision	Example
	Retirement
Chosen	Wanted next generation to have a chance at an academic teaching job. Don't believe I am owed a job for life despite tenure.
Forced	Retirement was kind of foisted on me; I had had surgery, was going to look for work, and then my husband was diagnosed with a brain tumor—not the time to look for a job.
	Remain working
Chosen	Commitment to my profession and feeling that I can still make a contribution in my professional work.
	My main reason for working is to be involved with people, children, learning, creativity.
Forced	Insurance, my partner needs health insurance.
	Money pretty much sums it up. I am hoping to be able to refinance in another year, but I am old.

degree, so we considered occupations that required a master's degree or higher, such as lawyer, physician, or professor, as professional. Nonprofessional occupations included personal trainer and travel agent.

Age, Health, and Income

As well as age, we included two further covariates: health and household income. The women's ages ranged from 60 to 83, with a mean of 69. Health was measured with a single item ("In general, would you say your health is excellent, very good, good, fair, or poor?") and rated from 1 (*poor*) to 5 (*excellent*), with 72% of the women rating their health as very good to excellent. Participants' total annual household income from all sources was rated from 1 (*under $40,000*) to 6 (*$400,001 and over*); the median income fell in category 3 (*$100,000–$200,000*).

Identity

To measure identity, we used a scale developed by Helson and Moane (1987): the Identity Certainty scale. This measure is actually a subscale from the Feelings About Life scale and has been used in research by Helson, Stewart, and colleagues (e.g., Miner-Rubino et al., 2004; Stewart et al., 2001; Zucker et al., 2002). Participants were given a series of statements, such as "A sense of being my own person" and "Feeling secure and committed," and asked to rate how descriptive each one was of their life, from 1 (*not at all descriptive*) to 3 (*very descriptive*). The overall mean for the resulting 8-item scale for this sample of women was 2.67 (*SD* = 0.30), and reliability was adequate (∂ = .67).

Analyses

We used both analysis of variance and analysis of covariance to analyze the data. On the basis of the literature, we expected that women who had chosen either of their work-related statuses would have higher levels of identity certainty than would their colleagues who felt they had less choice, and that professional women—especially those who chose to remain working— would also exhibit high levels of identity certainty. We present the results in the next section.

RESULTS

As expected, we found a significant difference in identity certainty between those who chose to retire and those who were forced to retire as well as those who were forced to continue working and no significant difference between choosing to retire and choosing to continue to work. Choosing retirement was related to the highest levels of identity certainty: On a 3-point scale, women who chose retirement (*M* = 2.75) scored higher than did women forced to retire and women forced to continue working (*M* = 2.54 for both). However, contrary to our expectations, there were no significant differences in identity certainty for those who chose to continue working (*M* = 2.69) compared with any of the other work-related statuses. This result did not change with the inclusion of the covariates (age, health, and income). Thus, identity certainty was highest in women who chose to retire, and this level was not significantly different for those who chose to remain working; levels of identity certainty in women forced to retire or to continue working were significantly lower than for those who chose to retire.

However, a slightly more nuanced picture emerged with the inclusion of the type of occupation (professional or nonprofessional). In this case, we found that there were few differences in identity certainty for both professional and nonprofessional women who chose to either retire or continue working, but identity certainty was comparatively low for those nonprofessional women who were forced to retire and lower still for professional women who were forced to remain working (see Figure 4.1). Thus, women, whether professional or nonprofessional, who chose to either continue

FIGURE 4.1. Level of Identity Certainty by Work-Related Decision

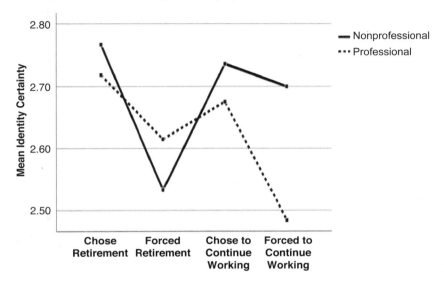

working or retire exhibited higher levels of identity certainty than did women forced to do either. Among women forced to retire or work, professional women forced to continue working showed lower levels of identity certainty compared with nonprofessional women forced to continue working; indeed, professional women forced to continue working exhibited comparatively the lowest identity certainty overall.

DISCUSSION

We examined levels of identity certainty as they relate to work-related decisions in a group of older women, taking into account whether the women perceived retiring or continuing to work as voluntary or involuntary. We also added the type of occupation as well as age, health, and household income. Our findings suggest that level of choice in whether to retire or continue working is associated with identity certainty for these women. For both professional and nonprofessional women, forced retirement was associated with relatively low levels of identity certainty. The largest difference in identity certainty was observed between nonprofessional women who chose retirement and professional women who were forced to remain working; there was also a large disparity in identity certainty between professional and nonprofessional women who were forced to remain in the workforce (i.e., they felt job-locked). In some ways, the most interesting finding is that professional women forced to remain working had the lowest sense of identity certainty.

With regard to interpreting the results, it is worth remembering that we included income and health as covariates and also asked specifically about the need to continue working because of financial or insurance needs. Additionally, few professional and even fewer nonprofessional women felt forced to continue working (14 and six, respectively). One might assume that after a long career, professional women would be less likely to need to continue working for either money or insurance. However, there are a plethora of potential reasons behind this finding, some of which we discuss below.

In light of the fact that many of the women in our study would have fought for and experienced greater educational and occupational opportunities through participation in the social movements of the 1960s and 1970s, having a sense of greater choice or control over work-related decisions might be particularly precious. Financial independence may be a choice for some, but for others, a necessity and/or reality: 35% of women in this study were currently not married, with 20% divorced, 10% widowed, and 5% single their entire lives. Does choice override personal resources such as financial success or health? Perhaps, given the evidence outlined earlier in this chapter (e.g., Everingham et al., 2007; Whiston et al., 2015). For example, our findings may be in accordance with Everingham and colleagues' (2007) transformative model of retirement, in which women can take on a working life subsequent to concluding a career but with greater control. In their study, women who had fewer rather than greater financial reserves put aside for retirement were more likely to follow this model; this might also be the case in our study, even for those women whose household income was above the current study's median, as we did not ask specifically about the size of retirement nest eggs.

Of course, there are many other reasons why women continue to work. For some women, the workplace may provide social structure and engagement; reasons can also be more complex than financial, insurance, or social, as evidenced by these responses to the open-ended question concerning other reasons to continue working: "I'm still working because it has many benefits and my husband can't easily travel or do sports. Work is the best diversion for me, and it pays (a little)." "I want to keep working because (a) I enjoy it and (b) there is no one to take on my role." "So I can give money away—Invest in my community/communities through philanthropy." "Being unmarried (divorced in 2011) I do not have a love of my life to share 'play time' with. Work is very engaging and feels useful." "The only power I have ever had in my job is the power not to retire. I enjoy using that." These responses highlight a number of themes: the diversionary nature of work, a sense of generative responsibility, philanthropic goals, feeling of use, and a slightly perverse (yet humorous) wish to wield what power one has to remain in the job. Many of the women in the present study also outlined multiple reasons for their work-related choices; very rarely was there only one reason.

In the current study, we measured an overall sense of identity certainty, one that Stewart and colleagues (Stewart & Ostrove, 1998; Stewart et al., 2001; Zucker et al., 2002) operationalized as a secure idea of one's self and where one fits in one's social world. Work identity—a high level of job involvement, working beyond the requirements of the job (Altschuler, 2004; Fisher et al., 2015)—is not specifically measured. However, work identity and a sense of certainty regarding who one is may be closely linked for many women. In 2018, 4 years later, we conducted a follow-up semistruc-tured interview study covering later-life transitions with 37 of the same women from the 2014 study outlined in this chapter. In their responses to open-ended questions, identity was spontaneously mentioned by many of the women, whether they had indicated in 2014 that they chose to retire or continue working or that they were forced to do either.

For example, one of the women who chose her work-related status (quoted below) was in the process of retiring when she was interviewed in 2018. She was aged 72 and single, had no children, and had indicated in 2014 that she was forced to continue running the agency she had founded 36 years previously. When asked in 2018 whether her retirement was planned or unplanned, she commented: "I had planned [retirement] out but it didn't turn out anything like I had planned [laughs] which is like most of life." In response to the question "Is there anything about the process or the approaching process that you want to tell me about?" she continued,

> I'm a little concerned because my work has been so much of my identity, and so much of my time. . . . I'm very concerned that I have to create a new identity for myself in a lot of ways . . . so, who am I going to be now that I'm not [a specialist in her field] you know? I have to create a new identity for myself. . . . I think I'll be alright. I've gone through a lot of life changes before, so, you know, I'm sure I'll adapt.

Issues of identity renegotiation were also evident for this next partici-pant, who in 2018 was 75 and divorced with two children as well as five grandchildren. She had indicated in 2014 that she chose to remain working. During the 2018 interview, when asked what she was looking forward to in retirement, she responded,

> I'm looking forward to reinventing myself, and not being [her current occupation] . . . not being identified in that context, because people make assumptions about [her current occupation] and what their motivations are and who they are, and they're money driven and always looking for business and I wanna shed that identity.

For one 75-year-old woman (widowed with two children and three grandchildren) who indicated in 2014 that she had chosen to retire in 2006, the identity–work link was something she perceived as gendered. Her comment came not in response to any of the work or retirement questions we posed but in response to the question "Do you think the process of aging is different for women compared to men?" To this she responded,

> Um, so, I think it's . . . this is a big generalization, but I think that, more often, men's identity is tied up to their job. I think that happens more with men than women. I think that's harder for them, that change in recognition, and appreciation, and competence, sort of, daily competence changes. I think that's hard for women, too, though.

Interestingly, none of the three women interviewed in 2018 who had indicated being forced to retire in the 2014 study mentioned any issues of identity when asked about work or retirement in 2018. Although all of them were in their early to mid-70s in 2018, these women differed on marital status (single, widowed, married) and family (no children, one child, two children, respectively), with two having retired in 2014 and one in 2003. For women who retired, whether forced to or by choice, perhaps the passing of time had distanced them from a preoccupation with work as a source of identity certainty, or they had had time to renegotiate or recalibrate their sense of self because that particular transition had occurred years before and was therefore less salient to them. Possibly other features of later life, such as downsizing, the process of aging, navigating relationships with adult children, or death of those close to them, were more closely linked to their sense of identity certainty; these issues often also spontaneously arose in the interviews.

What is evident from the data, theory, and previous research highlighted in this chapter is that work-related decisions remain complicated for women in later life. Also evident is the importance of examining these decisions within a life-course perspective (Elder, 1995; Settersten, 2003), taking into account personal resources, history, and social circumstances, as well as sense of control.

CONCLUSION

Transitions, such as those related to a lifetime of work, are complex. Holding on to, or revising, a sense of who one is and where one fits into society as a consequence of change in one's work role may be particularly difficult for many baby boomer women, whose work identities were often hard-won. Additionally, the freedom to make choices remains an important factor for all women as they continue to reassess and renegotiate their identities through the many transitions they will inevitably face with increasing age.

REFERENCES

Altschuler, J. (2004). Beyond money and survival: The meaning of paid work among older women. *International Journal of Aging & Human Development, 58*(3), 223–239. https://doi.org/10.2190/HNQH-BM29-KFB3-E461

Atchley, R. C. (1982). Retirement: Leaving the world of work. *The Annals of the American Academy of Political and Social Science, 464*(1), 120–131. https://doi.org/10.1177/0002716282464001011

Borrero, L., & Kruger, T. M. (2015). The nature and meaning of identity in retired professional women. *Journal of Women & Aging, 27*(4), 309–329. https://doi.org/10.1080/08952841.2014.950141

Calasanti, T. (2010). Gender relations and applied research on aging. *The Gerontologist, 50*(6), 720–734. https://doi.org/10.1093/geront/gnq085

Calasanti, T. M. (1996). Gender and life satisfaction in retirement: An assessment of the male model. *The Journals of Gerontology: Series B, 51B*(1), S18–S29. https://doi.org/10.1093/geronb/51B.1.S18

Calvo, E. (2006). *Does working longer make people healthier and happier?* (Issue Brief No. 5606). Center for Retirement Research at Boston College.

Clark, R. L., & Quinn, J. F. (2002). Patterns of work and retirement for a new century. *Generations, 26*(2), 17–24.

Coon, A. C., & Feuerherm, J. A. (2017). *Thriving in retirement: Lessons from baby boomer women.* Praeger.

Cooper, M. (1999). On retirement: A second life. In Z. Curtis (Ed.), *Life after work* (pp. 18–28). The Women's Press.

Czaja, S. J. (2006). Employment and the baby boomers: What can we expect in the future? In S. K. Whitbourne & S. L. Willis (Eds.), *The baby boomers grow up: Contemporary perspectives on midlife* (pp. 283–298). Psychology Press.

Di Gessa, G., Corna, L., Price, D., & Glaser, K. (2018). The decision to work after state pension age and how it affects quality of life: Evidence from a 6-year English panel study. *Age and Ageing, 47*(3), 450–457. https://doi.org/10.1093/ageing/afx181

Duncan, L. E., & Agronick, G. S. (1995). The intersection of life stage and social events: Personality and life outcomes. *Journal of Personality and Social Psychology, 69*(3), 558–568. https://doi.org/10.1037/0022-3514.69.3.558

Elder, G. H., Jr. (1995). The life course paradigm: Social change and individual development. In P. Moen, G. H. Elder, Jr., & K. Luscher (Eds.), *Examining lives in context: Perspectives on the ecology of human development* (pp. 101–139). American Psychological Association. https://doi.org/10.1037/10176-003

Erikson, E. (1959). *Identity and the life cycle: Selected papers.* International Universities Press.

Everingham, C., Warner-Smith, P., & Byles, J. (2007). Transforming retirement: Re-thinking models of retirement to accommodate the experiences of women. *Women's Studies International Forum, 30*(6), 512–522. https://doi.org/10.1016/j.wsif.2007.09.006

Fisher, G. G., Ryan, L. H., & Sonnega, A. (2015). Prolonged working years: Consequences and directions for interventions. In S. Leka, A. Jain, & G. Zwetsloot (Eds.), *Aligning perspectives on health, safety, and well-being* (pp. 269–288). Springer International Publishing.

Gibaldi, C. P. (2013). The changing trends of retirement: Baby boomers leading the charge. *Review of Business, 34*(1), 50–57.

Hammerman-Rozenberg, R., Maaravi, Y., Cohen, A., & Stessman, J. (2005). Working late: The impact of work after 70 on longevity, health and function. *Aging Clinical and Experimental Research, 17*(6), 508–513. https://doi.org/10.1007/BF03327419

Hartmann, H., & English, A. (2009). Older women's retirement security: A primer. *Journal of Women, Politics & Policy, 30*(2–3), 109–140. https://doi.org/10.1080/15544770902901932

Heckhausen, J., & Schulz, R. (1995). A life-span theory of control. *Psychological Review, 102*(2), 284–304. https://doi.org/10.1037/0033-295X.102.2.284

Helson, R., & Moane, G. (1987). Personality change in women from college to midlife. *Journal of Personality and Social Psychology, 53*(1), 176–186. https://doi.org/10.1037/0022-3514.53.1.176

Hollingshead, A., & Redlich, F. (1958). *Social class and mental illness.* Wiley. https://doi.org/10.1037/10645-000

Holstein, M. (2015). *Women in late life: Critical perspectives on gender and age.* Rowman & Littlefield.

Hutton, E. (1999). Retiring into the world. In Z. Curtis (Ed.), *Life after work* (pp. 54–63). The Women's Press.

James, J. B., Matz-Costa, C., & Smyer, M. A. (2016). Retirement security: It's not just about the money. *American Psychologist, 71*(4), 334–344. https://doi.org/10.1037/a0040220

Kim, J. E., & Moen, P. (2002). Retirement transitions, gender, and psychological well-being: A life-course, ecological model. *The Journals of Gerontology: Series B, 57*(3), 212–222. https://doi.org/10.1093/geronb/57.3.P212

Kojola, E., & Moen, P. (2016). No more lock-step retirement: Boomers' shifting meanings of work and retirement. *Journal of Aging Studies, 36*, 59–70. https://doi.org/10.1016/j.jaging.2015.12.003

Kroger, J. (2002). Identity processes and contents through the years of late adulthood. *Identity: An International Journal of Theory and Research, 2*(1), 81–99. https://doi.org/10.1207/S1532706XID0201_05

Kroger, J. (2016). Identity. In S. K. Whitbourne (Ed.), *The encyclopedia of adulthood and aging.* Wiley-Blackwell. https://doi.org/10.1002/9781118521373

Lachman, M. E., & Burack, O. R. (1993). Planning and control processes across the life span: An overview. *International Journal of Behavioral Development, 16*(2), 131–143. https://doi.org/10.1177/016502549301600203

Lodi-Smith, J., & Roberts, B. W. (2010). Getting to know me: Social role experiences and age differences in self-concept clarity during adulthood. *Journal of Personality*, *78*(5), 1383–1410. https://doi.org/10.1111/j.1467-6494.2010.00655.x

Miner-Rubino, K., Winter, D. G., & Stewart, A. J. (2004). Gender, social class, and the subjective experience of aging: Self-perceived personality change from early adulthood to late midlife. *Personality and Social Psychology Bulletin*, *30*(12), 1599–1610. https://doi.org/10.1177/0146167204271178

Moen, P. (2016). *Encore adulthood: Boomers on the edge of risk, renewal, & purpose*. Oxford University Press. https://doi.org/10.1093/acprof:oso/9780199357277.001.0001

Newton, N. J., & Stewart, A. J. (2010). The middle ages: Change in women's personalities and social roles. *Psychology of Women Quarterly*, *34*(1), 75–84. https://doi.org/10.1111/j.1471-6402.2009.01543.x

Newton, N. J., & Stewart, A. J. (2012). Personality development in adulthood. In S. K. Whitbourne & M. Sliwinski (Eds.), *The Wiley-Blackwell handbook of adulthood and aging* (pp. 211–235). Wiley-Blackwell. https://doi.org/10.1002/9781118392966.ch11

Ní Léime, Á. (2017). Older women public sector workers in Ireland: Decisions about retirement timing. *Journal of Women & Aging*, *29*(5), 392–404. https://doi.org/10.1080/08952841.2016.1196079

Osborne, J. W. (2009). Commentary on retirement, identity, and Erikson's developmental stage model. *Canadian Journal on Aging*, *28*(4), 295–301. https://doi.org/10.1017/S0714980809990237

Payne, S., & Doyal, L. (2010). Older women, work and health. *Occupational Medicine*, *60*(3), 172–177. https://doi.org/10.1093/occmed/kqq030

Price, C. A. (2000). Women and retirement: Relinquishing professional identity. *Journal of Aging Studies*, *14*(1), 81–101. https://doi.org/10.1016/S0890-4065(00)80017-1

Reitzes, D. C., & Mutran, E. J. (2006). Lingering identities in retirement. *The Sociological Quarterly*, *47*(2), 333–359. https://doi.org/10.1111/j.1533-8525.2006.00048.x

Settersten, R. A., Jr. (2003). Invitation to the life course: The promise. In R. A. Settersten, Jr. (Ed.), *Invitation to the life course: Toward new understandings of later life* (pp. 1–12). Baywood.

Shultz, K. S., Morton, K. R., & Weckerle, J. R. (1998). The influence of push and pull factors on voluntary and involuntary early retirees' retirement decision and adjustment. *Journal of Vocational Behavior*, *53*(1), 45–57. https://doi.org/10.1006/jvbe.1997.1610

Shultz, K. S., & Wang, M. (2011). Psychological perspectives on the changing nature of retirement. *American Psychologist*, *66*(3), 170–179. https://doi.org/10.1037/a0022411

Skaff, M. M. (2006). The view from the driver's seat: Sense of control in the baby boomers at midlife. In S. K. Whitbourne & S. L. Willis (Eds.), *The baby boomers grow up: Contemporary perspectives on midlife* (pp. 185–204). Psychology Press.

Stewart, A. J., & Healy, J. M., Jr. (1989). Linking individual development and social change. *American Psychologist*, *44*(1), 30–42. https://doi.org/10.1037/0003-066X.44.1.30

Stewart, A. J., & Ostrove, J. M. (1998). Women's personality in middle age. Gender, history, and midcourse corrections. *American Psychologist*, *53*(11), 1185–1194. https://doi.org/10.1037/0003-066X.53.11.1185

Stewart, A. J., Ostrove, J. M., & Helson, R. (2001). Middle aging in women: Patterns of personality change from the 30s to the 50s. *Journal of Adult Development, 8*(1), 23–37. https://doi.org/10.1023/A:1026445704288

Stewart, A. J., & Vandewater, E. A. (1993). The Radcliffe class of 1964: Career and family social clock projects in a transitional cohort. In K. D. Hulbert & D. T. Schuster (Eds.), *Women's lives through time* (pp. 235–258). Jossey-Bass.

Tangri, S. S., & Jenkins, S. R. (1986). Stability and change in role innovation and life plans. *Sex Roles, 14*(11–12), 647–662. https://doi.org/10.1007/BF00287695

Wang, M., Henkens, K., & van Solinge, H. (2011). Retirement adjustment: A review of theoretical and empirical advancements. *American Psychologist, 66*(3), 204–213. https://doi.org/10.1037/a0022414

Wang, M., & Shi, J. (2014). Psychological research on retirement. *Annual Review of Psychology, 65*, 209–233. https://doi.org/10.1146/annurev-psych-010213-115131

Whiston, S. C., Feldwisch, R. P., Evans, K. M., Blackman, C. S., & Gilman, L. (2015). Older professional women's views on work: A qualitative analysis. *The Career Development Quarterly, 63*(2), 98–112. https://doi.org/10.1002/cdq.12007

Whitbourne, S. K., & Skultety, K. M. (2006). Aging and identity: How women face later life transitions. In J. Worell & C. D. Goodheart (Eds.), *Handbook of girls' and women's psychological health* (pp. 370–378). Oxford University Press.

Zucker, A. N., Ostrove, J. M., & Stewart, A. J. (2002). College-educated women's personality development in adulthood: Perceptions and age differences. *Psychology and Aging, 17*(2), 236–244. https://doi.org/10.1037/0882-7974.17.2.236

5

PLENTY MORE AT THE FACTORY GATE

An Autoethnography of a Precarious Work (Life) in Progress

JACKIE GOODE

'. . . *still God knows in what Cabinet every seed Pearl lies (Donne, 1953–62, 8:98)' Once again, Donne returns to the image of dispersed body parts as so many minute pearls in the cabinet, a piece of Renaissance furniture that functioned both as a safe and a display case for wondrous and precious things. A hard exterior which held a hidden jewel, the cabinet was in fact a fairly popular metaphor for the body containing the soul.*

(Greteman, 2010, p. 38)

Autobiographical writing has a long history within a number of disciplines, but feminist reactions against a master narrative that constructed a universal (male) subject led postwar academic writers such as Walkerdine (1985) and Steedman (1986) to focus particularly on girls' and women's experiences—experiences that had hitherto been "hidden from history" (Rowbotham, 1973); furthermore, autobiographical texts were seen as a mode of writing through which to validate and make visible ordinary lives, including working lives. In the years that followed, however, autobiography/personal reflection

https://doi.org/10.1037/0000212-006
Older Women Who Work: Resilience, Choice, and Change, E. Cole and L. Hollis-Sawyer (Editors)

in academic writing was often criticized as narcissistic (see Walkerdine & Squire, 2010) and as such, it was seen as having little merit in terms of social, cultural, and economic analysis. Despite its status as a form of ethnography and despite the recent "turn to affect" and engagement with embodiment (also frequently accused of being characterized by "excess"; Wetherell, 2013), autoethnography has faced similar criticism. As Richardson (1992) observed, "for social scientists to ponder their lived experience, making that experience the centerpiece of an article seems Improper, bordering on the Gauche and Burdensome" (p. 126).

This view continues to have purchase within the editorial practices of some mainstream academic journals, where it is not uncommon to see critiques of autoethnography undertaken from a positivist standpoint. Indeed, one reviewer's comments on an earlier autoethnography of mine about dining out alone as an older woman (Goode, 2018a) included the observations that gender was not a dominant factor in this case because of the age factor interfering, that this was something that could have been foreseen before the research design had been drafted, that the setting was not representative enough for testing the phenomenon under study, and that the narrative segment is too polished and presented in a literary or feature-article manner, and thus very little heuristic value-added is brought by this approach. These comments reveal not only a misunderstanding of qualitative approaches in general but a failure to recognize the way auto-ethnography goes beyond the personal and individual. As Ellingson and Ellis (2008) observed, "Analytic autoethnographers focus on developing theoretical explanations of broader social phenomena" (p. 445). They contrasted this with evocative autoethnography, which focuses on "narrative presentations that open up conversations and evoke emotional responses" (p. 445). However, I prefer not to make this distinction.

My aim is to use autoethnography as a method of understanding how an individual life is connected through space and time to the lives of others in a way that evokes identification, opens up a conversation, and offers an analysis of wider social, cultural, and political issues. This chapter therefore offers an autoethnographic account of an academic life that began comparatively late and that continues post–official retirement. It aims to bring out the interweaving of biography and (institutional/ political) history by tracing experiences of precarity within the academy, that is, the state of having insecure employment or income, which prefigured what are now widespread conditions for most former and current colleagues.

WOMEN, "CAREER," AND CARE WORK

For British people of my age and background (those born in the late 1940s and early 1950s into working-class families), the apotheosis of one's beginnings as a bright grammar-school pupil of the 1960s might be seen as the achievement of a successful academic career—the onward movement of its subject through an uninterrupted linear trajectory to its summit before giving up paid work to enjoy a leisured retirement financed by a generous occupational pension. I should say that that narrative doesn't quite work for me. My entry into the academy as a paid-up "member"—that is, as a full-time researcher (albeit on a series of fixed-term contracts) for a period of 20 years—came late, and uncovering some of the reasons for that and its implications for my current experiences as someone still working goes some way toward explaining both the kinds and the meanings of my continuing participation in both paid and unpaid work, post–official retirement.

When I took up my first post as a full-time researcher on a project funded by the Economic and Social Research Council (ESRC),[1] which constituted the first step on my academic career, I had already qualified and worked for some years as both a probation officer and a teacher, and I was married with children. In light of my status at that time as a working mother, it is perhaps necessary to restate that all employees' participation in paid work is dependent upon some people's undertaking of unpaid or poorly paid care work and that those doing that care work are predominantly women. Furthermore, so much of care work in both employment and domestic settings remains invisible (De Vault, 1991). This is another common interpretive device used in our culture to explain women's lack of or delayed career success (where success is conventionally defined in terms of promotion through a career ladder): that we continue to carry an unequal burden in relation to child care responsibilities. Although I would argue that I did indeed take the major responsibility for either doing or organizing the child care in my family (with the support of day nurseries and child-minders, together with juggling my work commitments or working from home during school holidays), this narrative too doesn't fully work in an explanatory capacity in relation to my experiences of work for the majority of my working life and through into later life.

---

[1]The ESRC is the main government-funding body for the social sciences in the United Kingdom; highly competitive ESRC-funded projects are generally seen as the gold standard.

Problematizing the Notion of Work/Career Choice

The realities of women's (paid and unpaid) working lives are much messier, more complex, and more contingent than many theories capture. This is certainly true of Hakim's (2000) preference theory of women's workforce participation, in which women are divided into three lifestyle preference groups of work-centered, home-centered, or adaptive, with each having "a substantively different value system, as well as differing life goals" (Hakim, 2003, p. 55). Although the theory has been heavily critiqued (e.g., Leahy & Doughney, 2014), the particular conceptualization of the notion of choice inherent in it remains a powerful underpinning to neoliberal discourses and policies in relation to work and family life (as well as welfare). Just as the inseparable linkages between politics, economics, family, and work and the fact that we are all emotional as well as rational beings operate in the course of our paid working lives, so too these intersections and inter-actions carry through into later life, including for those like me who retain the privilege of some element of choice about whether, why, and what work they continue to do.

In telling a story of how this is the case in relation to my participation in work as an older woman, I am implicitly inviting the reader to problematize the model of choice in rational choice theory by looking instead at how, in lived experience, some things are afforded and some constrained, some become accomplished and some falter and perish—rather than patterns of working lives being chosen in the unproblematic way Hakim suggested, in which we are all levered into some ideal-type categorizations.

A Working Life Story

It is 1954.

"Is it *today* I start school? . . . Is it *today*?"

I have come with my mum down the stairs from the two-bedroom council flat in which my parents, my two sisters, and I live, into my father's butcher's shop. I am desperate to follow my big sisters into school. Once I do start, I love it. And when I'm not at school, I'm hanging around the shop, watching my dad at work, watching my mum helping out, watching them both inter-acting with customers—my dad who gets on with everyone, my mum who somehow conveys to me the subtle distinctions she makes between those customers who meet her aspirational criteria and those who are "common." When I'm older, I'll go on the rounds with my mum, delivering weekly orders to the customers on the back estate—more council housing built in the wake of postwar slum clearance from the West End of town—where those distinc-tions will be reinforced.

It is 1961.

We get my results on the 11-plus—the exam that takes you to grammar school. I've passed! I'm one of the select few. I start just as my eldest sister leaves, but she gives me all the low-down. She will soon start work in the library of the new technical center at British Rail, one of the biggest local employers, the other being Rolls Royce.

It is 1964.

I love school! I love "English Lang." I love English Lit. I *love* my English teacher. He has beautiful wavy hair just like my dad has in a photograph I've seen of him before I was born. School is my life, but if I want to buy the latest single or EP [extended-play record] to listen to on my big sister's new record player, I'd better get a Saturday job. My mother finds one through a customer—in a hardware shop at the other side of town. It's hard work, lugging heavy rolls of thick stiff linoleum around and cutting the required lengths with a Stanley knife. This is the real world and I'd better get used to it, "my girl," because all of a sudden in a way I don't understand, it seems I'm in danger of becoming "too clever by half" (Goode, 2019).

It is 1965.

I am devastated because my English teacher is leaving to take up a senior post at another school. My 15-year-old world collapses. I am in mourning. I fill my diary with outpourings of loss and longing.

It is 1966.

There's a battle on at home over my going into the sixth form next year, where after 2 years you take the exams that get you into university. This is a step too far for my mother, whose aspirations for betterment have apparently reached their limit, at least as far as her youngest daughter is concerned. She is somewhat mollified when I get a holiday job in the computer room at British Rail as a punch-tape operator, and at the end of the summer, she relents sufficiently to let me stay on at school after all (but there is resentment because, really, it's about time I left school and started "earning my keep").

It is 1967.

Application forms for university have been given out at school, and I carry mine around in my school bag for days, afraid to broach the subject at home. But then there is a careers evening at school, and my resulting thought of becoming a probation officer appears to be an acceptable choice to my mother. Rather inconveniently for her, however, it turns out that it is now a graduate profession. In fact, it requires a joint degree in sociology and social administration and then a postgraduate social work qualification. The whole subject is dropped at home, but at school, teachers keep asking me to return the completed application forms. I am embarrassed. I don't know what to say. I am between a rock and a hard place. Unholy rows break out at home. I am "selfish" and "ungrateful." At the last minute, my quiet father steps in—I am to be allowed to apply!

It is 1968.

My dad is so proud when I pass all of my first-year exams that when I get home for the summer, I see he has pinned a note congratulating me to the chimney breast above the fire.

It is 1969.

I am in my second year as an undergraduate. When I come home at Christmas, my dad is unwell but it's nothing serious. By the summer, though, he is in hospital. When I get home for the long vacation, there are daily visits. I am at his bedside when he dies. "He may have been your father," my mother tells me angrily, "but he was *my* husband!" And where was I anyway when he was ill? Away at university enjoying myself, that's where! I am not entitled to mourn him. I swallow my grief.

It is 1972.

I have got my degree and my certificate of qualification in social work. I have started work as a probation officer. I am given a caseload of more than 60 clients on my first day. I have a great bunch of colleagues. I love my work. I am good at it. I know this because my boss tells me so. He is very professionally supportive. He is a lovely man with thick wavy hair. A new colleague joins our team, and we start dating. After a year we get engaged.

It is 1975.

My lovely boss leaves. Something I don't understand happens; I don't seem to be able to face my clients. I can't bear the complexities of their lives or the painful stories they tell me. I can't face the responsibility I feel for making things better for them. I feel overwhelmed by everything. I sit in my office staring at the wall. I cry a lot. I decide I have to leave. My new middle-aged no-nonsense female boss tells me brusquely that I can do so if I choose but that I will discover there's nothing else I am capable of. A small spark of rebellion surfaces. I leave and retrain as a teacher. My fiancé isn't too happy about this. He seems disturbed by my deviation from the trajectory he had imagined for me. But I get a job as soon as I qualify.

It is 1979.

After 3 years of teaching, I am offered a paid studentship to do a full-time MPhil[2] at the highly esteemed local university. My husband appears to support the move, but my mother's criticism when I left Probation to

---

[2]In the United Kingdom, a master's of philosophy is a postgraduate degree by research only, with no taught component.

do (another?!) postgraduate qualification resurfaces with a vengeance. I'm almost 30—why am I not at home with a baby? (says the woman who has repeatedly issued me with the dire unspecified warning to "Just wait till *you* have children!"). In fact, after prolonged and painful discussions with my husband, I have been trying unsuccessfully to conceive for almost a year, but I don't tell her this. By the time the studentship has ended, my mother has died, and I am pregnant. I take a half-time job teaching in what is called a Disruptive (Pupil Referral) Unit while writing up my master's thesis. Upgrading to a doctorate is never discussed. Neither of my research supervisors has a PhD, and I am not aware this is even an option. (Many years later after we have become friends, my female supervisor will apologize, telling me how guilty she has felt all these years about her own ignorance of procedures at the time and about the opportunity for me to get a doctorate with very little extra effort she felt had been forfeited.)

It is 1991.

My second son is starting school. I have worked part-time since his older brother was born at the end of my writing-up period, and now I return to full-time work in a primary school in a deprived ex-mining area. It's really tough. The children are challenging, but it is the predominantly older female staff who are sitting out their time till their approaching retirement who make my life more difficult. They also seem to see me as "too clever by half." The head teacher who appointed me often goes AWOL [absent without leave]. The local education authority appoints a highly respected peripatetic deputy in an attempt to sort things out. He tries hard to do so—to be supportive to all the staff—but they continue to complain bitterly about everything while fiercely resisting change. He takes to discreetly chatting to me in the corridor after school. We are both struggling. After a year, he confides that he is leaving. He can't cope any longer with this toxic environment. He urges me to get out too if I value my own sanity. I take his advice. He goes on to a headship of an inner-city school in the next town, which goes from strength to strength under his leadership.

In (and Out) of the Academy
It is 1992.

I start my first job as an academic researcher. Over the next 8 years, I will work on a series of short-term contracts on a succession of funded projects that often have a focus on gender and that draw on the skills I have developed through both my social work training and practice and my MPhil research (although I am very clear about the boundaries between the two kinds of activities; see Goode, 2006).

I gain a reputation as a good qualitative researcher, but there is never time to apply for funding in my own right. And my name never comes first on the articles I write. At home, meanwhile, my marriage is deteriorating. My husband is unsympathetic to my own dissatisfactions with the institutionalized precarity I have, admittedly rather late in the day, come to understand and to the dissatisfaction I express about the lack of ownership of the products of my labors. He seems to feel vindicated when, after 8 years, the contracts come to an end, and I am made redundant ("Shame," says my head of department, "but plenty more at the factory gate"). I go on to secure research contracts elsewhere but occasionally still go back to the university where I spent 8 years to hear others give their inaugural lectures. After one such return visit, I write a poem about my initial entry into the academy as a researcher, about the growing industrialization of higher education that that "factory gate" reference signifies, and about trying to restore some agency to myself as I leave my original institution once more, after the lecture.

Woman Returner
At first it was like being back
at school. Back
with the clever ones. Back
where I belonged.
It felt like coming home.
But long absence
had left intellectual muscles wasted
analytic eye clouded
faculties dulled. I had failed to see
that the market had got in well ahead of me.
I thought I had kept one step ahead
jumping ship, breasting the waves from one sector
to another to reach a safe haven.
In mitigation for such naivete I offer,
on my own behalf, the ubiquitous rhetoric I met.
"Researchers are a precious resource. We value
and depend on them". The reverse, of course
was true. I was the dependent one. And, I put my hands up
to it, I colluded in the ensemble performance.
A daily tight-rope walker on the fine line between
that extinct old poodle collegiality
and subservience—

the oil that greased the wheels
of the new
academic production.
I served my mistresses well.
Crawled, hopped, and hauled through eight years,
five projects and so many contracts
I lost count. Lost too, along the way, some self-respect.
But kept a job.
When time was eventually called
off came the mask.
The bared teeth snarled:
"Researchers? Plenty more at the factory gate".
I sloped off still smiling, still doing the emotion work
for them as well as me. By then I'd honed my skills.
I saw all, heard all, but still said nowt.
Such wisdom was cold comfort.
Now when I go back with the retired
with those who made a more graceful and
well-earned exit, to attend long-overdue
inaugural lectures by my ex-colleagues (of sorts)
I slip unawares into including myself
Into saying 'we'
and talking about 'our' department
Redundant loyalty. Redundant me.
I see as I drive away again that I had been thinking
perhaps when I had served my time
in the wilderness they would let me back in.
Now, more contracts, more years on
I leave of my own free will.

It is 2002.

I have secured a post as the researcher on another high-profile interinstitutional ESRC-funded project, the fieldwork for which is, however, split between my home city and London. The principal investigators provide me with a hot desk at both universities but are also happy for me to work from home, which makes after-school child-care arrangements easier. My husband is not happy that I finance the purchase of secondhand office furniture out of the family budget to set up the spare bedroom as my office and that I can't claim for the work-related telephone calls I make from home; at the same time, the benefits to the family of my working from home for long periods over the following 2 years go unrecognized.

Losing the Plot

While my older son is negotiating his exams quite successfully, my younger son's ways of learning do not bring such effortless exam success, so my being there when he gets home from school during this period enable him to ask for support with homework and revision when he wants it.

My husband has been promoted once more, despite the Probation Service having changed direction in ways that are incompatible with his beliefs and values. He is permanently frustrated and angry—and certainly not inclined to be supportive to a wife struggling to maintain a balance between support and authority toward an adolescent son who is also often confused, frustrated, and angry.

My working from home may serve the family well but it requires even more juggling by me and is emotionally exhausting and personally isolating. I keep up the journal I have used for many years as a way of talking to myself. It records my travails as I try to face up to the increasingly undeniable knowledge that at some point I will stop trying to placate an angry husband and end my marriage. My still-precarious employment status is matched now by an increasingly precarious hold on my own ontological integrity, on my ability to stop everything falling apart, and on my ability to maintain a stable family life at least until my younger son (who has now passed all his exams and gone on to sixth form college) joins his older brother at university. If I can only secure a permanent post by then, I might be able to get the mortgage I would need to buy a small house in the same neighborhood, so that the children can maintain at least some continuity amid all the disruption that will ensue, when they come home. My nonacademic friends have always seen the fact that I have (almost) always managed to secure the next contract as evidence that I worry too much. But chronic insecurity has become what Williams (1961) called a "structure of feeling" that infuses my very being.

I do secure other projects, but when my marriage finally comes to an end, I am still on a fixed-term contract. A new ruling offers some hope of enhanced security for university researchers who have completed at least two 2-year contracts at the same institution. I qualify for this, but there is a get-out clause: The employer can terminate a contract anyway if they can identify a reasonable objection to renewal (e.g., if you haven't generated sufficient research funding to cover your own salary). But my younger son has followed his older brother in securing his place at university, so I initiate divorce after only 3 years' employment in the research institute whose head appointed me despite what he referred to at interview as my rather "hybrid" curriculum vitae ("Why *is* that?" "Er, because I'm a woman").

It is 2005.

My husband refers to this "hybridity," too, during the negotiations over our financial settlement. He is by now earning around twice as much as me in a secure senior management position, and he objects to my claim on half our combined pension pots. He sees his pension as his and makes clear what he thinks about the fact that although we started out equal in career prospects, I have brought in poorer earnings over the years and have ended up still in insecure employment. This has been my choice, he maintains, and I should bear the financial consequences. In a context in which I feel vulnerable in myriad ways, being a sociologist used to analyzing aids me not one jot in refuting this argument or in being able to offer any kind of counternarrative. Fortunately, recent legislation in relation to pensions is in my favor. And I do get a mortgage after all.

Choosing Work in Later Life

It is 2006.

In my own little house, and at the age of 56, a huge surge of energy and a new confidence in my own voice leads to a belated academic achievement. Having generated sufficient sole-authored articles that I worked on in my own time, I get my PhD-by-publication. The award of my doctorate feels like the validation of all my hard work that has been lacking for so long, institutionally and on the home front. Shortly after this, I get a permanent job in a research center at the university where I originally contract-hopped for 8 years before being made redundant.

It is 2007.

I am promoted for the first time in my academic career.

It is 2011.

The government funding on which the center largely relies has dried up, leading to successive rounds of redundancy. After a sustained period of more than 20 years as an academic researcher, I haven't been back at this university long enough to qualify for more than a month's salary as a redundancy payment, and I choose instead to take early retirement on a pension reduced by my part-time status during the children's preschool years, by my postgraduate training years, by short periods out of work, and by having to wait another 4 years for the postdivorce pension-sharing order to kick in. Over the next 5 years I supplement my pension with paid work of my own choosing, sometimes being invited back to my original department on projects requiring short fixed-term contracts and sometimes on a self-employed basis. The supplemental income funds attendance at conferences where I present the findings of small-scale research projects of my own design and execution. I make the kind of academic friends I've never had time to make and maintain before. Writing and publishing now is genuinely a pleasure.

It is 2018.

I am conscious of the irony inherent in being rewarded in my late 60s for the very hybridity that has arisen from my life of academic precarity— a precarity that has led of necessity to my becoming infinitely adaptable but that constituted a lack of career capital in an occupation in which expertise is defined as increasing specialization in increasingly niche areas. I am conscious too of how privileged I am in (so-called) retirement to have a pension that on its own affords me a much more modest lifestyle than my ex-husband now enjoys in his retirement but that nevertheless gives me security at last.

My grown-up sons, of whom I am immensely proud, have gone on to successful careers of their own. On my younger son's bedroom wall in his flat in London is a framed poster that reads in large font: "Work Hard and Be Nice to People." I mention it to my older son on one of his visits to me. "Not a bad motto to live by," I observe, adding, "I thought, when I saw it, that perhaps I'd got *something* right." He laughs. "That's what Dad said, too." I allow myself a slightly raised eyebrow that he acknowledges with another laugh. "When he said it," he continues, "I thought 'Yes—you gave me one of those, and Mum gave me the other.'"

That shuts me up. Not that I am not pleased that he feels I've passed on important values about kindness to others. But what about the feminism that I have never preached but that has informed so much of my research over the years and that has been the mood music of so many of my discussions with him from the time he was old enough to talk about gender issues? I am genuinely shocked that all the hard intellectual, physical, and emotional labor that has gone into producing and maintaining my own professional work identity (on which my sons continue to draw in various ways in their own working lives), not to mention my contribution to the family finances and all the family care work I put in, seems to have just disappeared in front of my eyes.

CONCLUSION

I return, finally, to Ettlinger's (2007) disinclination/inability to compartmentalize—that is, a disinclination to inflict symbolic self-harm by cutting out some parts of our selves and of our lives to privilege others (as in Donne's separation of body and soul). When applied in this context, it translates into a rejection of traditional, narrow definitions of *career* that leave out so much of the fabric of women's lives. So much of how life is for us now—including our participation in paid and unpaid work as older women—arises from our earlier life experiences. From my vantage point in later life, I see a number of interrelated factors at play in the choices I made in relation to my earlier working life. Many of these were to do with the reverberations of the dynamics of family relationships—which often remain hidden even to ourselves—such as the delayed grief reaction I now think propelled my leaving the probation service, such as the fact that I certainly wouldn't have gone to university in the first place had it not been for my father's support (see Goode, 2018b).

And then there are institutional factors. So, even with his support, it would have been inconceivable for a working-class girl to go to university without the availability of free tuition and a maintenance grant (followed by the Home Office stipend that financed my probation training). At the point at which I felt I needed to change direction, state provision played a part once more—a grant from my local education authority funded my teacher training. None of this, nor my ability to move with relative ease in and out of employment when my children were small, can be detached from the healthy state of the economy at the time. The fact that this worked not only for me but for the family was due not only to my ability to earn a salary sufficient to cover the cost of supplementary child care but also to my ex-husband's more sustained career, involving successive promotions and salary increases (together with the associated symbolic reward for him of status and the very tangible reward of future security).

In this gendered (main breadwinner/supplementary worker) model of workforce participation and family organization, one kind of contribution is more highly (publicly) visible and valued than the other and one kind of (privatized) work remains less visible and valued than the other. I had thought I was starting out on a late career in research but had no real grasp of the institutional organization of academic work with its flexibilized, casualized workforce of researchers. The fate of those who opt for a research-only path is to forfeit security of tenure. They have to try to secure end-to-end contracts, moving from project to project, and sometimes from institution to institution, to stay employed. The lucky few of us who manage to do this for any length of time inevitably accrue a wealth of experience of how research is organized and conducted in different contexts, a repertoire of skills, and a vast volume of data, some of which never sees the light of day.

All of those who use qualitative approaches to research will be familiar with the acquisition of this kind of material, but the whole process of deploying one's self in coproducing such data, living with it on a day-to-day basis, analyzing, interpreting, selecting from, and shaping it for various audiences, does not define their professional identity in quite the same way as it does for full-time contract researchers. The full-time researcher is permanently engaged in deploying herself in this way, creating intimate relationships that by their very nature are meaningful, before moving on to a new project with a new set of research subjects. The project constitutes its own bounded social world within which meaning is constructed, and we are required to parcel that meaningfulness up and leave it behind and to recreate ourselves anew in another (institutional and/or geographical) place or space. We have to constantly negotiate a series of beginnings and endings, and there is always a residue of data, always unfinished business. Of some significance for my sense of self-esteem was the fact that I had other professional identities on which to draw, even if the changes that fueled the development of these different selves arose out of shocks to my sense of ontological security.

By the time I washed up on the postretirement shore, a number of things had changed in ways that impacted even more negatively on the nature of academic work. The marketization of higher education and the introduction of austerity measures mean that the precarity I experienced as I tried to stitch together a curriculum vitae that had some semblance of coherence, while contract-hopping from one project and one institution to another, has spread to the whole academic workforce. We are (almost) all members of the industrialized academic proletariat now. Except of course that, thanks to a pension that may not be available to my younger British colleagues (and in defense of which they recently took to the picket lines), I am now in a position as a baby boomer in semiretirement genuinely free to choose whether and what work I do when my ex-colleagues, under the constraints of fast academia, are able to access a bit of funding and come looking for someone who can pick a brief up at short notice and deliver the goods.

And what about the nonpaid academic work I continue to do? Conference presentations and, more importantly, publications have become outputs to be counted and measured as part of the audit culture of higher education. But for me, just as much as for the occasional supplementary income it brings, it is the satisfaction I get in terms of pride in my accomplishments and in terms of finally belonging to a community that explains why I remain part of the academic workforce (on both a paid and a self-funded basis). Being an unsalaried visiting research fellow at the university where I spent most of my academic career is still a marginalized position but one that now benefits me in institutional terms. That sense of being overwhelmed by chronic insecurity that became a "structure of feeling" infusing my very being for so long has disappeared.

Sharma and Tygstrup (2015) observed that Williams's notion of structures of feeling has barely been theorized but what seems to be at its center is experience as lived presence within a time and place. They suggested he is asking,

> What does it feel like to be in a particular situation? How do our propensities for doing this and not that emerge? What fuels our enthusiasm or enhances our wellbeing? How do the little things pertaining to feeling, bodily sensation and atmosphere inflect . . . the ideas we proclaim and interests we pursue? (Sharma & Tygstrup, 2015, p. 1)

They called for a third layer to be built in to our analysis to complement the social and material infrastructure—that of an "affective infrastructure." And in doing so, they observed that Williams was prefiguring the affective turn in social and cultural studies. What these approaches share is

> a certain phenomenological awareness of how experience is articulated in a close and complex interaction between humans and their environments, how it is bodily mediated, how it plays out in a particular spatial framework, and how it is inextricably invested in and dependent on social relations between humans, and between humans and social institutions. . . . [Such approaches] expand our understanding of . . . the ways in which culture is continually reproduced (and gradually developed in still new dimensions) through the interaction between life forms and everyday practices on the one hand, and institutions and power relations on the other. (Sharma & Tygstrup, 2015, pp. 2–3)

And if so much of women's work—its social organization, its meanings, how it is experienced, how it is constitutive of our identities in important ways, and how it is inseparable from the rest of our familial, social, cultural and economic lives, all the way through into older age—still remains invisible (even to the sons we raised who have observed it at close quarters[3]), perhaps from the vantage point of an older working woman I can bequeath an autoethnographic account like this, which offers a degree of complexity in its retrospective analysis, compatible with the complexity of all working women's lived experience.

REFERENCES

De Vault, M. (1991). *Feeding the family: The social organization of caring as gendered work*. University of Chicago Press.

Ellingson, L., & Ellis, C. (2008). Autoethnography as constructionist project. In J. A. Holstein & J. F. Gubrium (Eds.), *Handbook of constructionist research* (pp. 445–466). Guilford Press.

---

[3] I am being unfair, of course. My son was, I think, drawing a contrast rather than devaluing my contributions to the worlds of paid and unpaid work. Still, stereotypes persist.

Ettlinger, N. (2007). Precarity unbound. *Alternatives, 32*(3), 319–340. https://doi.org/10.1177/030437540703200303

Goode, J. (2006). Research identities: Reflections of a contract researcher. *Sociological Research Online, 11*(2), 40–49. https://doi.org/10.5153/sro.1389

Goode, J. (2018a). Being one's own honoured guest: Eating out alone as gendered sociality in public spaces. *Sociological Research Online, 23*(1), 100–113. https://doi.org/10.1177/1360780418754566

Goode, J. (2018b). Exhuming the good that men do: The play of the mnemonic imagination in the making of an autoethnographic text. *Time & Society, 28*(4), 1645–1667.

Goode, J. (2019). Too clever by half. In J. Goode (Ed.), *Clever girls: Autoethnographies of class, gender and ethnicity* (pp. 89–113). Palgrave Macmillan. https://doi.org/10.1007/978-3-030-29658-2_5

Greteman, B. (2010). "All this seed pearl": John Donne and bodily presence. *College Literature, 37*(3), 26–42. https://doi.org/10.1353/lit.0.0117

Hakim, C. (2000). *Work-lifestyle choices in the twenty-first century: Preference theory*. Routledge.

Hakim, C. (2003). Competing family models, competing social policies. *Family Matters, 64*, 51–61.

Leahy, M., & Doughney, J. (2014). Women, work and preference formation: A critique of Catherine Hakim's preference theory. *Journal of Business Systems, Governance, and Ethics, 1*(1), 37–48.

Richardson, L. (1992). The consequences of poetic representation, writing the other; rewriting the Self. In C. Ellis & M. G. Flaherty (Eds.), *Investigating subjectivity, research on lived experience* (pp. 125–140). Sage.

Rowbotham, S. (1973). *Hidden from history: 300 years of women's oppression and the fight against it*. Pluto Press.

Sharma, D., & Tygstrup, F. (Eds.). (2015). *Structures of feeling. Affectivity and the study of culture*. De Gruyter.

Steedman, C. (1986). *Landscape for a good woman: A story of two women*. Virago Press.

Walkerdine, V. (1985). Dreams from an ordinary childhood. In L. Heron (Ed.), *Truth, dare or promise: Girls growing up in the fifties* (pp. 63–77). Virago Press.

Walkerdine, V., & Squire, C. M. (2010). Reading the rereadings: Valerie Walkerdine responds to the commentaries on 'Video Replay.' *Psychoanalysis, Culture & Society, 15*(4), 412–417. https://doi.org/10.1057/pcs.2010.24

Wetherell, M. (2013). Affect and discourse—What's the problem? From affect as excess to affective/discursive practice. *Subjectivity, 6*(4), 349–368. https://doi.org/10.1057/sub.2013.13

Williams, R. (1961). *The long revolution*. Chatto & Windus. https://doi.org/10.7312/will93760

PART II SOCIETAL ROLES OF AGING WOMEN WORKERS

INTRODUCTION

Societal Roles of Aging Women Workers

Chapters 6 through 9 relate to women's roles in the workplace and in their communities in later life. Societal expectations of older women's roles, from the workplace to the family, have evolved over time (Martin et al., 2019), but there are always issues of potential bias and barriers to access—such as discrimination in workplace training policies—in career development opportunities for older women of color and other related diversity issues (McGregor, 2018). Older women occupy many different roles by choice or need. These work-related roles may sometimes compete with or complement each other, but they ultimately affect one's physical and mental well-being in later life (e.g., women of color and the prevalent stress of a "superwoman schema"; Woods-Giscombé, 2010). Vives et al. (2018) reported that older Chilean women typically balance both unpaid and paid work roles into their later adulthood years, and older women's working environments can meaningfully impact both their health outcomes and work sustainability in many ways.

Older women past traditional retirement age may decide that they want to continue to work, but they may find that this contradicts filial or societal expectations of their societal role in their culture. The circumstances of this decision process have ramifications both for older women's quality of life (e.g., financial security) and for their personal relationships and/or social networks. As an example, Michel et al. (2019) discussed the needed social engagement of African grandmothers. The many challenges facing women in later life, from being an elder caregiver to being a female role model and mentor in the workplace, are significant factors to examine in understanding quality-of-life outcomes for diverse groups of older women who may otherwise feel invisible in society (Ainsworth, 2002; Harrison, 1991).

Older women past traditional retirement age have much to offer in terms of their wisdom, expertise, and cultural knowledge. Valuing their contributions through their continued societal roles would benefit these older women from diverse backgrounds and identities as well as society as a whole. The empowerment of older women of color and other aspects of diversity (e.g., sexual orientation, education background, and cohort membership) is crucial for the overall mental and physical health of societies undergoing aging growth trends in the coming decades (e.g., see a description of intersectionality of aging and lesbian, gay, and bisexual identity in Cronin & King, 2010).

In many cultures and contexts, older women are redefining what it means to be both an older worker and an older woman (Kautonen, 2008; Quéniart & Charpentier, 2012; Richards et al., 2012). Continuing to work in later life can be a quality-of-life issue for aging women across many cultures and communities (Choi, 2001; Kooij et al., 2008), especially in light of the new longevity of many populations across the world (Gratton & Scott, 2016). Economic security is certainly an aspect of this quality-of-life concern (e.g., "feminization of poverty"; Minkler & Stone, 1985). Beyond financial concerns, extending work engagement into later life can be a positive extension of self-identity and personal motivations for older women (McKenzie, 2018).

Acknowledging the ongoing balancing act of family role responsibilities and work activities for older women is a critical aspect of understanding their motivational needs to work past traditional retirement age (Hill et al., 2014; Jaslow, 1976; Majeed et al., 2017). One key aspect of continued work engagement is the need for older women to utilize and potentially redefine their skill set to maintain work viability within their community (Kasriel,

2017; Lössbroek & Radl, 2018). Working in later life can be an empowering experience for aging women and relates to their feelings of positive health, economic security, and self-esteem through proactive community and work-related engagement (Léime & Ogg, 2019; Lips & Hastings, 2012; Payne & Doyal, 2010).

Across the chapters in Part II, emergent themes reflect upon older women's working experiences. These include the following:

- coping in work (Chapters 6 and 9),
- work–life balance (Chapters 7 and 8),
- choosing to work instead of retire (Chapter 8), and
- circumventing ageism and sexism to thrive at work (Chapter 9).

REFERENCES

Ainsworth, S. (2002). The "feminine advantage": A discursive analysis of the invisibility of older women workers. *Gender, Work and Organization, 9*(5), 579–601. https://doi.org/10.1111/1468-0432.00176

Choi, N. G. (2001). Relationship between life satisfaction and postretirement employment among older women. *International Journal of Aging & Human Development, 52*(1), 45–70. https://doi.org/10.2190/2W25-DH9H-2F4D-7HWX

Cronin, A., & King, A. (2010). Power, inequality and identification: Exploring diversity and intersectionality amongst older LGB adults. *Sociology, 44*(5), 876–892. https://doi.org/10.1177/0038038510375738

Gratton, L., & Scott, A. (2016). *The 100-year life: Living and working in an age of longevity*. Bloomsbury.

Harrison, C. A. (1991). Older women in our society: America's silent, invisible majority. *Educational Gerontology: An International Quarterly, 17*(2), 111–121. https://doi.org/10.1080/0360127910170204

Hill, E. J., Erickson, J. J., Fellows, K. J., Martinengo, G., & Allen, S. M. (2014). Work and family over the life course: Do older workers differ? *Journal of Family and Economic Issues, 35*(1), 1–13. https://doi.org/10.1007/s10834-012-9346-8

Jaslow, P. (1976). Employment, retirement, and morale among older women. *Journal of Gerontology, 31*(2), 212–218. https://doi.org/10.1093/geronj/31.2.212

Kasriel, S. (2017, July 31). *Skill, re-skill and re-skill again: How to keep up with the future of work*. World Economic Forum. https://www.weforum.org/agenda/2017/07/skill-reskill-prepare-for-future-of-work

Kautonen, T. (2008). Understanding the older entrepreneur: Comparing Third Age and Prime Age entrepreneurs in Finland. *International Journal of Business Science and Applied Management, 3*(3), 3–13. http://hdl.handle.net/10419/190597

Kooij, D., de Lange, A., Jansen, P., & Dikkers, J. (2008). Older workers' motivation to continue to work: Five meanings of age: A conceptual review. *Journal of Managerial Psychology, 23*(4), 364–394. https://doi.org/10.1108/02683940810869015

Léime, Á. N., & Ogg, J. (2019). Gendered impacts of extended working life on the health and economic wellbeing of older workers. *Ageing and Society, 39*(10), 1–7.

Lips, H. M., & Hastings, S. L. (2012). Competing discourses for older women: Agency/leadership vs disengagement/retirement. *Women & Therapy, 35*(3–4), 145–164. https://doi.org/10.1080/02703149.2012.684533

Lössbroek, J., & Radl, J. (2018). Teaching older workers new tricks: Workplace practices and gender training differences in nine European countries. *Ageing and Society, 39*(10), 1–24.

Majeed, T., Forder, P. M., Tavener, M., Vo, K., & Byles, J. (2017). Work after age 65: A prospective study of Australian men and women. *Australasian Journal on Ageing, 36*(2), 158–164. https://doi.org/10.1111/ajag.12382

Martin, A. E., North, M. S., & Phillips, K. W. (2019). Intersectional escape: Older women elude agentic prescriptions more than older men. *Personality and Social Psychology Bulletin, 45*(3), 342–359. https://doi.org/10.1177%2F0146167218784895

McGregor, J. (2018). 3. Older women and career development: Double (triple) jeopardy plus or endless opportunities? In M. Adelina, S. Broadbridge, & L. Fielden (Eds.), *Research handbook of diversity and careers* (pp. 60–74). Elgar Publishing. https://doi.org/10.4337/9781785365607.00010

McKenzie, J. (2018). Loving your job matters. *Good Company, 12*(2). http://www.apaexcellence.org/resources/goodcompany/newsletter/article/860

Michel, J., Stuckelberger, A., Tediosi, F., Evans, D., & van Eeuwijk, P. (2019). The roles of a grandmother in African societies—please do not send them to old people's homes. *Journal of Global Health, 9*(1), 010306. https://doi.org/10.7189/jogh.09.010306

Minkler, M., & Stone, R. (1985). The feminization of poverty and older women. *The Gerontologist, 25*(4), 351–357. https://doi.org/10.1093/geront/25.4.351

Payne, S., & Doyal, L. (2010). Older women, work and health. *Occupational Medicine, 60*(3), 172–177. https://doi.org/10.1093/occmed/kqq030

Quéniart, A., & Charpentier, M. (2012). Older women and their representations of old age: A qualitative analysis. *Ageing and Society, 32*(6), 983–1007. https://doi.org/10.1017/S0144686X1100078X

Richards, N., Warren, L., & Gott, M. (2012). The challenge of creating "alternative" images of ageing: Lessons from a project with older women. *Journal of Aging Studies, 26*(1), 65–78. https://doi.org/10.1016/j.jaging.2011.08.001

Vives, A., Gray, N., González, F., & Molina, A. (2018). Gender and ageing at work in Chile: Employment, working conditions, work–life balance and health of men and women in an ageing workforce. *Annals of Work Exposures and Health, 62*(4), 475–489. https://doi.org/10.1093/annweh/wxy021

Woods-Giscombé, C. L. (2010). Superwoman schema: African American women's views on stress, strength, and health. *Qualitative Health Research, 20*(5), 668–683. https://doi.org/10.1177/1049732310361892

6

THE SECRET POOR AMONG US

Older Women Who Work to Make Ends Meet

MARY GERGEN AND ELLEN COLE

At 74 I can't retire. I couldn't live without my paycheck. But still, I'm enjoying my life right now, more than ever, really.

—Roberta

When we walk down the street, go into a supermarket, or get our hair cut, we usually mingle with strangers—people whose life stories mostly remain a mystery to us. We may exchange a bit of chitchat with the woman who waits on us in the dry cleaners or share a conversation at a local coffee shop with a talkative older woman. We watch a grandmother slowly getting off the bus with a toddler, wondering how she is managing with such an active child, given that she seems to need a cane to walk. Although we know almost nothing about these women, we usually do not suspect that they are living on the edge of financial collapse, even below the so-called poverty line. One may have $50 in her pocket, her spending money for the next month. One may be trying to figure out where to cut corners so she can buy her husband's cancer drug. Another is using a coupon she found in the

https://doi.org/10.1037/0000212-007
Older Women Who Work: Resilience, Choice, and Change, E. Cole and L. Hollis-Sawyer (Editors)

advertising flyer, good for one cup of coffee at the café. One is yearning for a nap, which may not be possible today.

Who are these older women who cannot take their rest? Who are those who keep going to work, making minimum wages, struggling to make ends meet? This chapter is not about the professional women who are enjoying their old age, engaging in their work with vigor and even fascination. We are not talking about the Ruth Bader Ginsburgs of the world. No, we are interested in the opposite end of the scale.

Sometimes it is hard to see these older working women. They may be right next to us as we go out into the world. When we meet them, what stories will they tell us? How will we come to understand how life came to be so difficult and how they manage in the face of such challenges? This is what engages us here, in this chapter. We decided we would let them share their stories with you. We take credit for their form within this chapter. We apologize for our editing. They are much more interesting than we can share.

But we leave them space, at least a little. Each of us first describes how we engaged with various women. And then we let them speak for themselves, in truncated form. At the end we share some of what we have learned through our excursions. We hope that you will also feel that you have discovered some insight into what it means to be a part of the secret poor. But first, we offer some background data for context.

A HISTORICAL JOG TO REMIND US OF THE ECONOMIC STATE OF OUR NATION TODAY

Most Americans today are well versed in the troubling state of our economy, in which the very rich have gotten richer and the rest of us have gotten poorer. We are also aware that when it comes to the distribution of wealth and poverty, we are not all equally likely to be climbing up the economic ladder or tumbling down. The gap between the rich and the poor has widened considerably over the years, and it is today at its greatest since the Roaring Twenties 100 years ago. Among those living below the poverty line, older people are among the most prevalent. The U.S. Census Bureau (2017) estimated that 16% of women age 65 and older live at or below the poverty line, compared with 12% of men. Older women of color experience poverty at significantly higher rates than do their White counterparts; Black, Hispanic, and Native American women are almost two times more likely to live in poverty than are older White women. Older nonheterosexual women also experience high rates of poverty due to historical discrimination. Nearly half of bisexual and transgender women live far below the federal poverty limit (Seegert, 2019).

Financially, various factors appear to impact older women more than they impact men. A highly significant activity concerns caregiving responsibilities that take women out of the labor force for months or years at a time. Childbirth and child care are demanding responsibilities, as is caregiving for spouses and older relatives. Marriage and having children at a young age, while forgoing further education, are significant factors in the lives of many women born between 1934 and 1959, including those in our study (Christ & Gronniger, 2018).

Women are often paid less than men for doing the same job, which creates special financial difficulties for women (National Partnership for Women & Families, 2020). Women are likely to receive less Social Security than are men and may be less likely to have pensions and other savings, such as individual retirement accounts, and because they live longer, they need money for a longer time as well (Kochanek et al., 2017).

Women too often rely upon their husbands as major breadwinners in a family. They are more likely to take part-time jobs and to sacrifice their career goals to support their better-paid husband's career options. If their marriage breaks up, the husband dies, or he loses his income through layoffs, health problems, or addictions, the financial status of the wife is grimly affected. Our study reveals how this circumstance plays out in various relationships.

Although the wage gap has been narrowing, a recent report by the American Association of University Women predicted that pay equivalency won't be realized until 2059. Women of color fare worse: Black women earn 61%, American Indian or Alaska Native women earn 58%, and Hispanic women earn 53% of White men's earnings. Lower wages and lower lifetime earnings mean that women save less for retirement (Miller & Vagins, 2018). Yet, women generally outlive men—81.1 years versus 76.1 years, according to 2016 mortality data (Kochanek et al., 2017). Seegert (2019) reported that married women generally fare better economically than do single women (never married, divorced, or widowed). However, as women age, they become more likely than men to be single. Only 15% of women over 85 are married, compared with 54% of men in that age group.

A BRIEF REVIEW OF LITERATURE ON OLDER WOMEN IN THE WORKFORCE

According to Altschuler (2004), older women engaging in paid work needed to have financial independence while often trying to compensate for lost dreams and regrets as well. The latter was based on having felt pressured as teenagers by cultural and family expectations or circumstances to marry and have children; some felt they had limited options and available resources. Many of them were sorry to be in the state they were in and wished they had made different decisions earlier regarding education and their careers. Discouragement was also voiced about discrimination in employment and difficulty finding appropriate paid work. Despite this, women reported working with exceeding determination and ambition while also caring for and being committed to others.

Fraser et al. (2009) reported that stress, physical limitations, lack of support, management issues, poor government initiatives, and societal perceptions of age act as barriers to paid employment for older workers, both women and men. Jaslow (1976) explored the relationships between work, retirement, health, and morale among women age 65 and older and found that those who continued to work reported higher morale than did those retired. Women who never worked reported the lowest morale of all. Payne and Doyal (2010) found that, overall, stress is the most common workplace health hazard for older women, associated with additional psychological and physical problems. This is especially true for older women who carry unpaid responsibilities outside of work.

What we found missing from these and other articles was information about older women who had to work, with no choice about it. Although we still do not have definitive data, it is our strongly held view, especially after completing this chapter, that many older women struggle to stay afloat and find they must work well into their so-called golden years to make ends meet. In the following pages we describe our process in identifying 10 such women, and then we share with you their stories.

ELLEN'S INTERVIEWS

The recruitment method I used to identify participants would be called a convenience sample. My task was to interview five women who continued to work after the age of 65 because they needed the money to pay their bills. I asked for suggestions from just about everyone I encountered, from my academic colleagues to bank tellers to cashiers at local markets and gas stations. Many told me no one would admit to needing to work for the money, but I knew that was not true. I heard the same refrain when I wrote my doctoral dissertation more than 40 years ago. My topic then was adult illiteracy, and I was told repeatedly that no adult would admit to being unable to read. I discovered then, as I rediscovered now, that people feel honored when they can tell their stories, without being judged, to someone who is truly interested in what they have to say.

I paid each participant $25, and our interviews lasted from an hour to an hour and 45 minutes. The interviews took place in a coffee shop, the participant's apartment or home, a convenience store with a few tables and chairs, and, in one case, my living room. Every interview had its painful and sad moments, and there was a lot of laughter. I thanked each participant at the end of our interview, and every one of them said something to the effect of "No, thank *you*. This was very meaningful to me, and I learned something new about myself. Thank you for listening." No one thanked me for the $25 (that did not seem to be their motivation), and in fact three of the five women did not want to take the money; I said they had to for the sake of the project. It was a very hot day when I met one woman at the convenience store. I told her I wanted to buy myself an ice cream cone and asked if I might buy her one, too. She was adamant. "Thank you, but no thank you." Each of these women was proud of her independence. Each one was dressed, in my opinion, elegantly. I found myself apologizing for my own casual attire. This was not the vision I had held of older women who had to work to pay the bills.

I decided not to record our interviews because I did not want to be distracted by any technological issues. Instead, I took notes and then immediately afterward wrote up as much as I could recall about each interview. I began by informing participants that all personal information would be presented anonymously in our chapter and asked each woman to give herself a new name.

Celestina, Housekeeper: "I'm not ready to be put on the shelf"

"Celestina," age 66, lives in a suburb with several generations of her family. She works 3 days a week cleaning houses, despite suffering from arthritis and diabetes, and she is often in pain. She was born in Texas to Spanish-speaking parents and calls herself Hispanic. She is proud of being bilingual. "It opens the door to different cultures." She attended school up to the ninth grade, married at 15, had her first baby at 16, and then went back to school and earned her high school equivalency certificate.

She and her husband, "Luis," had three daughters. They moved from Texas to the Midwest in 2000, and he died 2 years later, at age 54. Luis had been the breadwinner. Celestina, then 49, had never worked outside the home and "had to learn the hard way to be on a budget." She used a credit card for the first time in her life and naively racked up bills. "I had no income, no pension from my husband, and I had to wait until I was 55 to collect Social Security. So, I started cleaning houses." And now, many years later, "I still clean houses." She receives Social Security benefits now but needs to work "to make ends meet." "I'm still paying off credit card debts," she says, "and my medical expenses just about kill me—things I need for diabetes, like insulin pumps. The copays for medical supplies are sky-high." She says, "If I had to pay full rent, I wouldn't make it. I buy my own groceries, I don't have a car, I look for bargains. Every month I'm afraid I'll run out of money."

Although health issues make Celestina's physical work difficult, and I didn't get the sense that she enjoyed her work, her demeanor was upbeat. And, like others, she continues to work for more than the paycheck. She said, "My Dad worked until he died of old age. I never understood it until recently. If you sit still, you go downhill fast."

What does she do for pleasure? "I like to pamper myself. I go to TJMaxx for lotions and perfume, and I've been eyeing a little gold purse and a bling bracelet." "I love crocheting and old movies—Audrey Hepburn, Maurice Chevalier." Above all, volunteering for her church gives meaning to her life and "keeps my mind sharp." Her favorite volunteer activity is answering questions about the Bible.

When will Celestina stop cleaning houses? "If I get up one morning and I can't move, then I'll call it quits—especially if I can't get to the kitchen." "I know 100% that when I can't work, my daughters will take care of me."

What does she wish for: "It's just a fantasy, but I dream that the whole family moves together to Florida." What does she want people to know about her? "I'm not ready for a rest home; I want to take care of myself for as long as I can. I'm not ready to be put on the shelf."

Daphne, Art Restorer: "Good pedigree, but no money"

"Daphne" is a 67-year-old museum professional who has worked since 1979 at a world-famous museum in a West Coast U.S. city. I met her when she was visiting a neighbor of mine.

She described the upper-crust White family with a recognizable name that she married into as "good pedigree, but no money." Her husband, "Pearson," grew up in a "post–trust-fund Beatnik family." "His father used up the trust fund." Daphne met Pearson, a ceramic artist, after she graduated from college with an art history major. He worked part-time for a short while but "has always considered the studio his job." He has had an unpredictable income from sales of his ceramics and recently began teaching Introduction to Pottery at a community college. However, "he was in a serious accident resulting in health issues, and his future as an earner is more unpredictable than ever." Daphne has worked at "odd jobs" since the age of 14 and has been "the main breadwinner" of the family, "not by choice." Her husband "thought it was an imposition" to look for paid work.

Daphne grew up in "a large Catholic family of immigrants" from South America. She remembers living in a big house until she was 3 years old, when her family left a totalitarian regime to come to the United States. She knew no English, only Spanish, until she started school. She describes herself as "very awkward and shy" as a child, but she worked hard and was a good student. And this continues, she feels, to be an accurate description. More than anyone else I interviewed, Daphne is pleased with her professional accomplishments. She helped to "create a new field" in the art world. She says her work is "so, so interesting to me." "It gives me my identity."

Daphne and Pearson have three children. Prior to 1979 Daphne held a variety of part- and full-time jobs. When the children were small, she started a knitting business from her home. This experience "set the foundation" that she could "have kids, be a good mother and a serious professional."

From outside appearances, Daphne and Pearson live the good, even charmed, life. Their main residence is an apartment in a fixed-rent artists' working and living space. They also inherited a country home on a vast amount of land, one of several homes owned by members of Pearson's family. There is a barn with horses. She showed me photos, and the grounds are gorgeous. It is their responsibility to pay the taxes on the country home, and "this is an annual struggle." Daphne worries about her own mental health—"I'm so focused on survival."

When does Daphne plan to retire? "It depends on how much longer we live. A financial advisor told us that if I work until I'm 70, we'll have just enough to live on until we're 90. I want to work for 5 more years, but after that I'll still need a creative outlet. I want to keep on working at something creative, just not full-time in a building."

I asked Daphne about her joys, worries, and wishes. Joys: "Grandchildren." Worries: "I don't want to end up a crabby old lady, and I'm worried about Pearson's physical health. His life is so embedded in his studio that he forgets about it." Wishes: "I hope I can continue to have close relationships with my children and grandchildren, *and* I want to continue to be engrossed in my own work."

Linda, Executive Secretary to the Mayor: "As bad as the divorce was, it made me a better, stronger person"

"Linda" is a 69-year old White woman and works as executive secretary to her midsize town's mayor. She is paid for 20 hours a week, earning $11,500 annually, but most weeks she works many more hours. She says, "The financial compensation is not adequate, but it's what the town can afford." She is "reconciled to it." She also volunteers as chair of the town's political party that is not the same as the mayor's and is grateful for the open attitudes in her town that make this possible.

At age 19, Linda had to quit community college after only 2 months when her husband was drafted into the Vietnam War. For the next 10 years they lived on military bases and had two kids, and Linda occasionally earned money by babysitting. Eventually they moved back to the town where they were both born and where Linda now lives and works. When Linda was 32, her husband left her for another woman. "He gave me $65 a week for child support. I had to start cutting the bacon in half!" "I began to work for a local bank, started as a teller, and worked my way up to manager." She "worked there for 30 years, until the bank closed."

Linda no longer receives child support but does receive a "lifelong pension from the bank. But it's never been enough to make ends meet. I need my salary to pay the bills." "If I didn't work now I couldn't keep my house or have a newer car. I'd have a much more limited lifestyle. I couldn't *ever* buy things for my three grandkids."

Does Linda continue to work for reasons other than her salary? "I love helping people." When does she plan to retire? "Never!" "I'd be lost. I wouldn't know what to do." "I'm so grateful that I *can* work. If I didn't work, where would my self-worth come from?" Linda's weekly schedule: "Work, work, work, and take care of my grandkids (their parents work)." She is up at 5:30 a.m. and walks three houses down to wake up the kids and get them ready for school and onto the school bus. And then she is back by 3 p.m. to get them off the bus and make sure they have a snack and get their homework done. "Some days I take them to hockey practice or basketball." She spends "the middle of every weekday and some evenings in the office." I asked if she ever took a vacation: "I can't really take a vacation because of the grandkids, and I have a dog. One time I won a trip to anywhere in the United States I turned it down because there was no place I wanted to go." (Although this may sound sad to some readers, Linda told me this in an upbeat, matter-of-fact way.) What does she do for relaxation and fun? "Watch my grandsons' games. And I'm crew chief for a race-car driver." Linda's greatest joys, not unexpectedly, are her grandchildren. She worries about finances. And she wishes for better health. "I'd like to take a lot less pills, but I need them for AFib and prediabetes."

Linda became pensive at the end of our interview. "This makes me think about my life and the past, and I realize all I've gone through. As bad as the divorce was, it made me a better, stronger person. I have a good, fulfilling life now."

Living Comfortable, Hair Salon Helper: "Working at my age keeps me young"

The name my interviewee picked for herself is "Living Comfortable." I asked if she might prefer something like "Mary." She laughed, as she did throughout our interview, and said, "Nope, I like 'Living Comfortable.'" For brevity's sake, I will call her LC.

LC is soon to be 65. She identifies as Black; her father, whom she never met, "was Cherokee." We met in her apartment in an urban public housing complex, where she lives alone. She's never married but has had two "live-ins." LC has six adult children, 15 grandkids, and five "great grands." She loves living alone. "I don't have to share my closet. I like this freedom."

LC needs to work "to make ends meet." She "helps out" at a hair salon, earning minimum wage, 25 hours a week. In reality, she works far more hours. She gets up Tuesdays through Saturdays at 2:40 a.m., puts on water for tea and eggs to boil for breakfast, showers, makes her bed, and then prepares breakfast and lunch for that day's salon customers who placed their orders the previous day. She is out the door by 5:15 a.m. to take a bus to work (she does not have a car and does not know how to drive), carrying the prepared meals. She arrives at the salon at 5:45 a.m., where she turns on the lights, plugs in the stations, sets up the computer, and makes sure "everything looks good when the clients come in." She is home by 1 p.m. and in bed by 7.

What does LC do to relax after a pretty physical workday? "I listen to music and watch *Grey's Anatomy* or *Chicago P.D.* I take a little sip now and again—I love my vodka." "Not having money is the pits," she laments. "Social Security doesn't cut it." After rent, insurance, cable, a bus pass, food, and paying down outstanding bills at Target and Lane Bryant, she has $50 a month in her pocket. She is pleased to have finally learned "how to budget." She has no cushion because of bad choices in the past, including "enabling my kids." She felt responsible for them long after they became adults. One daughter declared bankruptcy, and LC gave her $800. Another son, now 46, "was always asking for money; now he works at a car wash, finally supporting himself." LC said, "My therapist taught me how to say no without feeling guilty."

Are there other reasons LC continues to work? "The main thing that keeps me working is that it gives my life meaning." "Not having a job could kill me!" "I need to stay busy." "I meet different people, I hear interesting stories. I put a smile on people's faces." "Working at my age keeps me young." "I have to look presentable when I go to work, and that makes me feel good." What would the alternative be? "If I'm not working, my kids would want me to babysit, run errands, cook for them. I love my family, but I'd rather go to work." Long-term security: "I'm trying to build a security blanket." "I'm trying to put money in the bank so I can retire at 85." "My arthritis is getting bad, my knees are bad—I worry I won't last that long."

What is her biggest wish? "Increased finances. More money. Yes!" And what does she want people to know about her? "I always liked to work. I've never wanted a handout. I'm not lazy." And, it seems to me, she is full of good-natured laughter!

Roberta, Liquor Store Cashier: "The only dignified thing I have in my life is my new car"

"Roberta" is 75 years old and tells me in a conspiratorial tone that she is a "Jewish lesbian" who now lives alone after her partner of several decades passed away. She describes herself as a "small old woman." We used to live in the same town, and I know others have described her as "tough as nails" and, affectionately speaking, "that crazy hat lady." She is a character.

I met Roberta 3 years ago, when she worked at a cement factory, not as a secretary or cashier or receptionist but on the floor of the plant, loading heavy bags onto front-end loaders and then going back for more, the only woman in sight. Before the cement plant, Roberta held a variety of jobs, including running a house-cleaning business and selling at flea markets. For a decade she directed activities at a nursing home. By the time of our interview she had left the cement plant, saying that after 6 years the strenuous work started to get to her. She noticed that her physical powers were "beginning to wane." She now works 32 hours a week at a wine and liquor store, sometimes at the checkout counter, sometimes mopping the floor. She earns $11.10 an hour and is "okay with that, satisfied."

Why does she still work at her age? "I had to buy a new car; I totaled my last one. The only dignified thing I have in my life is my new car. I don't have much of anything else." "I like to pay my bills down. And I like the luxury of going out to eat every once in a while." And there is another reason. "I like having a reason to get up in the morning. It gives me a schedule, structure in my life. I like being around people. When I was between jobs, I sat in front of the TV and drove myself crazy."

What about pensions or savings that carry many through their later years? "It's my own stupid fault that I have to work, even though I still choose to. I was frivolous. I wasn't frugal. I've worked hand-to-mouth my whole life. I've never saved. If I had any extra money I'd spend it. I would do things like buy a new computer I didn't need; propane bills went to the side."

When does she plan to retire? "When I'm no longer of use." "When I can pay off my car and my credit card." "Right now, I'm viable. I laugh a lot. I bring people out of their shells, make them smile. I have a gift." But Roberta does have concerns about the future. She says, "I wonder if I'm going to get sick, what will I do then?" "I would love the satisfaction of not having debt."

What does she want others to know about her? "I am an older woman who must work, and I want to work. I'm enjoying my life at this time. I have a greater acceptance of myself and my life, more than I did when I was 50."

MARY'S INTERVIEWS

When Ellen and I decided to interview women who needed to keep working into their late 60s, 70s, and 80s because they could not survive on Social Security and other savings alone, I knew it might be hard to find the ones we had envisioned in my suburban neighborhood. What ended up happening was that I found people who fit our criteria, but what was striking was that these women were what we came to call the secret poor. These women appeared on the street to be middle class and certainly not living on the edge of financial disaster. Surprisingly, two of my interviewees were college-educated; most had issues related to the men in their lives. As Ellen did, I used a convenience sample to identify participants. When asking the women to participate, I never was precise as to why I wanted to interview them, but I did say my colleague and I were doing a study of women who were working past 65. I did interview one woman who was highly involved in working at 82, but she seemed to be working for the fun of it; she also had two widow's pensions, plus Social Security, so I had to eliminate her from the study for lack of financial distress. I discovered, as did Ellen, that people feel honored when they can tell their stories, without being judged, to someone who is truly interested in what they have to say.

I tried to pay each participant $25, but one would not take it. I took another one out to lunch at an upscale restaurant in our area, which I thought would please her more than the cash, and later she sent me an elegant thank you note, which ended: "It was a super fun and thoughtful time—anytime!!" My interviews lasted from 1 to 2 hours. I interviewed Courtney in my home. I interviewed Barbie in hers. Two were interviewed in a friend's home. As with Ellen's group, each of these women was proud of her independence.

Like Ellen, I did not record our interviews. Instead, I took notes and then immediately afterward wrote up as much detail as I could recall about each interview. I began by informing participants that all personal information would be presented anonymously in our chapter, and I gave each one a new name.

Courtney, Master's Degree From Smith: "Life can be so unfair"

"Courtney" is 64 and took her Social Security early, at 62. It saved her from living on the street. Courtney was working as a pet sitter and a gardener when my husband and I met her about 5 years ago. She had taken a job caring for a woman with chronic illness, and after Courtney lived with her for 2 years, the woman died. Courtney had no plans for what she would do after the woman died, so she just kept living in the woman's house. The son of the woman, who inherited the house, wanted to remodel and sell it. She stayed in the house with her cat, despite his urgings that she move out. Basically, one could call her a squatter. She had nowhere to go and no prospects. The son shut off the electricity and tried to force her out. As she often worked for us, we invited Courtney to come live in our house, where she could garden and care for our cats when we were out of town. It seemed like she had no other plausible alternative. What she earned would be about equal to her rent. She was then able to collect Social Security and also do work for other people, gardening, pet sitting, and then doing part-time work at a local day care.

Eventually she was able to move back to the city into a special housing unit designed for very poor people, often those who are mentally ill, homeless, disabled, addicted, or otherwise incapacitated. Although she had looked forward to this move, when she finally moved in she came to dislike it, quite intensely. The living quarters are very small, there are limits to what one can do there (e.g., cooking must be done in a communal kitchen), and she finds the people there often highly offensive and sometimes frightening. She is looking to move to another place, which may not be much better.

Courtney comes from a large Irish Catholic family in Boston. She has hardly any contact with them. She has a master's degree from Smith in social work and did have social work jobs in her early career. She moved to Philadelphia to work and to follow a medical resident, with whom she was having a relationship. After a time, they separated. Later she worked as a court reporter, and she did this until carpal tunnel syndrome overtook her, and she had to quit. After this she became a caretaker for elderly people.

Courtney is very small. She is about 4′10″ and weighs 96 pounds. Clothes she can afford do not come in her size, so she buys her clothes in the boys' departments of stores. She is quite fussy about her hair and chooses her hairdressers with care. Her hair is a beautiful mix of black and grey, thick and always stylish. It is her one extravagance. She has had little extra money to spend but is fanatical about eating organic foods, mostly vegetables. She is in need of dental work, which she has not been able to afford. She is looking forward to saving up enough so that she can go to the dentist. Courtney has never married nor had any children. She says that she prefers animals as companions. She is quite cynical about the world and suspicious of many things and people. She is well-read, is politically liberal, and has a biting sense of humor. She is frequently offended by the encounters she has with public assistance employees, and she often feels "ripped off." She continues to search for work, as she wants to earn money and be accepted into society as a full-fledged member. Even without a job, she feels on firmer ground today for getting by than she has in a long time.

Daisy: "Without my gambling winnings, we couldn't afford Nick's medicine"

"Daisy" came from a divided family, with her mother from a big Italian family and her father from a big Irish family. The narrative Daisy tells is that each side looked down on the other until her mother proved what a wonderful caring person she was to his family. Daisy is 79 years old but described herself as "having great heredity." She has even-toned porcelain skin with few wrinkles, which she credits to a favorite facial cream she uses every day. She graduated from high school in 1958 and got a job at a big insurance company. She did office administrative work and really loved her job. She also met Nick, a guy who was "crazy about her." He courted her by bringing her a cocktail and a snack every day after work (and continued to do so for the next 55 years, until he was too ill, 3 years ago). After working for a few more years at the insurance company, Daisy married Nick and she had her first child at 22. She stayed home with her children for several years but returned to the workforce when her fourth child turned two. It was then that Nick had his first heart attack. Daisy realized she needed a better paying job to help support the family. She found one at a family-run beer distributing company.

The beer company promoted Daisy, who had been at the lowest level of employment, and trained her to do the accounts payable. She worked there as a valued employee for 30 years. When the company was sold, Daisy was unceremoniously let go on the first day. She was "hauled into the conference room" with six people from sales, the new owner, and the sales manager. All seven people were told they were not needed and that this was their last day. The other six people, ranging in age from 30 to 52, were given 20 weeks of pay, and Daisy, at age 78, was given 7 weeks of pay. She was in shock, as she had no intention of leaving, and she loved her job. Daisy needed to work to receive the medical benefits from her job, both for Nick and for her medical prescriptions. She had planned to stay until age 80.

Until Nick's more recent health issues that keep him from driving and traveling, they would go to Atlantic City to gamble. They had all kinds of comps (free rooms, shows, restaurants). It was a wonderful hobby, she said. Now, they can no longer go, but Daisy has taken up gambling online. She was always successful at it, and her last win (the week before she was let go) was for $43,000! To make up for lost wages, Daisy also has been selling things on eBay.

Today Daisy takes care of Nick and her pets (six cats and two dogs). Two days a week, she also cares for her teenage granddaughter and her great-granddaughter. Over the past years she has cared for her daughter's ex-husband, their children who have been in trouble, and her son's wife in a time of crisis. There is always someone coming to Daisy. She thought she would have more time since her recent forced retirement, but other people seem to need her right now. She considers online gambling to be her rest. She doesn't sleep well.

In addition to Nick's cancer treatments, their monthly medical bills include a $149 ointment. Because Daisy no longer has health coverage through her work and Nick cannot work, she foots the bill for Medicare for both of them, at more than $400 monthly. They could not afford the ointment that Nick needs without her recent gambling winnings.

Life has changed since she had to stop work. She is trying to think about the positive aspects of this. "I no longer have to worry about driving in the bad weather or on the highway, and that alleviates a lot of stress." "My biggest worry is that Nick is going to die." She will just continue to take him to appointments and care for him and keep winning at gambling. Her goal is to start to enjoy not going to work, to let it sink in.

Barbie, the Introverted Artist: "I feel cheated in my life."

After 16 years of marriage, "Barbie" was in desperate circumstances and needed to find a job. During her marriage, she had three children. Her first child was born with a severe disability and died at age 8. She then had another girl and a boy. Her husband, Dan, was a stockbroker she met at her first job after college at a brokerage firm. "Dan was an orphan and never had a real sense of family," she said. He was charming and bold and liked to put on a big show of how successful he was, but his finances were a disaster, and she had to get a job. Barbie rented a typewriter, went to secretarial school, and learned to type. Her parents helped to support her during this difficult time, and eventually, with the insistence of her father, she divorced Dan. He had basically mortgaged everything, including their house; sold stocks that belonged to her by fraudulently signing her name; and went deeper into debt, living a high life on his own (e.g., a 3-week trip to Scotland to play golf).

She found a job at the local college. After some years, she became the assistant to the head of the Facilities Department. Here she stayed until she retired at 65. She retired as a matter of course, without considering the financial ramifications. Dan had given her very little in child support and was rarely in touch. She was dependent on herself. "After I retired, I stayed home and slept for a month." After 6 weeks, her old boss called her and asked her to come back part-time. They needed her badly. She did return and eventually she ended up working almost full-time. Because of the persistence of her boss, her salary was raised, her health benefits were paid, and she was given an individual retirement account. She worked another 18 years and quit last August at 82 years of age. She said that if she had not gone back to work, she "wouldn't have made it financially." She was not financially viable when she quit at 65. By going back for 18 years, she was able to keep her house and her "place" in her suburban locale.

At the end of the interview she showed me around her house, which is overstuffed with her art projects. She does not want to take any art classes or join the art center. In the afternoons she takes naps. She likes to read, and she was reading two different books on introverts. She said every line describes her. Asked about friends, she mentioned people she had known—"some are dead, some are demented, some moved away. I have no friends."

Asked about volunteering, she gave a horsey laugh. "Hah. My whole life I was a volunteer. No more. I feel cheated in my life. Didn't get to have what I wanted and deserved." Some days for fun she will go from store to store, buying the sale items. "Avocados for 39 cents." She gets a kick out of saving money.

One of the drains on her money has been her daughter, Jan. She went to the University of Vermont and never left. "If you live in Vermont, you gotta drink." Jan was married and divorced, with two kids. She gets into scraps with the police. "She gets very angry when she is drunk." Barbie bails her out of jail and pays her fines.

At 82, Barbie looks younger than her years, with long blond-brown hair; she is tall, slim, and agile. She goes to her balance class, which she loves, and her morning yoga. "I hate the idea of getting fat." She had a hip replacement years ago. She has pain in her knee, and it bothers her on her walks.

She said, "I must rise above my pain." She has a ready laugh, likes to say rather outrageous things, and has been on antidepressants for decades. She started on Prozac. "I can't say how many years ago. Now I'm on something else." Without work she gets depressed. "Retirement has been a struggle." She said she did not really retire. "I quit because they were running the place in such a stupid way I couldn't stand it. Now I am without an agenda, and I don't like it."

Julie, Style Setter: "Disappointing Life Story"

Almost 60 years ago, "Julie," a Swedish-American beauty queen, married an Olympic star. They settled in a community near where he grew up—the Italian district of Philadelphia—and he created a small construction company. When the economy was good, life was very good for them. They had two children, a girl and a boy. She decorated, entertained, and was a remarkable cook. Julia Child was her guru. He oversaw his construction projects, played tennis, and was admired by the ladies.

Before her marriage, Julie had had a lively and diverse career in New York City. She worked in fashion houses, at magazines, and in the film industry, mostly as an administrative assistant. Her position and her pay were at the lowest levels. She had many suitors. Barry, her future husband, hung around with his Olympic team, most of whom were from wealthy families. Although he was handsome, charming, and athletic, he was not rich.

Julie did have a taste for elegant things, and she also had the skills of sewing, knitting, and designing clothes. She developed a line of clothing under her name. Over time she had shows in stores in the East Hamptons, New York City, and Philadelphia. Her other love was gardening, and her yard contained fascinating and unusual plants. She joined the community group that tended to local public spaces. She was never paid to do this, and she still works many hours a week as a volunteer. Her two children chide her for having a full-time job, without pay. Today she does not feel respected by her children, and this erodes her own self-respect.

Over the years, as the economic tides rose and fall, the income of Julie and her husband vacillated. About 14 years ago Barry was out running on the track when he suffered a stroke. He has not totally recovered. In the past 6 months Julie thinks he has really slipped, both physically and mentally. He is terribly depressed and longs to have some work again. It is not clear he could manage working, either physically or mentally. Shortly before the stroke, Barry had gotten contracts to build five "McMansions." He managed to build four of them, with increasing help from Julie. On the last house,

Julie said she had to take over the job, as he was unable to continue. She said she was driving the pickup truck and was in charge of the project.

Overall, she said, they never planned for their future. They had no savings. Barry never made much in investing and had lost some money on one venture. She described her husband as a "passive aggressive Peter Pan," always imagining that things might be better. She said his passivity had destroyed their marriage.

Julie said they live on Social Security, though it is not clear how much they might receive, given their employment histories. I asked her how they make ends meet, and she said, "I don't really know. He writes the checks, and I don't keep track." Julie is trying to make money, restarting her fashion business. She has some connections in various stores, and she has made a bit of money with her knitting. She showed me a consignment slip for $84 for a couple of things that were sold in a downtown boutique. She doesn't want to be responsible to keep their "ship afloat," but it isn't clear that Barry can do so. Neither child is helping out, nor does she expect it.

She cannot imagine moving, in part, because their house is stuffed with her things: yarn, materials, sewing machines, and finished items she has never sold. She is not clear about how she might support the two of them in the future. She does not really know what their circumstances are but suspects the worst and frequently feels disappointed. She tries not to think about it.

Leah, House Cleaner, Babysitter, Caretaker: "I never had a dream for myself."

"Leah's" family, as she describes it, was a bad one. Her father was an alcoholic who beat her mother in front of her. Finally, her mother left him and moved back with her parents, who were originally from Italy. In 12th grade Leah became pregnant and dropped out of school. She married her boyfriend. Her daughter was born when she was 17, and then at 23 they had a son. Leah's husband was very controlling, would not let her work, except with his mother, and was an alcoholic as well. At 26, with two children, she divorced him.

Leah lived without a partner for 5 years, and after a few lengthy relationships, married Bob, whom she deeply loved. The biggest issue was that he had health problems. They would have celebrated their 20th anniversary this year, but he passed away 2 years ago.

When she left her first husband, she began cleaning houses to make ends meet. She was on welfare for medical reasons and worked part-time at the YMCA. She started her own house-cleaning company but did not declare her income for tax purposes. She did two houses a day, 6 days a week. She still runs this business but has cut down to five houses twice a month, and she collects Social Security and a pension left behind by Bob.

Besides cleaning homes, Leah babysits children and elderly patients so that their caretakers can do their shopping and errands. This income is also under the table. She doesn't make enough working these jobs, so she also has worked as a ward assistant keeping watch over patients in a mental hospital. She takes whatever money she makes and divides it into weekly envelopes. They are designated for mortgage/car/gas/insurance/home repairs/emergency credit card payments. She also sets the day/time she works. She has lived through cancer for 7 years and recently had a knee operation. This knee continues to give her issues—infections and falling—but she continues to work.

She said that she loves working. She loves rearranging people's spaces and things, and she enjoys how surprised and delighted they are when they see what she has done. She takes pride in her cleaning and work ethic. Leah said, "I never had a dream for myself. I'm not educated, not smart, I'm dumb, in fact, and probably could never be anything else. I do have 'street smarts.'" She said, "I don't like myself very much, so I don't do nice things for myself." She said that she loves to care for others.

As for retirement, Leah, 71, said, "I will work until I can't do it anymore. I am hoping to get another 10 years in." Her biggest worry is not having an emergency fund.

DISCUSSION AND CONCLUSION

When we first discussed collaborating on the topic of women over 65 who must, rather than choose, to work, we imagined women who were bone tired, who were perhaps suffering from declining health, and who would surely have retired by now if they could. We assumed that older women who had to work would prefer not to. Our original working title was "When Just Getting By Is Getting Old: Women Working in Later Life to Pay the Bills." We expected it would be easy to identity this population: the slow-moving food server at the local diner or the gray-haired woman who works at night cleaning hospital rooms came to mind.

Now, there is no doubt that the women we imagined do exist. We know from the data presented earlier in this chapter that a substantial percentage of older women struggle financially. But our interviews introduced an unanticipated reality. Of the 10 women we interviewed, not one would have been easily identified as poor, despite being financially vulnerable.

They did not say they resented their work lives; instead, without sentimentality, they told us of their resolve in, and acceptance of, the lives they had. They struggled financially, but they were not bowed by their circumstances. Often there was pride in their voices, describing how they had overcome difficulties and how they had improved their circumstances. Often they acknowledged mistakes made in the past and described their determination to manage and plan for a better future. And nearly all of them wanted to continue working. Their greatest fear was that they could not achieve their future goals. What follows are the themes that stood out for us, as we read and reread and reflected upon the stories of the lives that our participants shared with us. We end this account with lessons learned.

Themes

Some of the following themes that emerged in our interviews have overlapping edges, but each seemed to us to have a distinctive essence. Each was described with passion, in multiple interviews.

Needing to work "to make ends meet" was a common phrase. There was no doubt that earning money was a necessity for each of them.

"Love and marriage and the baby carriage" compelled many of the women in our sample to leave school, not get further education, and think not of careers but only of love, marriage, and having babies. Each put her faith in her husband, and when he failed to keep up his end as a breadwinner, oops—the family became economically endangered. Husbands may have been beloved or scorned, but they were always a significant factor in the economic fates of their wives.

Identity and self-esteem: "My work is so interesting to me; it gives me my identity." "I'm so grateful that I *can* work. If I didn't work, where would my self-worth come from?" Every woman defined herself, in no small part, by what she did for work.

Purpose: "The main thing that keeps me working is that it gives my life meaning." "I need to stay busy." One woman said she never wants to retire. Without her work "I'd be lost. I wouldn't know what to do." "I like having a reason to get up in the morning. It gives me a schedule, structure in my life. I like being around people." "When I was between jobs, I sat in front of the TV and drove myself crazy." "I need an agenda." Every woman we interviewed appreciated the motivation that their work provided.

Accomplishment: "I want to continue to be engrossed in my own work." "Right now, I'm viable. I laugh a lot. I bring people out of their shells and make them smile. I have a gift." Our interviewees felt pride in their achievements.

Pleasure: "Working at my age keeps me young." "I love my family, but I'd rather go to work." "I meet different people, I hear interesting stories." "I love helping people." Work is enjoyable.

Need for independence: "I'm not ready for a rest home; I want to take care of myself for as long as I can. I'm not ready to be put on the shelf." Our interviewees did not want to be taken care of by a family member or anyone else, but they did worry about becoming needy at a future time.

Long-term security/fear about the future: "I'm trying to build a security blanket." "I'm trying to put money in the bank so I can retire at 85." "My arthritis is getting bad, my knees are bad, I worry I won't last that long." One interviewee said she worries about her mental health because "I'm so focused on survival." "I wonder if I'm going to get sick, what will I do then?" "I would love the satisfaction of not having debt." Fear about the future, especially financially, applied to each woman we interviewed.

Lessons Learned

As we became more familiar with the stories of our 10 participants, we realized that the poor older women among us are often not easily identifiable. Each of the women we interviewed seemed to take pride in being socially acceptable members of their communities and went to some lengths to present themselves as socially appropriate. We were surprised by the pleasure that nearly all of our respondents experienced through their work. At the same time, there was near panic when our respondents discussed the future. Only one thought she had a safety net: Celestina believed her daughters would take care of her if or when she became too frail to clean houses. The rest lived in fear that they might become the "bag ladies" of the street.

A subtle but significant fear expressed by some of the women we interviewed, and surprising to us, was that if they did not work or if they had to retire, their family members would take advantage of them in several ways. Family members might see them as free to babysit, offer housing, take care of pets, care for other relatives, and be somehow available to be a resource for others. Having work to do provided a shield against the demands of the rest of the family. One woman, for example, commented that she thought she would have a lot more time for herself after she retired but feared that family obligations would take over. Without a work world, poor, older women fear they will find themselves "mugged" by members of the family and have no recourse to escape their influence. Several respondents noted that even now, as they struggle to make ends meet themselves, children and grandchildren expect financial help as a matter of course.

One of the conclusions we draw from these lessons is that governmental changes could do much to relieve the impact of poverty on older women. Although currently there are concerns about the future viability of Social Security, it must be preserved to protect the lives of older people. In addition, more credit should be given in the system for caregiving, and health care, including vision and dental care, must become easily available and affordable. Ways for reducing domestic violence, addictions, and legal penalties should be enhanced. There should be ways of supporting less disparity between the wages earned for jobs that women often do and the wages earned for jobs men do, and a higher minimum wage for all. We advocate for a public educational curriculum that includes financial information for teenagers so that they become aware of the economic costs of adult life and the nature of financial planning. Girls, especially, must become aware that wearing princess dresses in childhood does not guarantee a Prince Charming when they graduate.

We realize that we have captured a moment in time, when most women now over 65 never envisioned themselves as having well-paid careers or even a long-sustaining career of any kind. It is our hope that current and future generations of women will be less naïve and will honor their own development and be more able to take their economic security into their own hands. They will make plans for their long-term futures, with more awareness that how they plan for themselves in their younger years will reverberate in their later ones. Although this was a hope that we brought to this analysis, we recognize that we may have been overly optimistic. High school graduation rates, especially among minority girls, fall far below 100% (U.S. Department of Education, 2017–2018).

Without a high school diploma, the likelihood of economic success in the job market is grim. The repetition of the lifestyles of today's older poor women may well be repeated, with the attendant disappointments and financial struggles. Societal efforts to remediate these conditions are desirable, but optimism may not be realistic. With adequate educational opportunities and job training, perhaps change can be accomplished.

And, finally, our central takeaway from completing this chapter is that we need to go beyond stereotypes of frail, needy, cranky, and irrelevant women who continue to work after the age of 65, whether they need to or not. Instead, our biographical vignettes suggest determination, resourcefulness, self-reflection, and an ethic of care for themselves, others, and the world-at-large. At the same time, we sincerely hope that stories of being a poor old woman will become a rarity, that women will have the choice to work or not after the age of 65, and that being comfortable and confident until the end of life will become the norm.

APPENDIX 6.1

INTERVIEW QUESTIONS

1. Demographic Information: First name or made-up name of her choice; Age; Contact—email, text, or phone #.

2. What do you do for your paid employment? Where? Full-time or part-time, one or more jobs? History of working at this/these or other jobs? Do you feel the financial compensation is fair, adequate?

3. Why do you still work at your age? [Try to understand how life went that she is still working, even if she would rather not work. Choices made in the past—bad marriage, no marriage, little education, illnesses, immigrant status, care for others? Maybe she likes working, even if she must. Maybe it makes her feel productive, alive, active.]

4. When do you plan to retire? Is it possible? How do you imagine life will change for you when you stop working? [Residence, money, move to another area?]

5. Weekly life schedule: Working hours, caring for self, and others [who are they?]. Volunteer work, church work? Housework? Rest and relaxation time? Travel among various places? Time off, vacation time?

6. Final Questions: (a) Joys of life—e.g., grandchildren, friends, church, hobbies? (b) Worries? (c) Wishes—e.g., increased financial security, health care, better family relations?

7. Anything else you think we should have asked, or you'd like to say?

REFERENCES

Altschuler, J. (2004). Beyond money and survival: The meaning of paid work among older women. *International Journal of Aging & Human Development, 58*(3), 223–239. https://doi.org/10.2190%2FHNQH-BM29-KFB3-E461

Christ, A., & Gronniger, T. (2018). *Older women & poverty.* Justice in Aging. https://www.justiceinaging.org/wp-content/uploads/2018/12/Older-Women-and-Poverty.pdf

Fraser, L., McKenna, K., Turpin, M., Allen, S., & Liddle, J. (2009). Older workers: An exploration of the benefits, barriers and adaptations for older people in the workforce. *Work, 33*(3), 261–272. https://doi.org/10.3233/WOR-2009-0874

Jaslow, P. (1976). Employment, retirement, and morale among older women. *Journal of Gerontology, 31*(2), 212–218. https://doi.org/10.1093/geronj/31.2.212

Kochanek, K. D., Murphy, S. L., Xu, J., & Arias, E. (2017). *Mortality in the United States, 2016* (NCHS Data Brief No. 293). U.S. Department of Health and Human Services, Centers for Disease Control and Prevention, National Center for Health Statistics.

Miller, K., & Vagins, D. J. (2018). *The simple truth about the gender pay gap*. American Association of University Women. https://www.aauw.org/app/uploads/2020/02/AAUW-2018-SimpleTruth-nsa.pdf

National Partnership for Women & Families. (2020, March). *America's women and the wage gap* [Fact sheet]. http://www.nationalpartnership.org/our-work/resources/workplace/fair-pay/americas-women-and-the-wage-gap.pdf

Payne, S., & Doyal, L. (2010). Older women, work and health. *Occupational Medicine*, *60*(3), 172–177. https://doi.org/10.1093/occmed/kqq030

Seegert, L. (2019, January 8). New reports paint a grim picture of older women in poverty. *Covering Health*. https://healthjournalism.org/blog/2019/01/new-report-paints-a-grim-picture-of-older-women-in-poverty

U.S. Census Bureau. (2017). *The Supplemental Poverty Measure: 2016* (Current Population Reports No. P60-261). https://www.census.gov/content/dam/Census/library/publications/2017/demo/p60-261.pdf

U.S. Department of Education. (2017–2018). *Consolidated State Performance Report, 2016–2017*. https://www2.ed.gov/admins/lead/account/consolidated/index.html#sy06-07

7
WORK-LIFE BALANCE AND THE OLDER WORKING WOMAN

H. LORRAINE RADTKE AND JANNEKE VAN MENS-VERHULST

It's hard to be a woman. You must think like a man, act like a lady, look like a young girl, and work like a horse.

—Anonymous

The issues we take up in this chapter involve the relationship between an older woman's paid work activities and, for want of a better expression, the rest of her life. Variously referred to as work–family conflict, work–life balance, work life balance, and work–life integration, it has been extensively researched and remains a concern for employers, governments, and individual women and men. However, emphasis has been placed on young adulthood and midlife, especially in relation to women as mothers, with only recent and very limited interest in the older woman.

Two historical developments have inspired us (and others) to pursue this line of inquiry. First, the growing health benefits that are at least partly responsible for the increasing longevity experienced particularly in the wealthier parts of the world have extended the phase of women's lives in which they retain many capabilities. Second, we live in a time when the

https://doi.org/10.1037/0000212-008
Older Women Who Work: Resilience, Choice, and Change, E. Cole and L. Hollis-Sawyer (Editors)

members of the baby boom, post–World War II generation of nations such as Canada, the Netherlands, and the United States are beyond midlife. In many places in the world, then, there is now a large number of women who are at, or beyond, statutory retirement age and have been negotiating the multiple demands of daily living that include paid employment for most or all of their adult lives. This is an opportune moment to explore the meaning of work–life balance for the older working woman who remains in the labor force or may be grappling with the question of whether to stay or leave.

We address this issue by critically examining existing literature, both empirical and theoretical. We approach this through a social constructionist lens (Burr, 2015) and therefore pay attention to how the conceptualizations of issues related to work–life balance enable and limit women in their everyday activities. Importantly, often gender is ignored or treated as an individual difference variable to be controlled (e.g., Wayne et al., 2017). We adopt a contrary position and foreground the perspectives of, and on, women, especially older women. Furthermore, we care more about the situation of the older woman than we care about the interests of her employer. Nevertheless, we recognize that how work–life balance is conceptualized as a problem for the older woman worker will have implications for the structure of work and the policies that guide workplace practices. Our sensitivity to time and place, which reflects our feminist, social constructionist perspective, means that we have paid particular attention to knowledge generated in Canada and the Netherlands, the places where we have lived and worked our entire adult lives.

As a final introductory comment, we want to highlight that our interest in the topic is simultaneously academic and personal. It is academic, as we already conducted some investigations of the identity construction of "third age" women, that is, older women who have left the labor force, are no longer responsible for dependent children, and remain healthy and active (Radtke et al., 2016; van Mens-Verhulst & Radtke, 2013). Our research showed that in constructing their identities, older Canadian women who fit the criteria for being third-age women drew from four pairs of contradictory meanings of aging. One set of meanings captured negative aspects of aging—physical deterioration, cognitive decline, social marginality, and inevitability of its effects—whereas the other set included meanings through which the women could constitute themselves as "not old" and establish continuity between their past and present selves—physically capable, time of wisdom, deserving of special treatment, and a process requiring adaptation with the possibility of transcendence. Although this chapter directs the spotlight to older women who remain working, we assume that they share many of the deliberations, worries, and aims of third-age women, and when they imagine what is possible for them, they will be constrained by the same meanings of aging, both positive and negative, as were our third-age participants.

Our personal interest stems from our positions in life. Janneke retired from academic life 13 years ago but continues academic pursuits on a voluntary basis. Lorraine will be retiring from academic life this year and is already past the age when one is eligible for the government retirement pension. Both of us are partnered, are mothers and grandmothers, and have many friends and acquaintances who have retired, plan to retire, or continue preretirement work on a paid or voluntary basis. All in all, we have come to understand the meaning of work–life balance for the older woman worker as involving a variety of pushes and pulls or forces that she negotiates in her everyday life and have some effect on whether she remains in the workforce or leaves.

UNPACKING THE MEANINGS OF WORK–LIFE BALANCE

Although the historical record shows that women have struggled with combining work and the rest of life since at least the 1800s (Phipps & Prieto, 2016), the need for concepts such as work–life balance originated with the economies in the global north, where women's participation in the paid workforce has been contingent on national economic interests. For women, then, access to paid work historically has been precarious but also has led to the second shift (Hochschild, 1989) insofar as expectations that they should devote themselves to domestic tasks and motherhood remain a looming presence. Research interest in the topic arose in the 1960s (Williams et al., 2016) and has remained steady since the 1990s (Özbilgin et al., 2011). Today, as the large baby boomer generation has approached statutory retirement age, economies in the global north need them to remain in the workforce longer as the generations behind them are not sufficiently large to fill the gap. Thus, the older woman in Canada and the Netherlands experiences the pull of this demand, which we elaborate upon later. For their part, researchers have become interested in work–life balance and the older worker in the context of how to keep older women in the labor force (e.g., Edge et al., 2017). Our focus, however, is on the perspectives of the older women who now confront this political moment. Before we move on to this, however, we offer a brief, critical review of the history of the concept.

Work and Life as Conflicting Domains

Initially, the problem for women was constructed as the reciprocal impact of work on family life and vice versa. In her classic book, *Work and Family in the United Sates: A Critical Review and Agenda for Research and Policy* (1977/1988), Rosabeth Moss Kanter criticized the myth of work and family as separate spheres, noting that it had been shaped historically by workplaces wanting committed workers and shored up by gender norms that associated family concerns with women, married with children of course, and the emphasis on individual achievement in American culture. Yet, there was clear evidence that the two domains were interdependent. The earliest theories of work–life balance attempted to elucidate that interdependence and its consequences by focusing on interrole conflict, that is, the proposal that conflicting role expectations of work and life lead to stress and strain (Greenhaus & Beutell, 1985) and "spillover" that could be positive or negative from the work domain to the family domain or vice versa (Staines, 1980). Some examples of more recent theoretical developments involve directing attention to work and family as domains with borders that are traversed by workers (Clark, 2000) and to cognitive processes entailed in thinking about how work and life are related that then affect whether an individual experiences work–life conflict (Leslie et al., 2019). These latter theories, however, are gender-blind and thus contrast with the earlier notions of role conflict that emphasized women's role as unpaid care workers within the family.

An important debate erupting in the 1980s centered on claims that women's taking up of multiple roles was a problem ("you can't dance at every wedding" or more formally, the scarcity hypothesis, which proposes that women possess a finite amount of energy that can be divided only so many ways). This was countered by the claim that there are many benefits of multiple roles for women, including enhanced well-being (the expansionist hypothesis; Barnett & Baruch, 1985). At stake was women's right to paid employment combined with family life (Williams et al., 2016); the debate pitted feminist arguments about equality and economic independence for women against traditionalist arguments that ideally it was in everyone's best interests for women (i.e., particularly women of privilege) to devote their lives to motherhood and other domestic duties. Notably, years of empirical research continue to provide support for both views, and as a way out of this morass, some have recommended that we consider the matter of how women are able to navigate their many responsibilities from political and ethical perspectives (Febbraro, 2003; Phipps & Prieto, 2016; Sørensen, 2017). Today, we would argue, these contradictory positions continue to shape, at least implicitly, research agendas and everyday conversation about women and paid work. Furthermore, they contribute to the pushes and pulls that encourage women to remain at work, a point we elaborate on at the end of this section.

Extending the "Problem" of Work–Life Balance to Older Women

Overall, researchers have located the problem of work–life balance in middle age, when the majority of women are caring for dependent children, and in domestic life specifically (i.e., family; e.g., Keeney et al., 2013; Kelliher et al., 2019; Özbilgin et al., 2011). Among the critical responses to this relatively narrow view, Kelliher et al. (2019) called for an expansion of the meanings of *work* to include deviations from the model of full-time, permanent employment and the meanings of *life* to include more than caring for children. Furthermore, Gardiner et al. (2007) and, more recently, Biggs et al. (2017) proposed that we need to recognize the multiplicity of people's activities that change throughout the life course and the tendency to judge ourselves and be judged by others solely based on our engagement in paid work. In particular, Biggs et al. questioned the very premise that ideally healthy older women and men should spend their extended lifespan continuing with the paid work they did in middle age. They discussed the commodification of time and argued that care work and volunteer work are recognized as work-like and get recognition from policymakers (and we would add researchers) because, like paid work, they potentially can be given a monetary value and are thus a productive use of time. Less commodifiable activities, however, remain unseen. Thus, this societal focus on using one's time efficiently and productively encourages the extension of one's working life and marginalizes other activities that offer only personal fulfillment.

Rethinking the metanarrative of commodification may lead to a new vision of what older workers can contribute. As an example, Denmark et al. (2015) identified a variety of leadership opportunities for older women interested in "encore careers," such as mentor, coach, political office, and self-employment, activities befitting a "sage" (Denmark & Williams, 2012), third-age women (Radtke et al., 2016; van Mens-Verhulst & Radtke, 2013), or women who have achieved gerotranscendence (Torenstam, 1996). As well, an alternative view of life as "more than" is also more inclusive of older people who live as singles, do not have children, or identify as a sexual minority and are managing multiple interests and responsibilities on a daily basis. Older women as a group reflect this heterogeneity, with some being always single and others widowed or divorced; some being (grand) mothers and others not; some identifying as sexual minorities and others as heterosexual; and so on. As Gardiner et al. (2007) noted, an intersectional approach is called for.

Resisting Individualizing Meanings of Work-Life Balance

Adopting an intersectional approach means, among other things, seeking upstream explanations (Cole, 2009) for older women's experiences of work–life balance. Such explanations are rooted in history, culture, laws, and policies related to labor force participation and the practices of organizations. One such explanation centers on the workplace as structured around masculine norms, with the ideal worker constructed as devoted to work and always available (Williams, 2010; Williams et al., 2016). In its most extreme form, the work devotion of the ideal worker entails working long hours with little time off, a pattern characterizing those participating in professional and managerial occupations and hence also tied to social class. Of course, the ideal worker conflicts with the ideal woman, who is devoted to her family and always available to them, positioning women as inevitably struggling with work–life balance. For the older working woman, to remain working she must have adapted to the masculinist work environment and successfully negotiated conflicts between work and life that preexisted her becoming older. Older women having higher education in a field with a hidden curriculum that encourages adaptation to masculinist norms, single women, or women with few family responsibilities are likely to be the most adapted. They will be open to the pulls of work, such as work satisfaction, high self-esteem, and appreciation for one's abilities and skills. However, the older woman worker will continue to negotiate between her devotion to work and forces that pull her to other facets of her life, such as the expectations associated with the ideal woman. Having reached old age, though, she may redefine her devotion to work perhaps by working part-time. The possibility of making such a "choice," however, will depend on circumstances, such as her financial needs and whether or not her employer is supportive.

Yet another critique highlights how work–life balance has itself become a commodity, with individual women held accountable for achieving it and status accorded to those who can offer a satisfactory biographical account (Schilling, 2015). In this study of older professional women aged 54 to 61 years, the biographical narratives showed how external forces affected women's feelings of work–life balance and the meaning of success was altered over time.

The capabilities framework, developed by Hobson (2014) and colleagues, is one way to view work–life balance (Hobson prefers *work life*, without the dash, arguing that there are no boundaries between the two) in terms of how it can be achieved and the constraints around what is possible. Strengths of the framework are that it is gender sensitive (e.g., it incorporates forms of gender inequality such as the division of household labor), treats care as a value (i.e., as something to be achieved), and recognizes gendered norms as part of the institutional context that shapes what women and men imagine as possible. The basic idea is that work–life balance is something women and men want to achieve because it fosters well-being. Factors at three levels—individual, institutional, and societal—influence available choices and the freedom to choose. With a focus on welfare societies primarily in Europe and working parents, the framework offers great promise for understanding how work–life balance may be achieved and what holds back progress on that front. Similar to the other theoretical perspectives highlighted in this section, Hobson's framework takes a broad view on what contributes to an individual's experience of the interdependence of work and life.

PUSHES AND PULLS OF WORK-LIFE BALANCE

Inspired by the capabilities framework, we conceive of the older working woman as acting to remain at work in the context of pushes and pulls, sometimes contradictory, that direct her to paid work or to other life activities, envisioning these pushes and pulls as layered. We identify the layers as cultural, social, and personal. At the cultural level, the pulls toward employment may include the value accorded to those who earn money, whereas the pushes toward employment may include ageism that shores up a youth-oriented culture, with participation in paid work as a strategy for offsetting marginalization and invisibility (Radtke et al., 2016). At the social level, the pulls may include the status one is accorded through one's employment (e.g., as a professional), whereas the pushes may include ambivalence about, or even rejection of, expectations that she parents her grandchildren in retirement. At the personal level, the pulls may include the satisfaction she derives from her work and investment in a career (Fideler, 2012), whereas the pushes may include apprehension about being bored when no longer working. The pulls toward life at the cultural level may include the "discourse of a restful retirement" that constructs an idyllic life of leisure beyond paid work (Lips & Hastings, 2012, p. 149); pushes may include discourses of gender that position women as natural caregivers and emotion workers (Sørensen, 2017). At the social level, pulls toward life may include feeling undervalued at work or at a dead end (e.g., being positioned as "past their peak"; Lips & Hastings, 2012, p. 149), whereas pushes toward life may include having insufficient access to resources to support the care of a partner who is chronically ill and therefore having to do the care work herself. At the personal level, pulls toward life may include a passion for specific hobbies, whereas pushes may include a desire to care for a loved one suffering from a terminal illness.

Furthermore, a variety of contextual factors, such as her work history, health, financial circumstances, and educational level, affect the relevance and impact of the pushes and pulls on the older woman's actions. Access to financial security afforded through retirement, for example, is subject to government and employer policies that restrict older women's freedom to continue in paid work or retire, as is the case in Canada and the Netherlands. Furthermore, continuing with paid employment to help out adult children financially may seem necessary in a world where precarious employment and the cost of housing are challenges for the younger generation (Fideler, 2012). There is also the gender order at work, at home, and in their communities. At work, women are more likely to be consigned to low-paid, low-status positions (Loretto & Vickerstaff, 2015). At home, they are likely to have been the primary caregivers of children and other family members, with the prospect of continuous parenthood as they care for grandchildren, elderly parents, aging spouses, and perhaps other extended family members. More privileged women with the financial resources to outsource some of the care work have the luxury of deciding how to prioritize work, home responsibilities, and other pursuits (Fideler, 2012). Flexibility in the workplace, about which we say more below, may allow women to negotiate between expectations at work and the demands and interests of life.

In the remainder of the chapter, using pushes and pulls as our conceptual lens, we consider first the relatively small empirical literature relevant to our topic and, second, what is known about older working women in the Netherlands and Canada. In some cases, research is gender-blind or has reported no sex/gender differences, but we include it when it seems reasonable to assume that it may apply to women.

OLDER WOMEN AND WORK IN THE NETHERLANDS AND CANADA

Both the Netherlands and Canada are members of the Organisation for Economic Co-operation and Development (OECD), which promotes the objective of encouraging longer working lives for women and men to counter the gap of an aging population. A recent report (OECD, 2018) congratulated the Netherlands on taking a number of important steps to increase the employment rate of older women and men by, for example, making the public aware of the issues and emphasizing the potential for older women and men to contribute to society and the economy. At the same time, it emphasizes the need to do more, such as discouraging mandatory retirement. This constitutes a significant change from the start of the 21st century, when Dutch employers encouraged workers to retire early by offering them incentives that were difficult to refuse; changes to the law beginning around 2006 have served to deter an early exit (Damman, 2014; Damman et al., 2015). In the case of Canada, a 2013 report following up the 2006 OECD report *Live Longer, Work Longer* noted that the percentage of workers aged 50 to 64 years had increased between 2005 and 2011 and was 5.4% above the OECD average (OECD, 2013). It attributed the increase to initiatives of the Canadian government, such as changes to the national pension plan that include allowing individuals over the age of 65 years to collect their government pension and continue to work. Thus, in both countries, there is a strong pull at the institutional level for older women to remain working.

Not surprisingly, a strong pull toward life in both countries comes from cultural recognition of women as care workers. This of course sets up an opposing force that works against older women remaining in the workforce. As Bendien (2015) pointed out, the ideal housewife, who devotes herself to motherhood, has not yet fallen out of favor within Dutch society. The Dutch women of interest to us are the generation that led the way in remaining in the labor force, albeit largely as part-time workers, throughout their adult years and into old age. In negotiating work–life balance with part-time work, they have created a compromise position. Similarly, in Canada, a 2013 report of the National Seniors Council, which was commissioned by the federal government, identified caregiving duties as a possible barrier to paid employment for the older worker. Without doubt, this impacts women significantly. In a Canadian study employing a nationally representative sample of women and men, aged 55 to 69 years (i.e., between the age of eligibility for early access to one's pension and the age just before one is required to take one's pension benefits), women engaging in high-intensity caregiving (i.e., 15 or more hours per week) was associated with not working or working reduced hours (Jacobs et al., 2014). The demands of such caregiving may well serve to push the older woman toward employment as a means of escaping the stresses, that is, as a form of respite. In both countries, then, the cultural meanings of womanhood that equate it with caregiving pull women of all ages toward life, but then, faced with the actual demands of caregiving, women negotiate a balance that may involve remaining at work or not.

Older Women Remaining at Work as a Growing Trend

Older women participate less in the labor force than do older men. In the Netherlands in 2018, 10.3% of women aged 65 to 69 years of age were employed in the labor force (compared with 23.8% of men in the same age range; Centraal Bureau voor de Statistiek, n.d.). For those aged 70 to 74 years, the employment rate dropped to 3.9% of women and 10.8% of men. In Canada in 2019, older women's employment rate was somewhat higher at 22.7% for ages 65 to 69 years and 5.1% for age 70 years and over (Statistics Canada, 2020).

A relevant but understudied phenomenon is *bridge employment*, that is, paid work taken up postretirement or when receiving a pension and covering the time in between official retirement and actual retirement. This is a growing trend in the United States and OECD countries generally. Unfortunately, the available data for the Netherlands and Canada point to this trend but do not provide a full picture. In the Netherlands, the percentage of those 65 to 70 years of age who participate in bridge employment, working at least 12 hours per week after ending their career employment, increased from 3.4% in 2001 to 8.6% in 2014 (de Wind et al., 2016). Recent research with a large sample of retirees reported that one quarter of them participated in bridge employment (Dingemans et al., 2016). In Canada, among women aged 50 to 66 years who left a long-term job in the late 1990s and early 2000s (86% reported leaving voluntarily), 51% were reemployed by the following year (that percentage drops to 41% when considering women aged 60–64 years only; Bonikowska & Schellenberg, 2014). Of the women who left their long-term job at age 60 to 64 years, 25% continued to work for 6 or more years, which was well beyond the average retirement age (Bonikowska & Schellenberg, 2014). Taken together, these data suggest that maintaining employment even when receiving a pension is not uncommon among older women.

Notably, in the Netherlands, women's median intended and actual retirement age between 2001 and 2011 was 60 years, which is well below the age at which they were eligible for a public pension (i.e., 65 years; Damman et al., 2015). However, women who became mothers after age 27 years (i.e., they were "late" mothers at the time), with children living at home, remained in the workforce longer. As well, women who had been divorced retired later than did women who had been continuously married, although those repartnering did not differ from the continuously married. Similarly, Canadian research reported that women who left a long-term job at age 50 years or later were more likely to be reemployed if they were separated or divorced and less likely if married (Bonikowska & Schellenberg, 2014). Clearly, remaining at work is more common among older women living in particular circumstances (i.e., late motherhood, dependent children, divorced), and the common context is likely their financial situation. Financial need may lead older women to prioritize work over retirement, but how they then negotiate the combination of work and life is another matter.

Older Women Remaining at Work: Reasons and Supporting Conditions

Several recent studies conducted in the Netherlands have explored factors that contribute to older workers remaining at work, albeit using different kinds of samples, research designs, and measures. Two large-sample studies reported that women were less likely to engage in bridge employment but otherwise reported no differences between women and men in terms of what contributes to remaining at work (de Wind et al., 2016; Dingemans, 2016; Dingemans et al., 2016). Three supporting conditions associated with remaining employed were identified in some or all of the studies. These included good health (de Wind et al., 2016; Dingemans, 2016; Dingemans et al., 2016; Sewdas et al., 2017), financial need (de Wind et al., 2016; Sewdas et al., 2017), and flexibility in the work environment, most commonly meaning the opportunity to work part-time (Sewdas et al., 2017).

Among the pulls toward employment (i.e., characteristics associated with older women and men remaining at work) was *work engagement* (i.e., whether individuals rated themselves as having sufficient energy and mental resilience, strength and fitness, stamina, enthusiasm, inspiration, pride, and job satisfaction; de Wind et al., 2016), satisfaction derived from using knowledge and skills but also the opportunity to learn new knowledge and skills (Sewdas et al., 2017), and having worked in a high-level job or a supervisory position before retirement (i.e., jobs that are engaging, may have flexible time schedules, and are associated with status and respect; Dingemans et al., 2016). Related to this, women and men who reported more preretirement disengagement from work were less likely to remain working (Dingemans et al., 2016). As well, a relationship between participation in volunteer work and bridge employment (de Wind et al., 2016) is suggestive of social engagement that may be a pull toward employment and life. Other pulls related to the social level included being recognized by coworkers and clients, the social contact with others (for some, younger colleagues were particularly important), and remaining relevant to society (Sewdas et al., 2017). A push at the social level was not spending a lot of time alone (this was relevant whether or not participants had partners; Sewdas et al., 2017). Another pull at the personal level included maintaining continuity with the daily routines of life (e.g., getting ready for work at a certain time), whereas a push at the personal level was anxiety about losing one's purpose in life. Overall, this research begins to give us some sense of how work–life balance may figure in older women remaining in paid work—her engagement with her work, relationships with others, and social standing and contributions to society are important pulls; loneliness and concerns about having a purpose in life constitute pushes. Importantly, it is also consistent with research conducted in other parts of the world, such as Australia (Shacklock et al., 2009). Missing, of course, are the pushes and pulls of life.

To date, Canadian researchers have not studied the reasons associated with older women remaining at work, other than financial considerations. One study, however, has explored work–life balance dissatisfaction among Canadian workers 55 years of age and older (Uriarte-Landa & Hébert, 2009) and reported that working older women were more likely to be dissatisfied than were working older men. There were no sex differences in the factors that contributed to dissatisfaction, however. Those factors that increased dissatisfaction included having a disability, being an elder caregiver, having a managerial job, and working long hours. Those that decreased dissatisfaction included having an employed partner, enjoying one's job, and being self-employed. Caring for children had no impact on dissatisfaction with work–life balance. Furthermore, there are some consistencies between the Dutch research and the Canadian research. The negative effect of a disability is consistent with good health as a necessary condition to even consider that one's work and life are balanced. Similarly, the working environment— long hours (meaning lack of flexibility) and being self-employed (meaning flexibility)—either enables balance or not. As a point of difference, the pull toward life of caregiving for an elder is not something that has been explored in Dutch research; however, there is ample evidence that it occupies a considerable amount of older women's time (de Boer et al., 2019; Plaisier & Schijns, 2015).

ENVISIONING WORK-LIFE BALANCE AMONG OLDER WOMEN

The older women of concern to us and represented in the research cited are primarily part of the baby boom generation. Compared with younger generations in the United States, baby boomers may experience the least conflict between work and family (Bennett et al., 2017), although within the baby boom generation, there may also be considerable variation due in part to shifts in the legal and policy environment (this, however, has yet to be studied). Because older adults have had lengthy careers, they are likely at a point where they have flexibility in their jobs, little expectation of travel for work purposes, and leave time, all of which would benefit them in relation to balancing work and family responsibilities. The success of the baby boom generation in establishing work–life balance appears to be at least somewhat generalizable as similar results were obtained in a large sample study of older workers in Finland, Lithuania, and Sweden (Richert-Kazmierska & Stankiewicz, 2016). Consistent with this, in a study of professional, managerial, and executive employees of IBM in Europe, the United States, Asia–Pacific, Latin America, and Canada, older workers (age 55 years and older) had the most job responsibility, the highest morale, and the most caregiving responsibilities and yet were most able to manage work and family responsibilities (Hill et al., 2014). Furthermore, older women had greater awareness of, and used to a greater extent, work–family programs compared with older men. Although older women had fewer family demands in terms of being less likely to have dependent teenage children than did older men, they also had fewer resources to assist with this—that is, compared with older men, they were less likely to have a spouse and a spouse who worked part-time. Not surprisingly, older women reported more family–work conflict than did men. For both women and men, however, flexibility such as the possibility to work at home or vary one's work schedule and the option of working part-time contributed to work–life balance.

The most detailed picture of older working women's work–life balance can be found in Fideler's (2012) study of 155 employed, professional women, aged 60 to 84 years, in the United States. She described the women as prioritizing work, something they can do at this stage of their lives. Furthermore, she attributed the greater flexibility in the work environment that is associated with technological innovation as contributing to better work–life balance than was previously possible. One pull of employment for these high-achieving women is the personal satisfaction and wellness that they derive from work. A common regret was insufficient time for life (i.e., family, friends, nonwork activities)—the pull of relationships and personal interests—but few were caregivers for grandchildren, which means many successfully resisted the cultural discourse that could consign them to "eternal parenthood." Nevertheless, more than half reported that they volunteered, displaying the kind of social engagement reported by de Wind et al. (2016) among older Dutch workers. Other pulls to employment that are consistent with the Dutch and Canadian research include a desire to contribute and intense work engagement. A pull at the cultural level may be their emphasis on economic independence, although in the Dutch context the concept of the *ideal housewife* remains a compelling force in women's lives (Bendien, 2015). Naturally, there was variability in how the women negotiated among the various pushes and pulls.

Research investigating work–life balance and retired, professional women in the United States has confirmed what the studies of older women remaining at work have concluded—the pull of employment provides a purpose in life and structure to one's time (Loe & Johnston, 2016). In this study, some of the retired women regained a sense of being valued, a cultural pull, through engaging in bridging employment. Importantly, an aspect of work–life balance that was stressed in this study but is missing entirely from the research focused on women who remain at work is the renegotiation of personal relationships and care work. A question worth pursuing is how personal relationships and care work are affected when older women continue with their paid work.

Altogether, the small amount of available research supports the conclusion that the many older women who remain working, whether out of necessity or out of personal need, have substantial experience and skill at creating a balance among the many demands and opportunities in life. At an older age, they no longer have dependent children, but they may have a partner or elders in need of their help. How they balance will depend in part on access to resources to support their caregiving. Whether paid work gives way to caregiving or some other arrangement will also depend on other pulls and pushes, which in turn depend on a woman's work history, life history, and current circumstances.

IS A FLEXIBLE WORK ENVIRONMENT THE SOLUTION?

Flexibility in the work environment is frequently touted as a solution to conflict between work and life throughout the life course. One radical suggestion is to abolish retirement at a specific age and replace it with a system that allows temporary exit from employment at needed points in the life course (Alfageme et al., 2012). Such proposals are forward-looking in drawing attention to potential structural changes in light of women's (and men's) increased longevity and in undermining the construction of age as the criterion used to offer and restrict opportunities (Riley & Riley, 1999). Greater flexibility over the life course in choosing when to pursue education, be a mother, focus on a career or job skill development, and engage in leisure activities is afforded by such longevity and could become normative as more and more older women remain in the workforce.

To date, flexible work environments among older workers appear to be relatively uncommon and limited in nature. In their study of factors that support 50- to 64-year-old workers in the United Kingdom remaining in the labor force, Loretto and Vickerstaff (2015) reported that the incidence of flexible working was low, and the most common form was part-time work. As expected, women were more likely to work part-time than were men. The older women, however, still looked forward to being released from paid work as freeing them from jobs that did not bring them satisfaction. Thus, having the flexibility afforded by part-time work was not sufficient as a motivation for remaining in the labor force. In general, the older participants focused on flexible work as a means of fitting work into the rest of life, a reversal from their previous priorities.

Consistent with what has been documented elsewhere, many of the women who participated in Loretto and Vickerstaff's (2015) study were caring for elderly dependents or ill partners, but flexible work was not seen as sufficiently flexible. After all, the demands of such care work are unpredictable and not likely to be supported by an employer. Older women were not inclined to talk about flexible work as a choice, except in the case where they rejected it with the aim of continuing to build their careers. Typically, these were "late starters" (i.e., women who had focused on raising children but who now enjoyed their work and foresaw opportunities in the future). Thus, older women may consciously opt to remain in the labor force as a matter of personal fulfillment (Fideler, 2012). On the other hand, many women viewed their flexible work (part-time or retired) as "helping out," allowing them to do unpaid work that involved assisting elderly people, daughters working full-time, neighbors, and friends. Hence, what seems like a straightforward approach to enabling older women to remain in the workforce is far from simple. Attending to intersectionality and how women are positioned with respect to income and pension security, relationship status, motherhood, and other caregiving burdens will be important in determining the kinds of flexibility needed to manage the multiple demands of everyday life. Women, it seems, negotiate flexibility for themselves throughout their working lives. Employers and policymakers may well learn something useful about creating flexible work environments by listening to women's perspectives.

CONCLUSION

Our efforts to shed light on the meanings of work–life balance for older working women have been hampered by a lack of research that is directly relevant to the topic. Hence, from the rather large, interdisciplinary literatures on work–life balance, older women and work, and retirement, we have drawn from sources that we deemed to be most relevant and most recent. We focused on the Netherlands and Canada, which have similar national agendas for socioeconomic development but still retain some of the social safety net associated with welfare states. Although the claims we make are likely to hold beyond the borders of these two countries, a suspicion that is supported by research conducted elsewhere and cited here, nevertheless, we cannot assert that our conclusions hold universally.

Utilizing a work–life balance perspective from which to address women working beyond the statutory retirement age has allowed us to see the complex array of pushes and pulls that are potentially relevant to any decisions they might make about continuing to work or fully retire. These forces operate at cultural, social, and personal levels. Furthermore, they are constrained by a context that includes their work and educational history, financial circumstances, and qualities of the work environment, such as the possibility of part-time employment. An intersectional perspective is clearly needed as there is unlikely to be one set of recommendations for older women for whom work is a necessity and/or personal commitment.

REFERENCES

Alfageme, A., Pastor, B. G., & Viñado, C. (2012). Temporary exit from employment throughout the life course: An alternative to retirement to challenge ageism and sexism. *Critical Social Policy, 32*(4), 696–708. https://doi.org/10.1177/0261018312449810

Barnett, R. C., & Baruch, G. K. (1985). Women's involvement in multiple roles and psychological distress. *Journal of Personality and Social Psychology, 49*(1), 135–145. https://doi.org/10.1037/0022-3514.49.1.135

Bendien, E. (2015). Ambiguities of work satisfaction for middle-aged and older career women in the Netherlands: Stretching a tradition. *European Journal of Women's Studies, 22*(1), 84–98. https://doi.org/10.1177/1350506814529938

Bennett, M. M., Beehr, T. A., & Ivanitskaya, L. V. (2017). Work–family conflict: Differences across generations and life cycles. *Journal of Managerial Psychology, 32*(4), 314–332. https://doi.org/10.1108/JMP-06-2016-0192

Biggs, S., McGann, M., Bowman, D., & Kimberley, H. (2017). Work, health and the commodification of life's time: Reframing work–life balance and the promise of a long life. *Ageing and Society, 37*(7), 1458–1483. https://doi.org/10.1017/S0144686X16000404

Bonikowska, A., & Schellenberg, G. (2014). *Employment transitions among older workers leaving long-term jobs: Evidence from administrative data*. Statistics Canada. https://www150.statcan.gc.ca/n1/pub/11f0019m/11f0019m2014355-eng.htm

Burr, V. (2015). *Social constructionism* (3rd ed.). Routledge. https://doi.org/10.4324/9781315715421

Centraal Bureau voor de Statistiek. (n.d.). *Labor participation; key figures.* https://opendata.cbs.nl/statline/#/CBS/en/dataset/82309ENG/table?ts=1561141478550

Clark, S. C. (2000). Work/family border theory: A new theory of work/family balance. *Human Relations*, *53*(6), 747–770. https://doi.org/10.1177/0018726700536001

Cole, E. R. (2009). Intersectionality and research in psychology. *American Psychologist*, *64*(3), 170–180. https://doi.org/10.1037/a0014564

Damman, M. (2014). *From employee to retiree: Life histories and retirement in the Netherlands*. Amsterdam University Press.

Damman, M., Henkens, K., & Kalmijn, M. (2015). Women's retirement intentions and behavior: The role of childbearing and marital histories. *European Journal of Population*, *31*(4), 339–363. https://doi.org/10.1007/s10680-014-9335-8

de Boer, A., Plaisier, I., & de Klerk, M. (2019). *Werk en mantelzorg: Kwaliteit van leven en het gebruik van ondersteuning op het werk* [Work and informal care: Quality of life and the use of support at work]. SCP.

Denmark, F. L., Goldstein, H., Thies, K., & Tworecke, A. (2015). Older women, leadership, and encore careers. In V. Muhlbauer, J. C. Chrisler, & F. L. Denmark (Eds.), *Women and aging: An international, intersectional power perspective* (pp. 71–88). Springer International Publishing.

Denmark, F. L., & Williams, D. A. (2012). The older woman as sage: The satisfaction of mentoring. *Women & Therapy*, *35*(3–4), 261–278. https://doi.org/10.1080/02703149.2012.684543

de Wind, A., van der Pas, S., Blatter, B. M., & van der Beek, A. J. (2016). A life course perspective on working beyond retirement—results from a longitudinal study in the Netherlands. *BMC Public Health*, *16*, 499. https://doi.org/10.1186/s12889-016-3174-y

Dingemans, E. A. A. (2016). *Working after retirement: Determinants and consequences of bridge employment*. Rijksuniversiteit Groningen.

Dingemans, E., Henkens, K., & Solinge, H. (2016). Access to bridge employment: Who finds and who does not find work after retirement? *The Gerontologist*, *56*(4), 630–640. https://doi.org/10.1093/geront/gnu182

Edge, C. E., Cooper, A. M., & Coffey, M. (2017). Barriers and facilitators to extended working lives in Europe: A gender focus. *Public Health Reviews*, *38*, 2. https://doi.org/10.1186/s40985-017-0053-8

Febbraro, A. R. (2003). Alpha bias and beta bias in research on labor and love: The case of enhancement versus scarcity. *Feminism & Psychology*, *13*(2), 201–223. https://doi.org/10.1177/0959353503013002005

Fideler, E. F. (2012). *Women still at work: Professionals over sixty and on the job*. Rowman & Littlefield.

Gardiner, J., Stuart, M., Forde, C., Greenwood, I., MacKenzie, R., & Perrett, R. (2007). Work–life balance and older workers: Employees' perspectives on retirement transitions following redundancy. *International Journal of Human Resource Management*, *18*(3), 476–489. https://doi.org/10.1080/09585190601167904

Greenhaus, J. H., & Beutell, N. J. (1985). Sources of conflict between work and family roles. *Academy of Management Review*, *10*(1), 76–88. https://doi.org/10.5465/amr.1985.4277352

Hill, E. J., Erickson, J. J., Fellows, K. J., Martinengo, G., & Allen, S. M. (2014). Work and family over the life course: Do older workers differ? *Journal of Family and Economic Issues*, *35*, 1–13. https://doi.org/10.1007/s10834-012-9346-8

Hobson, B. (Ed.). (2014). *Work life balance: The agency and capabilities gap*. Oxford University Press.

Hochschild, A. (1989). *The second shift: Working parents and the revolution at home.* Avon Books.

Jacobs, J. C., Laporte, A., Van Houtven, C. H., & Coyte, P. C. (2014). Caregiving intensity and retirement status in Canada. *Social Science & Medicine, 102,* 74–82. https://doi.org/10.1016/j.socscimed.2013.11.051

Kanter, R. M. (1988). Work and family in the United States: A critical review and agenda for research and policy. *Family Business Review, 2*(1), 77–114. https://doi.org/10.1111/j.1741-6248.1989.00077.x

Keeney, J., Boyd, E. M., Sinha, R., Westring, A. F., & Ryan, A. M. (2013). From "work–family" to "work–life": Broadening our conceptualization and measurement. *Journal of Vocational Behavior, 82*(3), 221–237. https://doi.org/10.1016/j.jvb.2013.01.005

Kelliher, C., Richardson, J., & Boiarintseva, G. (2019). All of work? All of life? Reconceptualizing work-life balance for the 21st century. *Human Resource Management Journal, 29*(2), 97–112. https://doi.org/10.1111/1748-8583.12215

Leslie, L. M., King, E. B., & Clair, J. A. (2019). Work–life ideologies: The contextual basis and consequences of beliefs about work and life. *Academy of Management Review, 44*(1), 72–98. https://doi.org/10.5465/amr.2016.0410

Lips, H. M., & Hastings, S. L. (2012). Competing discourses for older women: Agency/leadership vs. disengagement/retirement. *Women & Therapy, 35*(3–4), 145–164. https://doi.org/10.1080/02703149.2012.684533

Loe, M., & Johnston, D. K. (2016). Professional women "rebalancing" in retirement: Time, relationships, and body. *Journal of Women & Aging, 28*(5), 418–430. https://doi.org/10.1080/08952841.2015.1018047

Loretto, W., & Vickerstaff, S. (2015). Gender, age and flexible working in later life. *Work, Employment and Society, 29*(2), 233–249. https://doi.org/10.1177/0950017014545267

National Seniors Council. (2013). *Older workers at risk of withdrawing from the labor force or becoming unemployed: Employers' views on how to retain and attract older workers.* https://www.canada.ca/content/dam/nsc-cna/documents/pdf/policy-and-program-development/publications-reports/2013/older-workers-risk/older_workers-en.pdf

Organisation for Economic Co-operation and Development. (2006). *Live longer, work longer: A synthesis report.*

Organisation for Economic Co-operation and Development. (2013). *OECD thematic follow-up review of policies to improve labour market prospects for older workers: Canada.* https://www.oecd.org/els/emp/Older%20workers_Canada-MOD.pdf

Organisation for Economic Co-operation and Development. (2018). *Key policies to promote longer working lives in The Netherlands.* http://www.oecd.org/els/emp/Netherlands%20key%20policies_Final.pdf

Özbilgin, M. F., Beauregard, T. A., Tatli, A., & Bell, M. P. (2011). Work–life, diversity and intersectionality: A critical review and research agenda. *International Journal of Management Reviews, 13*(2), 177–198. https://doi.org/10.1111/j.1468-2370.2010.00291.x

Phipps, S. T. A., & Prieto, L. C. (2016). A discovery of early labor organizations and the women who advocated work–life balance: An ethical perspective. *Journal of Business Ethics, 134,* 249–261. https://doi.org/10.1007/s10551-014-2428-9

Plaisier, I., & Schijns, P. (2015). Hulp delen [Share help]. In M. de Klerk, A. de Boer, I. Plaisier, P. Schyns, & S. Kooiker (Eds.), *Informele hulp: Wie doet er wat? Omvang, aard en kenmerken van mantelzorg en vrijwilligerswerk in de zorg en ondersteuning 2014* [Informal help: Who does what? Scope, nature and characteristics of informal care and voluntary work in care and support 2014] (pp. 103–120). SCP.

Radtke, H. L., Young, J., & van Mens-Verhulst, J. (2016). Aging, identity, and women: Constructing the third age. *Women & Therapy, 39*(1–2), 86–105. https://doi.org/10.1080/02703149.2016.1116321

Richert-Kazmierska, A., & Stankiewicz, K. (2016). Work–life balance: Does age matter? *Work (Reading, Mass.), 55*(3), 679–688. https://doi.org/10.3233/WOR-162435

Riley, M. W., & Riley, J. W. (1999). Sociological research on age: Legacy and challenge. *Ageing and Society, 19*(1), 123–132. https://doi.org/10.1017/S0144686X9900731X

Schilling, E. (2015). 'Success is satisfaction with what you have'? Biographical work–life balance of older female employees in public administration. *Gender, Work and Organization, 22*(5), 474–494. https://doi.org/10.1111/gwao.12097

Sewdas, R., de Wind, A., van der Zwaan, L. G. L., van der Borg, W. E., Steenbeek, R., van der Beek, A. J., & Boot, C. R. L. (2017). Why older workers work beyond the retirement age: A qualitative study. *BMC Public Health, 17*, 672. https://doi.org/10.1186/s12889-017-4675-z

Shacklock, K., Brunetto, Y., & Nelson, S. (2009). The different variables that affect older males' and females' intentions to continue working. *Asia Pacific Journal of Human Resources, 47*(1), 79–101. https://doi.org/10.1177/1038411108099291

Sørensen, S. Ø. (2017). The performativity of choice: Postfeminist perspectives on work–life balance. *Gender, Work and Organization, 24*(3), 297–313. https://doi.org/10.1111/gwao.12163

Staines, G. L. (1980). Spillover versus compensation: A review of the literature on the relationships between work and women. *Human Relations, 33*(2), 111–129. https://doi.org/10.1177/001872678003300203

Statistics Canada. (2020). Unemployment rate, participation rate and employment rate by sex, annual (Table 14-10-0327-02). https://www150.statcan.gc.ca/t1/tbl1/en/tv.action?pid=1410032702

Torenstam, L. (1996). Gerotranscendence: A theory about maturing into old age. *Journal of Aging and Identity, 1*, 37–50.

Uriarte-Landa, J., & Hébert, B-P. (2009, October). Work–life balance of older workers. *Perspectives on Labor and Income*, 17–28.

van Mens-Verhulst, J., & Radtke, L. (2013). Women's identities and the third age: A feminist review of psychological knowledge. *Tijdschrift voor Genderstudies, 16*(2), 47–58. https://doi.org/10.5117/TVGEND2013.2.MENS

Wayne, J. H., Butts, M. M., Casper, W. J., & Allen, T. D. (2017). In search of balance: A conceptual and empirical integration of multiple meanings of work-family balance. *Personnel Psychology, 70*(1), 167–210. https://doi.org/10.1111/peps.12132

Williams, J. C. (2010). *Reshaping the work–family debate: Why men and class matter.* Harvard University Press.

Williams, J. C., Berdahl, J. L., & Vandello, J. A. (2016). Beyond work-life "integration." *Annual Review of Psychology, 67*, 515–539. https://doi.org/10.1146/annurev-psych-122414-033710

8 WHAT, RETIRE? NOT NOW— MAYBE NOT EVER

PATRICIA A. O'CONNOR

One's philosophy is not best expressed in words; it is expressed in the choices one makes.

—Eleanor Roosevelt

Working people, both men and women, generally aim to retire at what society or they consider an appropriate age, typically age 65. Research on retirement centers largely on the individual's financial preparation for retirement (Jefferson, 2009; Lee, 2003; Sunden & Surette, 1998; Tompor, 2019) and, somewhat secondarily, on the psychological and social consequences for retirees. The lack of financial preparation results in women working into older ages out of necessity, that is, to pay the bills, a group examined elsewhere in this book.

For women, retirement is frequently associated with poverty (Lee, 2003). However, women with sufficient financial resources pre- and postretirement are able to engage in chosen activities but may have other issues with the status of being retired. This less frequently researched area includes a focus

https://doi.org/10.1037/0000212-009
Older Women Who Work: Resilience, Choice, and Change, E. Cole and L. Hollis-Sawyer (Editors)

on the psychological and social consequences of retirement on the retirees. These have been explored by Price (2000), who found that women experience a loss of their professional identity after retirement. Somewhat more recently, Sherry et al. (2017) examined women's apprehensions about retirement, including their conflicting feelings about the potential freedoms and changes in relationships that are likely to occur. The changes are documented by Cole and Gergen (2012) and Loe and Johnston (2016), who noted the ways in which retired professional women cope with the multiplicity of issues that naturally occur.

Increasingly, women are working past their expected retirement age, some for financial reasons as noted above, but others simply because they enjoy their work and careers and/or want to continue to contribute (Dendinger et al., 2005). Frieze and colleagues (2011) explored factors that would predict the decision to retire among still-working MBA graduates. Women in their study were less likely to consider retirement if they enjoyed their work, if their husbands planned to work past retirement age, or if they felt their work made a contribution.

That women are working longer is well-documented (Hill, 2002; Satter, 2017), and there is also evidence of the difficulties associated with retirement among women (Loe & Johnston, 2016; Price, 2000; Sherry et al., 2017). However, what propels women to continue working into their 70s, though they are financially able to retire, has received much less research attention. The aim of this chapter is to determine whether specific factors are associated with these women's decisions to continue working, postponing retirement, or even rejecting its possibility. My particular interest in conducting this pilot study stems from my own decisions regarding retirement.

METHOD

For this qualitative study, two methods were used to identify women who were 70 years of age or older and still employed, the combination of which yielded a relatively small sample of women. The first method was an email sent to an electronic mailing list of a committee of self-identified older women in a professional organization/association; the list comprised more than 200 email addresses, but the number of those women who were 70 years of age or older and were still working was unknown. One person indicated a willingness to participate. The second method employed snowball sampling: I solicited potential participants among friends and colleagues, which yielded 11 working women 70 years of age or older for a total of 12 women available for interviews. One woman who initially agreed to participate was not available for the interview.

The interview for this study comprised four straightforward domains: What do you do? Why continue? Are your loved ones affected by your continuing to work? Do you have retirement plans? Respondents were also asked their age, ethnicity, and geographic location and about their relationships (married/partnered, single/widowed) and the presence of children (or not). The actual questions are in Appendix 8.1.

Participants were interviewed by phone ($n = 8$) or in person ($n = 2$); one completed the interview via email. All phone-interviewed respondents except one were interviewed at the first phone call; the single interview completed by email was scheduled as such because the respondent was out of the country. Interviews took approximately 20 to 40 minutes to complete.

RESULTS

These 11 women ranged in age from 71 to 77 ($M = 74.8$). Five are married or in a stable relationship, and six are single; one self-identified as widowed, and two others self-identified as divorced. Three self-identified as lesbian. Nine of the 11 have children more or less regularly in their lives; at least two have children living in other countries. Seven of these women live on the East Coast: five toward the north and two in the south. Three live in the Midwest and one on the West Coast. All self-identify as Caucasian, two as Italian descent and one as Jewish. All are well-educated with 4-year college degrees; additionally, two have master's degrees and two have doctoral degrees.

Most ($n = 10$) of these respondents either own their own business or manage a private practice of some sort of independently organized and managed work. Three are currently working in full-time positions, with two leading their own/family businesses; only one is employed full-time by a large organization. The other eight work part-time or work with great flexibility; for example, one works as a consultant 2 days a week but can change those days if necessary. Another example of the available flexibility is those who teach classes (e.g., art, yoga) or who work with individuals in some manner of helping. One of the two who are full-time in a family business would prefer to be part-time, but family pressures preclude that.

Nearly all, married/partnered and single, reported that their working is not a problem for family or friends. The exception was one single person who described that her last relationship ended because the partner wanted her to retire or at least work less. Only one reported that continuing to work full-time limits her activities, but that seemed to be less of a problem and more of a simple fact. Another noted that friends recognize the importance of her work and that she does not "stay friends if they don't get it."

All but two of these women value their continuing engagement in work of their choosing. One of the two, who is unable to leave the family business and is not happy about that continued involvement, illustrates the consequence of not having a choice, and the other works solely to support her interest in extensive travel. The nature of her part-time work permits her to visit other countries and take extensive trips to visit family living abroad. When she stops traveling, she expects that she will likely stop working.

Among the nine who appreciate, even cherish, their ability to stay engaged in their preferred work, two particularly value being involved and working with the younger generation or just younger people. One described simply not being ready to retire, in part because her partner is much younger. Another noted that "it's fun to work" but with the caveat that it would be "scary not to be" working. A third stated, with a tone of certainty, "I like to solve problems." Most also find that working keeps them connected to other people, though there may be leisure activities that could achieve that same outcome. Several indicated that they intend to work until they are unable to do so because of health or mobility problems (e.g., being unable to drive). Six emphasized the passion involved in their chosen work:

- "I love what I do and cannot imagine an avocation that would be as enjoyable."
- "[Working] gives me meaning, identity, structure."
- "My brain wants to keep working and figuring out how to make the world a better place."
- "[My] mind is better challenged."
- "[This is] my lifelong passion."
- "[I] can't not do it [my work]."

DISCUSSION

The central question for this study—why financially stable women who could be retired continue to work—emerged as a compelling topic for me because I am in my mid-70s and continue to work full-time as an academic. The simple answer, from this small sample and my own experience, is that women working into their 70s by choice are generally passionate about what they do, as am I. Moreover, they find meaning in their lives by continuing to engage in that passion, similar to the findings of Frieze et al. (2011). Their work can generally be defined as central to who they are as individuals (Schmidt & Lee, 2008).

There is a societal expectation that being retired is better than working and, therefore, people working past retirement age present a confusing, even contradictory image for that expectation. Only one of the 11 women in this small sample named an unfortunate consequence of not fulfilling the retirement expectation: loss of a relationship. But that person did not express regret at continuing to work. Two others indicated some conflicting instances of pressure from friends to retire or, maybe more accurately, pressure to have the availability that retirement may offer. One noted limited time for activities, and another noted that friends who make those kinds of demands are no longer her friends. A third, avoiding the conflict, relied on friends who could accommodate her continuing to work, though she was also able to accommodate their plans by changing her work schedule.

The question "When are you going to retire?" that is frequently posed to working people of retirement age seems similar to the "When are you going to get married?" or "When are you going to have children?" questions that are associated with other expected stages in life. Stepping outside the societal norms and expectations can be difficult, but clearly for these women and for me, the benefits that accrue from decisions not to retire (yet) outweigh the difficulties associated with following the norms and expectations.

A serious limitation is that these results stem from a small sample of women who are all Caucasian and all college-educated. Furthermore, these are women who are choosing to work, who are specifically not working to pay the bills. Working for them is a choice, and the existence of that choice allows them to pursue their passions. These results, then, are not applicable to the many women who were or are unable to be financially prepared for retirement.

Two threads emerge from this exploratory study for future research. First is how these women, and women like them—women who are working by choice—came to understand that they could pursue their passions. That is, they could ignore the societal expectation, and even the social pressure, that retirement was their next step. Second is identifying the kinds of contributions these women can and do make. Most of them noted their interest in continuing to make a difference or a contribution to their local communities and beyond. One specifically noted the possibility of giving back to the community financially. These women generally have multiple resources, including their own time, energy, and expertise, to give. We need a more in-depth understanding of their contributions and the support that making those contributions may require.

APPENDIX 8.1

INTERVIEW QUESTIONS

1. Can you tell me about your current occupation, including how long you have been in that occupation?
2. Did you have a time when you changed careers (from what to what)?
3. A simple question: Why do you continue to work when you could be retired?
4. Are you married, or do you have a significant other? (yes or no)
5. How about children? (yes or no)
6. Does that work, or that you are working, affect that or those relationships? In what way?
7. Do you have other older friends/relatives who are still working or are retired? How does your working affect those relationships?
8. Do you have retirement plans? (Please explain)
9. Anything else that would be helpful for me to know?
10. A little information about yourself:

    Age _____ Ethnicity _____ Location of residence _____

REFERENCES

Cole, E., & Gergen, M. (Eds.). (2012). *Retiring but not shy: Feminist psychologists create their post-careers*. Taos Institute Publications.

Dendinger, V. M., Adams, G. A., & Jacobson, J. D. (2005). Reasons for working and their relationship to retirement attitudes, job satisfaction and occupational self-efficacy of bridge employees. *International Journal of Aging & Human Development, 61*(1), 21–35. https://doi.org/10.2190/K8KU-46LH-DTW5-44TU

Frieze, I. H., Olson, J. E., & Murrell, A. J. (2011). Working beyond 65: Predictors of late retirement for women and men MBAs. *Journal of Women & Aging, 23*(1), 40–57. https://doi.org/10.1080/08952841.2011.540485

Hill, E. T. (2002). The labor force participation of older women: Retired? Working? Both? *Monthly Labor Review, 125*(9), 39–48.

Jefferson, T. (2009). Women and retirement pensions: A research review. *Feminist Economics, 15*(4), 115–145. https://doi.org/10.1080/13545700903153963

Lee, W. K. M. (2003). Women and retirement planning: Towards the "feminization of poverty" in an aging Hong Kong. *Journal of Women & Aging, 15*(1), 31–53. https://doi.org/10.1300/J074v15n01_04

Loe, M., & Johnston, D. K. (2016). Professional women "rebalancing" in retirement: Time, relationships, and body. *Journal of Women & Aging, 28*(5), 418–430. https://doi.org/10.1080/08952841.2015.1018047

Price, C. A. (2000). Women and retirement: Relinquishing professional identity. *Journal of Aging Studies, 14*(1), 81–101. https://doi.org/10.1016/S0890-4065(00)80017-1

Satter, M. Y. (2017, February 15). Older women working longer. *BenefitsPRO*. https://www.benefitspro.com/2017/02/15/older-women-working-longer/?slreturn=20200703120833

Schmidt, J. A., & Lee, K. (2008). Voluntary retirement and organizational turnover intentions: The differential associations with work and non-work commitment constructs. *Journal of Business and Psychology, 22*, 297–309. https://doi.org/10.1007/s10869-008-9068-y

Sherry, A., Tomlinson, J. M., Loe, M., Johnston, K., & Feeney, B. C. (2017). Apprehensive about retirement: Women, life transitions, and relationships. *Journal of Women & Aging, 29*(2), 173–184. https://doi.org/10.1080/08952841.2015.1113728

Sunden, A. E., & Surette, B. J. (1998). Gender differences in the allocation of assets in retirement savings plans. *The American Economic Review, 88*(2), 207–211.

Tompor, S. (2019, January 23). The depressing truth about women and retirement. *The Tennessean*, p. A1.

9 "YOU'RE TOO YOUNG/OLD FOR THIS"

The Intersection of Ageism and Sexism in the Workplace

RUTH V. WALKER AND ALEXANDRA I. ZELIN

People's bodies are not marked or experienced as "old" in a universal manner but rather the perception varies by gender, race, ethnicity, class, and sexual orientation.

—Toni Calasanti (2005, p. 10)

Of the 72,675 complaints filed with the U.S. Equal Employment Opportunity Commission (EEOC) in 2018, complaints of discrimination due to race, gender, age, and disability status were the most prevalent (EEOC, n.d.-b). A total of 32.4% of workplace discrimination complaints were attributed to sex-based discrimination, and 21.4% were attributed to age-based discrimination. These statistics give a limited view of the true prevalence of workplace discrimination based on gender and age. Although an individual can file a discrimination complaint for more than one reason (i.e., experiencing both age- and sex-based discrimination), the EEOC does not report the numbers

We thank the members of Ruth's dissertation committee for their valuable insight and feedback on the larger study from which the data for this chapter was taken: Toni Bisconti, Kathryn Feltey, Katherine Judge, Jennifer Stanley, and Harvey Sterns.

https://doi.org/10.1037/0000212-010
Older Women Who Work: Resilience, Choice, and Change, E. Cole and L. Hollis-Sawyer (Editors)

of cases alleging both types simultaneously. Furthermore, nationwide surveys suggest the EEOC complaint statistics dramatically underestimate the prevalence of age- and gender-based discrimination in the workplace (Parker & Funk, 2017; Perron, 2018). Researchers at the Pew Research Center found that 42% of women reported experiencing discrimination in the workplace due to their gender, and the percentage of women reporting gender discrimination did not vary with age (Parker & Funk, 2017). A national study by the American Association of Retired Persons found even higher levels of age discrimination, with an estimated 61% of respondents to their survey reporting either experiencing or witnessing age discrimination in the workplace; however, only 3% filed a formal complaint with their employer or a government agency (Perron, 2018).

Experiences with age discrimination are significantly more common among middle-aged and older women as well as people of color (McGann et al., 2016; Perron, 2018). Duncan and Loretto (2004) investigated experiences with age discrimination across gender and multiple age groups. One of the notable findings from their study was evidence of a u-shaped trajectory, such that participants reported significantly higher rates of age-based discrimination in both emerging adulthood (16–24 years old) for being "too young" and mid- to late adulthood (45 years and older) for being "too old." Although Duncan and Loretto did not find gender differences in the number of negative experiences with age discrimination for being "too young," women were significantly more likely to report discrimination for being "too old" or for being both "too young" and "too old" at the same time and to begin reporting age discrimination for being "too old" as early as their 30s. McGann et al. (2016) also found evidence women began experiencing age discrimination for being old at younger ages than did their male counterparts.

Previous researchers have generally investigated experiences with discrimination in workplace by age and gender separately (for exceptions, see Duncan & Loretto, 2004; Granleese & Sayer, 2006; Jyrkinen & McKie, 2012; McGann et al., 2016); however, our goal was to look at the impact of both of these identity categories in tandem. Furthermore, the available quantitative evidence does not tell the full story. Although Parker and Funk (2017) did not find differences in the proportion of women reporting gender discrimination by age, it is unknown if those experiences differ qualitatively by age group. To address this limitation, we utilized data related to participant experiences with ageism and sexism in the workplace context extracted from a larger qualitative study. The larger study focused on exploring how experiences with ageism vary by both age and gender across the lifespan. These experiences will be positioned within the extant literature to answer the following questions: (a) What prescriptive age and gender expectations exist in the workplace? (b) What are women's experiences with ageism and sexism in the workplace? (c) How do these experiences with ageism and sexism vary across the lifespan? (d) How are women's experiences with ageism in the workplace unique from men's? (e) How do women cope with and resist these experiences with discrimination?

STUDY METHOD

The data presented and discussed in this chapter are drawn from a hermeneutic phenomenological qualitative study of 70 participants, 22 to 87 years old—43 women and 27 men. Purposeful sampling techniques were utilized to ensure participants represented various different races and socioeconomic status. Please see Table 9.1 for more participant information. For the purposes of this study, we categorized age into young adulthood (18–39 years old), middle age (40–64 years old), and older adulthood (65 years old and up). This study included two phases: (1) nine story circles segregated by gender and (2) eight in-depth interviews. Story circles and interviews allowed us the opportunity to explore participants' experiences with ageism and to make comparisons across age and gender. Our two-phase approach of utilizing both informal story circles followed by in-depth interviews with select participants who had experiences with gendered ageism aligns with Moustakas's (1994) recommendations for phenomenological research and has been employed successfully in previous exploratory qualitative research (Walker et al., 2017).

DEFINING PRESCRIPTIVE WORKPLACE EXPECTATIONS BY AGE AND GENDER

Defining how individuals are expected to perform in the workplace is complicated. Expectations for performance vary by industry, company, and the individual's role within that company, among other factors (e.g., experience, level of compensation). When those factors are held constant, we can see how differences in workplace expectations vary by age and gender as well. These workplace expectations go beyond simple descriptions of responsibilities associated with an individual's role to include generally unspoken and unwritten components tied to their age and gender. Numerous researchers have demonstrated how both women and older adults are disadvantaged in

TABLE 9.1. Demographic Information for Study Participants

Interview method	Age range	Race	Income	Education
		Female story circle participants		
Story Circle 1 (34.52 minutes) N = 6	27-40	White (6)	$20,000–$29,999 (1) $40,000–$49,999 (1) $70,000–$79,999 (1) $80,000–$89,999 (2) $100,000–$149,999 (1)	Vocational (2) Some college (1) College degree (2) Graduate degree (1)
Story Circle 2 (85.57 minutes) N = 7	23-64	White (7)	NA (1) < $10,000 (1) $30,000–$39,999 (1) $50,000–$59,999 (1) $60,000–$69,999 (2) $100,000–$149,999 (1)	High school (2) Vocational (1) Some college (1) College degree (3)
Story Circle 3 (54.08 minutes) N = 6	51-72	White (6)	NA (2) $60,000–$69,999 (1) $90,000–$99,999 (1) $100,000–$149,999 (1) $150,000 or more (2)	College degree (4) Graduate degree (2)
Story Circle 4 (78.31 minutes) N = 9	31-78	White (9)	NA (2) $60,000–$69,999 (1) $90,000–$99,999 (3) $100,000–$149,999 (1) $150,000 or more (2)	NA (1) College degree (6) Graduate degree (2)
Story Circle 5 (60.07 minutes) N = 8	43-77	White (6) Black (2)	NA (1) < $10,000 (5) $10,000–$19,999 (2)	Middle school (1) High school (1) Vocational (1) Some college (2) College degree (3)

Group	Age	Race	Income	Education
Story Circle 6 (63.44 minutes) N = 7	44-87	NA (1), White (2), Black (4)	NA (1), <$10,000 (5), $20,000-$29,999 (1)	NA (1), High school (3), Vocational (1), College degree (2)
Male story circle participants				
Story Circle 7 (79.03 minutes) N = 6	39-69	White (6)	NA (1), $80,000-$89,999 (1), $90,000-$99,999 (1), $150,000 or more (3)	Grade school (1), Some college (2), College degree (1), Graduate degree (2)
Story Circle 8 (50.77 minutes) N = 11	22-78	White (6), Black (4), Multiracial (1)	<$10,000 (5), $10,000-$19,999 (5), $20,000-$29,999 (1)	Middle school (2), High school (5), Some college (1), College degree (1), Graduate degree (2)
Story Circle 9 (58.22 minutes) N = 8	27-45	White (6), Hispanic (2)	$70,000-$79,999 (1), $80,000-$89,999 (1), $100,000-$149,999 (3), $150,000 or more (3)	Some college (1), College degree (4), Graduate degree (3)
Female interview participants				
Interview 3 (100.42 minutes)	64	White	$30,000-$39,999	Vocational education
Interview 4 (97.17 minutes)	32	White	$100,000-$149,999	College degree
Interview 5 (77.88 minutes)	67	White	$10,000-$19,999	College degree
Interview 6 (51.75 minutes)	37	White	$20,000-$29,999	Vocational education
Interview 7 (88.13 minutes)	74	Black	<$10,000	College degree
Male interview participants				
Interview 1 (62.58 minutes)	65	White	$20,000-$29,999	Vocational education
Interview 2 (60.25 minutes)	30	White	$60,000-$69,999	Vocational education
Interview 8 (56.57 minutes)	37	White	$150,000 or more	Some college

Note. NA = not available.

the workplace in terms of hiring, performance evaluations, promotions, and training opportunities (Duncan & Loretto, 2004; Finkelstein et al., 1995; Gordon & Arvey, 2004; Gordon et al., 1988; Heilman & Chen, 2005; Heilman & Okimoto, 2007; Lyness & Heilman, 2006; Parker & Funk, 2017). When both age and gender are considered, younger women are more likely to report bias in pay, benefits, and promotions; older women are more likely to report barriers to accessing promotions (Duncan & Loretto, 2004). Bias based on age and gender in the workplace illustrates how expectations for performance are tied to the stereotypes and expectations held for individuals due to both their age and their gender.

Prescriptive stereotypes dictate how an individual is expected to act based on these social characteristics and can be divided into positive prescriptive stereotypes and negative proscriptive stereotypes. Positive prescriptive stereotypes dictate that certain behaviors are approved and promoted in certain groups but not others (Koenig, 2018). Negative proscriptive stereotypes are behaviors that are viewed unfavorably, in general, but a disproportionate amount of disapproval is assigned to certain groups compared with others (Koenig, 2018). For instance, men are expected to behave in ways that demonstrate confidence, aggression, assertion, intelligence, independence, and ambition (Fiske et al., 2002; Koenig, 2018). Women are expected to engage in behaviors that emphasize more stereotypically feminine qualities, such as showing affection, sympathy, kindness, and caring for others and being passive (i.e., communal, relational characteristics; Fiske et al., 2002; Koenig, 2018).

There are fluctuations in the strength of these gender-based prescriptive stereotypes by age. Although men are, in general, viewed as more agentic from elementary school through older adulthood, other prescriptive stereotypes start later in the lifespan and do not necessarily last throughout older adulthood (Koenig, 2018). Independence and dominance expectations begin earlier in the lifespan but are not expected in men in later life. On the other hand, intelligence is still expected in older men but is not expected until young adulthood. For women, prescriptive stereotypes for being communal and weak begin early and are expected across the lifespan. Expectations for being emotional and shy also begin early but are not expected in older women. Surprisingly, gender-based expectations for being likeable were found only for adolescent girls, not for women in adulthood and older adulthood.

Participants in our study explicitly and implicitly described how their experiences with discrimination were rooted in both age- and gender-based expectations in the workplace. In alignment with positive prescriptive stereotypes, the female participants in the present study who worked in "pink collar" industries (i.e., teaching) generally described feeling respected and appreciated in the workplace, across the lifespan. However, participants stressed the importance of matching gender, industry, role, and behavior in being viewed as meeting societal expectations. For example, in an all-male story circle, a young male participant working in sales discussed how he is expected to be aggressive when trying to close sales with clients. "The leadership was expecting an aggressive . . . reaction from me." He described how his quiet and responsive approach to sales is interpreted by leadership as a lack of skills. "They may take it as you're just not seasoned enough; you should've fought for this." In this industry and role, aggression is viewed positively for him as a male. Those in a position to evaluate his workplace performance viewed his lacking an aggressive approach as not meeting this expectation.

Aggression is not viewed similarly for women in the workplace, even when they are employed in the same industry, company, and role. Representing negative proscriptive stereotypes, a young man in the same story circle and industry described how he saw a middle-aged woman treated in the workplace when she exhibited the same aggressive behavior that was promoted in men:

> All these opportunities would come up and she would try, she is a very aggressive person, but she never got anything. In addition, I think many people did not like her because, or do not like her I should say, present tense, because she is so aggressive. I think actually it hurt her in the work environment. However, I think she is probably one of the best people I have ever worked with. Smart. And she's aggressive for a reason, and most of the time it's probably the right tactic.

The men in this story circle discussed generational differences in terms of the amount of aggressive behavior exhibited by women in industries that are traditionally male-dominated. They noted seeing higher levels of aggressive behavior in middle-aged and older women in the field—noted that it was appropriate for the industry, company, and role—but discussed how this behavior is viewed negatively because of their gender. As one participant explained, "The decision makers are mostly men, and in my limited experience with women there, because there's not many, I have seen that aggressive women don't do—they aren't appreciated as much." Although coworkers can learn to appreciate women displaying negative proscriptive stereotypical behavior, participants noted that clients and customers have a difficult time overcoming the biases associated with these prescriptive and proscriptive stereotypes. However, the men noted that when they acted outside of the prescriptive stereotypes defined by their gender (i.e., not displaying aggression in sales), their clients and customers appreciated that behavior from them even if their colleagues and company leadership team did not. With women, clients and customers did not appreciate that behavior, and most colleagues view them negatively even if they acknowledge their approach may be appropriate.

The differences in experiences described by women and men by age and gender in this study illustrate the importance of person–job fit and evidence of a gender-role congruity bias. A meta-analysis of 136 independent experimental studies found that men are at an advantage during the selection process for male-dominated fields; however, there is no evidence that women have an advantage during the selection process for female-dominated fields (Koch et al., 2015). Not only are women at a disadvantage during the selection and hiring process, but they also suffer in evaluation and promotion decisions. Lyness and Heilman (2006) found that women whose job role did not align with gender-based prescriptive stereotypes were evaluated more negatively and had more barriers to promotion when compared with their male colleagues. Furthermore, they are rated as less likeable, more hostile, and less desirable as a manager (Heilman & Okimoto, 2007). This finding is supported by a national survey conducted by the Pew Research Center (Parker, 2018). Although sexual harassment was noted as an issue throughout the workforce, 62% of women working in a male-dominated field said sexual harassment is a problem in their industry and 49% said it was a problem in their workplace; this is a significantly larger proportion of women compared with those not employed in a male-dominated work environment.

Beyond industry, participants—namely, male participants—described how an individual's role in the workplace is associated with their age. Alternately, for women, the identity that was often noted as the most salient for them in the workplace was their gender rather than their age. This identity marker was stressed particularly for women not working in a traditionally pink-collar industry. Entry-level positions are assumed to be occupied by young adults, and leadership positions are associated with middle-aged and older adults. Regardless of age, both men and women noted experiencing difficulty and frustration with their treatment in entry-level positions because of assumed lack of knowledge and experience in their field. One woman described how this issue was heightened for her when she began an entry-level position in a new industry at the age of 57. She described how her younger supervisor treated her and her coworkers: "She did always make the ones of us who were older feel stupid, like, you know, we didn't know anything, and we're dumb, and like you know she was younger and she had work experience." Similarly, one middle-aged man described how workplace reactions to his age have changed over time: "Like, 15 years ago it was, 'how old are you?' I was like how old am I? [laughing] The context changes a little bit, um, early on was more impressed that you can do whatever you were doing, now it's [a] surprise that you're not doing more than you are." As a middle-aged man, he feels like he was expected to go farther with his career. Thus, the experience of employees being treated as if they are incompetent may be more related to their role within the company; however, these experiences are more likely to be reported by young adults, as they are more likely to work in entry-level positions.

In this way, age and how others treat people may be relative to the age of an individual's colleagues in similar roles. For example, a 30-year-old male participant discussed being treated as "too old" by his younger colleagues in the military. Meanwhile, an older teacher did not feel old because of the range of ages of her colleagues. Another participant noted that his coworkers see him as younger than his age because he has an entry-level position in his company. Another participant noted he is viewed as younger because of his technological expertise, a skill his coworkers associate with youth. Thus, individual age, colleague age, individual gender, colleague gender, role, company, and industry are integrally tied together to impact how we expect people to behave and how we feel about behavior that does not meet our expectations.

UNDERSTANDING EXPERIENCES OF WORKPLACE DISCRIMINATION

Participant experiences with workplace discrimination based on their age and gender can be divided into four subcategories. Three subcategories describe interpersonal forms of ageism: (a) competency challenges, (b) preference for youth, and (c) sexualization and desexualization of women. The fourth subcategory describes institutional forms of discrimination (e.g., pay and promotion); however, it is not expanded upon in the following section because it was not discussed to the extent that forms of interpersonal discrimination were discussed during the story circle and interview process. This may be due to a variety of factors, including that this form of discrimination is more difficult to prove, it may be more likely to be questioned by participants, or interpersonal forms of discrimination may have been more salient when asking for participants to describe their experiences with a given phenomenon.

Competency Challenges

Both ageism and sexism are maintained by stereotypes that question the competence of the recipients of each form of discrimination. One of the most prominent stereotypes about older adults in the workplace is that they are no longer able to perform their job role as competently as does a younger employee (Ng & Feldman, 2008); however, a meta-analysis of 438 independent samples did not support the stereotype that age negatively affects job performance. Sexism also supports the idea that women are not competent enough for the workplace, although it does so via two pathways: Hostile sexist ideals note that women should not be in the workplace at all, whereas benevolent sexist ideals denote the need for a man's assistance and supervision in the workplace while women hold gender-stereotypical roles that align with prescriptive stereotypes (Barreto & Ellemers, 2005; Glick & Fiske, 2001; Lee et al., 2010). Notably, men and women support both hostile and benevolent sexism ideals (Becker, 2010; Fowers & Fowers, 2010; Glick & Fiske, 1996, 2001, 2011; Glick et al., 2000; Young & Nauta, 2013); however, women are more likely than men to reject hostile sexist beliefs (Barreto et al., 2010; Fowers & Fowers, 2010; Glick & Fiske, 2001). With stereotypes questioning the competency of both older workers and women across the lifespan, it is no surprise that the participants' most commonly mentioned experience with discrimination in the workplace was dealing with treatment related to the assumption they were incompetent. Participants viewed this assumption of incompetency as being caused by multiple factors: age, gender, industry, and job role.

Women and men who participated in the study noted feeling, as young adults, like their knowledge or expertise was questioned. They described being treated as if they were incompetent by others because of the perceived lack of experience in the field that comes with being new, being young, and being in entry-level positions. One middle-aged woman who noted she had a "baby face" explained, "There would be times I would come home crying, they would be so mean to me. In addition, you know, it was, 'Well you don't know what you're doing. You know, you're too young.'" This idea that age is equated with presumed knowledge was mentioned by several male participants who were regularly questioned about their age. In fact, in one story circle, all eight male participants said they had been asked how old they are by colleagues or supervisors at work. Notably, none of the female participants reported ever being questioned about their age. Furthermore, when men discussed having their competency questioned when they were younger, new to their company, or in an entry-level position, they also described how those competency challenges eventually ceased as they grew older and gained more experience. For women, it varied by industry. Women in pink-collar jobs such as teaching felt like it got better, until they were once again assumed incompetent in old age for their lack of knowledge of new technology and innovations in their field. For other women, particularly those in male-dominated fields, it did not stop when they grew older and gained more experience.

Another notable difference between the women and men in this study was that none of the men reported challenges to their intellectual competency in the workplace as a middle-aged or older man; when middle-aged or older men were questioned in regard to their competency, it was due to the belief they were not capable of completing physical aspects of their jobs. However, women reported challenges to their intellectual competency across the lifespan. A young woman described the way male clients did not take her as seriously as they did male colleagues:

> Sometimes talking to men, they feel as though it's more of a conversation. . . . Like oh yeah whatever, she is just coming in here to talk about coffee or it is a casual conversation. Not to where, hey, let's get down to business and actually talk numbers.

A young male participant described how he sees clients treat young women in the field working in sales positions. He noted that it was difficult to put this type of discrimination into words, given that the behaviors are not as readily noticeable until compared with how young men are treated:

> I've travelled with uh guys that are fresh out of school going to visit a dealer versus women that are just out of school also and it's night and day difference response from the dealers. Wish I could put—which is what you are looking for, to be able to put it in words. . . . It is just the demeanor. They feel like it is more, um, it is less formal if a woman walks in. They feel like they can just kind of kid around and um, we don't really need to talk about business.

Thus, even though many participants noted feeling as if their competency was questioned as a young adult in the workplace, participants of both genders noted that it was more difficult for a young woman than for a young man. One male participant explained this difference within the context of working in the car industry: "Even though I may be young, I didn't have to go make credibility about knowing automotive." Although he admitted, "I know nothing about cars . . . but you're assuming that I do know because I'm a man. While a woman is like they will assume they don't know." He went on to explain that "women have to demonstrate that there was an interest or even pretend that they didn't know cars and allow the customer to teach them."

Male participants discussed how they have witnessed not only the credibility of women questioned more than that of their male peers but also how successful women were subjected to questioning about how they achieved their roles. In the words of one young man, "I actually believe I wouldn't have the opportunities I've received if I had been a woman. I think they would have double questioned my motives." This was reiterated by another participant who said, "There's a—a clear-cut instance in our area with rumors flying about how one person got their job, and it's a woman, of course." Similarly, another young man explained in his interview how women in the military are viewed and treated:

> Women in the military get looked at as if they did favors or they were, they obtained a certain rank because they did something for someone or that they are just being privileged and it's not looked at as if they worked hard to get where they did. Even if they did. In addition, sometimes they uh, are put into situations where they cannot be successful in their career. Which is so frustrating to see happen. Um, we will get, uh, a woman come into the shop and she will automatically be put behind a desk working on computer things. Um, you know administrative type things when that is not the main focus of our job.

Both older adults and women stereotypically are often treated in a paternalistic manner because of the combined effect of viewing them as simultaneously high in warmth and low in competence (Fiske et al., 2002). This paternalistic behavior can look benevolent—or helpful—in nature and underlies both benevolent ageism and benevolent sexism (Cary et al., 2017). In the workplace this benevolent behavior can lead to an assumption that a worker cannot complete their job responsibilities, which in turn can result in overhelping, exclusion from training and networking opportunities, denial of promotions, lower wages, and more (Cary et al., 2017; Jones et al., 2014; King et al., 2012). There are similarities and differences in how women and men view this benevolent behavior, particularly in how they attribute the intentions behind these helping behaviors. An older man described helping behavior in the workplace as a sign of "respect." He went on to explain that younger workers view it as "You're old now, you've put in your time and I'm going to do this for you." One young man, who is considered old for his workplace, noted that he used to think younger coworkers offered help because of his status and rank but has changed his view after reflecting on the activities they offer him assistance with:

> Before really thinking about it I had always attributed it to, um, a bit higher of a rank and not as much as age, um, although hindsight I'm starting to think there is bit more of a connection there. Um, simple things like, uh, like taking out trash, or I guess any action that would be [sighs] really anything with lifting, carrying anything that might be heavy, um, I'll have one of the, uh, the younger guys come over and offer help.

Thus, because his younger coworkers are helping when a task requires a physical component, rather than a mental component, he sees it as more related to his age. The tasks the middle-aged and older men described younger adults assisting them with were also physical in nature. Participants in a study by McGann and colleagues (2016) described a similar bias for men in working-class occupations. An older appearance for them and the men in this study implied they were not as physically capable of completing their work.

Alternately, women noted receiving offers to open doors, carry items, and serve as a protector. This behavior was credited not to their age but rather to their gender because of the presence of this behavior across the lifespan. A middle-aged woman in academia described how her male colleagues feel the need to protect her from her male students:

> I have one professor standing outside my door, like listening, waiting for some-
> one to give me a hard time, and I walk out and I said, "Steve, can you go back
> to your office? Because I don't really need you here."

She also noted that a male frequently calls her "honey" and "sweetie" when in fact she is an administrator at her university. Older teachers in the K–12 school system noted how they appreciated the offers of assistance from their younger colleagues to teach them how to use new technology and tech-niques in the classroom. Thus, for women in pink-collar jobs (i.e., teaching), offers of assistance were interpreted differently depending on whether they were coming from a male or a female colleague. Middle-aged and older women in male-dominated industries did not describe being the recipient of benevolent acts by their colleagues. According to the Stereotype Content Model, recipients of paternalistic or benevolent behavior are often associ-ated with higher levels of perceived warmth and lower levels of perceived competence (Fiske et al., 2002); middle-aged and older women working in male-dominated industries are often not perceived as "warm," which may explain why they did not report similar experiences.

Preference for Youth

Although the participants in this study did not elaborate on this at length, other researchers have found evidence of a preference for youth that is particularly dominant in industries that place an emphasis on appearance such as front office, customer service, and even teaching roles (Granleese & Sayer, 2006; Handy & Davy, 2007; McGann et al., 2016). Women in previous research studies have described engaging in beauty work to hide the signs of aging to gain more visibility in the workplace and to be taken more seriously (Granleese & Sayer, 2006; Hurd Clarke & Griffin, 2008).

In the current study, participants in workplaces that valued abilities associated with youth (i.e., physical prowess, speed, appearance, techno-logical knowledge) described this phenomenon. Although both women and men described experiencing this, their descriptions varied. Both young and old men in physically demanding jobs described the preference for youth because of the perception they are better able to handle physical aspects of their work. Alternately, women described a preference for youth because of the desire for speed, appearance, and technological knowledge. As one older woman stated, "My age—it's not the image that the company wants to project." Her employer would specifically choose young men to represent the company when potential clients visited, even though she was more knowledgeable and experienced and held a higher position. They did not want clients to see an employee that did not meet their prescriptive stereotypical expectations.

Women in the health care field described the preference for youth by both their employer and their patients, as youth was equated with speed; however, you could not be too young:

> If you go into the nursing home or hospital . . . if you look like you're 18 they'll—a lot of people will send you out of the room. Well you are new; you do not know what you are doing really. However, if you walk in their mid-20s, they will have you do it. Later years they'll be like okay you can do it, but we have to have more time . . . they think that you're going to do it slower.

If workers look too young, they are viewed as unqualified by patients; however, workers who are middle-aged and older are viewed as being competent but slow. In this participant's experience, only workers deemed to be the "right" age were treated favorably by their patients.

Sexualization and Desexualization of Women

The sexualization of women in the workplace described by participants in this study and others falls under the sexual harassment umbrella. A Pew Research study found that 59% of women reported experiencing sexual harassment, and 69% of those women noted it happened in the workplace (Graf, 2018). Comparatively, 27% of men reported experiencing sexual harassment, with 61% reporting they experienced it in the workplace. Female participants reported this as occurring, most often, in their youth. They also generally reported their harassment as coming not from their colleagues but from their clients, customers, students, and patients. A young woman in sales described a common occurrence with potential male customers:

> I've been given phone numbers before on the back of a business card. Alternatively, on a business card specifically said, you can reach me on my cell phone, available at all times. So it's typically been more sexual . . . flirty, comments that I've received.

She noted that at times the behavior of the male clients she works with has made her feel so uncomfortable that she walks away from their business;

however, she noted that if their business would provide a large enough commission, she decides whether she can overcome her discomfort rather than incurring the financial loss associated with walking away from a sale.

As women age in the workplace, there is a change in the way their sexuality is viewed. A couple of middle-aged women noted that the sexual comments they receive in the workplace have decreased as they get older. As one woman who works as a physical therapist explained, "When I was younger they—everybody wanted me to flirt. Now everybody doesn't want me to flirt." She explained that rather than being free of sexual comments from her clients entirely as she has aged, the age of the men that flirt with her has simply changed. Young male patients no longer make sexually suggestive comments to her, but her middle-aged and older male patients still do. As another woman explained, "We get a lot of like, sexual innuendos and stuff. . . . It is getting probably less . . . it does as you get older. Less and less." Past researchers have noted how this relief from sexual objectification can come as a double-edged sword. Although the lack of sexual objectification with age is welcomed by some women (Isopahkala-Bouret, 2017), the perception of older women as lacking sexual desirability may also serve to make other women feel invisible, undesirable, and like they have less power (Hurd Clarke & Bundon, 2009; Hurd Clarke & Griffin, 2008; Hurd Clarke & Korotchenko, 2016).

METHODS OF MANAGING WORKPLACE DISCRIMINATION

Participants described reacting to workplace discrimination in multiple ways: coping, advocacy, and questioning. Women in this study went into the most depth describing how they reacted to and coped with workplace discrimination. They were also more likely to question one another in the story circles about how they handled the situations they described in their stories. Older women, particularly those in the male-dominated industries, described more advanced methods for managing and preventing workplace discrimination. Younger women were more likely to describe more superficial methods as they are still acquiring the knowledge and experience necessary to develop those methods.

Coping

Participants discussed utilizing four main coping techniques for managing their experiences with workplace discrimination: (a) avoidance, (b) reframing, (c) support seeking, and (d) denial. For many participants, they relied on more than one coping technique. For example, one young woman who experienced competency challenges in a male-dominated industry explained how she adjusted her professional behavior to avoid further discrimination in the future. Furthermore, her explanation demonstrates that she also reframed the situation to position the experience as a beneficial learning experience that contributed to her professional growth:

> I learned that I need to, to let them talk about their business and not kind of go in strong headed and with ten different suggestions to make the business better, but really listen to what they had to say what they were doing and build off that. Make little suggestions. It got me prepared for this industry. And I, see it all, all over the place in tire world, so um, yeah it, I think it was definitely, I needed to learn it and it's good that I learned it.

This participant experienced pushback from the men to whom she was trying to sell her company's merchandise because of her heightened visibility as a woman in a male-dominated industry. In response, she adopted a strategy of making herself less visible by putting the focus on her male clients, allowing her male customers to dominate the conversation and "teach" her, an approach that was more acceptable and a better match to the gender expectations her clients had for her.

An older woman discussed a variety of methods, particularly support-seeking from her colleagues, to make herself more visible and competent to men who would not recognize her authority when working as a computer consultant. She sought support from her male colleagues, working out a system whereby she would signal them to make an excuse to leave the room or endorse her as a source of knowledge. She said that with her male colleagues in the room, "They [male clients] would not look at me; they would not talk to me." She described how precarious this process of increasing her visibility as a knowledgeable consultant was because "you have to find a way to do it without ticking them off, blow the sale."

Although some younger women in sales discussed how they walked away from sales when male customers were sexually suggestive, middle-aged and older women described feeling more confident handling these situations. One middle-aged woman in particular noted that she adopted a strategy of mirroring their sexually suggestive remarks rather than getting uncomfortable:

> When I was much younger, if I was treating a guy, and if a guy would say something like sexual, teasing or whatever I'd be like real nervous you know and I'd be like, "Oh I've got to get out of this room." I would be like, "I can't treat him anymore!" But now like I will banter back and forth. I do not care if they say something, I am saying it right back! And I am not like embarrassed about it at all!

Advocacy

Although only women discussed many of the coping mechanisms above (i.e., support seeking), several young men reported colleagues advocating on their behalf, without being asked, to vouch for their credibility. This form of interpersonal advocacy was reported by multiple young men who had their competency challenged:

> When we go into customer visits and I'm meeting them for the first time, they always half-joking ask how old I am. It happened last week with, with a gentleman who I'd say is twice my age, and he kind of laughed at the guy and said, um, "You know, you don't need to worry about that. From what I've felt already, he'll be able to help you more than I ever could."

Although none of the women mentioned their colleagues or supervisors spontaneously advocating for them, two older women stressed feeling like they had the support of their employer or their colleagues. For example, one of them had a man she supervised complain to upper management about the feedback he received on the quality of his work and said, "They backed me a hundred percent." Older women were also the only participants to note engaging in interpersonal advocacy on behalf of others. One older woman discussed how she created a safe work environment for the women at her work by confronting sexual harassment head on, firing problematic employees, and taking the time to mentor female employees. All of this was possible only because she had been promoted to a supervisory role within her company through which she had the power to enact these changes. This difference in advocacy by age for women may be due to differences in the level of confidence and support they feel they have in their workplace (i.e., perceived organizational support), which in turn impacts their job satisfaction, performance, and commitment (Rhoades & Eisenberger, 2002). Alternately, for men, their relative position of power may blind them to the awareness that their advocacy is even needed.

The majority of participants described other forms of advocacy that occurred at the personal level, including assertiveness, boundary setting, and formal avenues of protest. Assertiveness was the most common form of advocacy. Several participants, both women and men, said that they worked harder to prove themselves in response to having their competency questioned. They described either verbally defending or demonstrating their competence. One young woman in sales learned ways to highlight her knowledge about her clients' industries as part of her sales pitch. She did not have a sales partner to vouch for her, so she had to find other ways to assert her competence:

> I try to, if I have a fact that can prove that I know what I'm talking about, I'll try to state a fact. Or, um, if they're in a certain type of a field, I will say like, "Oh

well most people in your field do this blah blah blah," so that they can relate and be like, oh okay she actually does know what she's talking about because other people in my field do this, and hey, we do this as well. So I try to make them understand that I do know what I'm talking about and maybe I'm not old enough and haven't experienced all of these things over years, but I do have some experience and I, and I am knowledgeable.

Both women and men utilized this method of assertiveness and proving their competence in the workplace across the lifespan, just for different reasons. For example, the 30-year-old male participant who felt his physical abilities were questioned by his younger military colleagues described how he felt the need to maintain and demonstrate his ability to competently engage in physically demanding tasks when challenged:

> I think that it influenced, um or at least pushed me to work harder from time to time to make sure that I always stayed ahead. Especially physically, especially physically. . . . Grandpa will still whoop your butt, or grandpa will still run faster than you, or grandpa will still outperform I suppose. So, I guess I relate it a lot to a performance level on if I can still keep up with, or do everything the younger guys can do. I do not know how I would feel about it if I could not. I think I would be less comfortable being called an "old man."

He went on to describe other assertive methods he uses to respond to the ageism he receives because of the perception that, at the age of 30, he is "old" in the workplace. When younger coworkers offer him help when he is performing a physical task, he will counter their behavior either with an assertive retort, such as "I'm not broken, get the fuck away from me" or by saying, "All right, here you go" if he thinks the task is too difficult for them to complete. He said he will "then watch them not be able to do it and then I'll pick it up and do it anyways." This attitude varied greatly from the older men who choose to cope by reframing similar experiences as demonstrations of veneration and respect by their colleagues.

Boundary setting was another method several participants utilized to advocate for themselves in the face of ageism. Although women across the lifespan discussed this method, only one man (a young adult) mentioned it. Women spoke about refusing to work with clients who sexually harassed them as young adults, threatening retirement when treated unfairly as older adults, and working to establish ground rules across the lifespan. Specifically, one older woman discussed that when she was young establishing ground rules was important because "I was going to be the one training and if you don't establish that at the very beginning, you're dead meat. They're not going to learn from you. You're not going to do anything for them." She noted that, in some ways, the need to establish firm boundaries and expectations with clients has not changed after 30 years in the computer industry.

Specifically, she discussed how establishing ground rules is important when working with young men:

> Then you got the younger ones. So yeah, when I go back I'm ya know I'm giving them the proposal next week and they're going to have to get used to seeing me and sometimes it becomes very disconcerting for the younger men.

Another older woman reiterated this sentiment: "I get a lot of bad times because of that, because all the men that work with me are all younger and having an older woman tell—whether it's a woman or what it is—they don't like it." She went on to state that "I have actually fired more people than the other supervisors there, because I won't take the stuff that they give out." She also explained how she uses her position as a supervisor and woman to advocate on behalf of the other women that she works with:

> The girls who work with me at night liked working with me at night because I was safe; it felt safer and more secure. Umm there were a couple of guys that were a bit forward with the one girl, and I told them that they needed to stop—that that was harassment. And if they continued with it, I would walk them out the door. End of discussion.

She was able to use her position of power as a supervisor to make the workplace safer for the women she worked with. When she was asked if a male supervisor would have intervened to protect this young woman, she noted that they would not have.

A young man recalled setting boundaries at one place of employment. When he heard that he might be passed over for a promotion in favor of an inexperienced but older colleague, he said, "I met with HR [human resources] and everything and I, I you know basically told them I said if I don't get this position, I'm done." He not only set boundaries with that employer but also used formal channels (i.e., talking to human resources) to express his displeasure. Other participants, all women, discussed filing reports, making complaints to supervisors, and engaging in legal disputes when treated unfairly by others.

Questioning

The last type of short-term reaction to ageism in the workplace, described solely by the female participants, was questioning. This reaction occurred across the lifespan when participants were either unsure whether it was appropriate to label their experiences as discrimination or unclear of the motivations underlying their experiences. For example, a young woman said, "If I was male or if I was older or if I had my PhD or you know. . . . What would make it different to where you really would think that what I'm saying is true?" She questioned whether the challenges to her competency in the workplace would be different if she was a different gender or age or if she had a higher level of education. Another young woman recalled, "I'm sitting here thinking like did he call me that because I was young or did he call me that because I'm a girl?"

Although middle-aged women also described questioning whether they had experienced discrimination at times, they generally did not question why they experienced it. They generally attributed their experiences with discrimination in the workplace to their gender rather than their age, with one exception. An older woman described how she was treated after she began a new job when she was middle-aged: "We were wondering why we are, you know, being picked out of a couple being picked out. Does it have to do because we're new, or age, or what?" Although she was middle-aged, for that entry-level role, she was considered old and felt that her treatment by her supervisor was due to their perception that she was incompetent because of either her age or her level of experience; however, she was not sure which.

This questioning was unfortunately evident even for participants who had positive experiences in the workplace. After an older woman was promoted to a supervisory position at work, she questioned why she was given that responsibility:

> Do they have me on third shift 'cause I'm a woman and nobody else will take it? Uh, or is it really, because they have a competence for me to run the whole shop and quality and everything, or are they taking advantage of me, you know?

Although she was promoted, she was not certain if it was because her employers had faith in her competence or because they were taking advantage of her willingness to work the overnight shift. This suspicion was bolstered with the knowledge that she was making $4,000 to $8,000 less than did her male counterparts in the same role. For this woman, she was concerned that her employers were manipulating her; alternately, male participants described the common perception that women manipulate employers to get a promotion: "There's a clear-cut instance in our area with rumors flying about how one person got their job, and it's a woman, of course."

PRACTICE APPLICATIONS

Workplace discrimination is expensive. In 2019, the EEOC estimated that $75.7 million in monetary benefits was paid out because of age-based discrimination complaints (EEOC, n.d.-a), and $244.7 million was spent due to sex-based discrimination complaints, not inclusive of the money paid out during the litigation process (EEOC, n.d.-c). Thus, it is in the best interest of both the employer and the employees to invest in efforts to prevent it from occurring. Participants in this study discussed interrelated strategies that can be implemented at the institutional level that they have found to be effective, including (a) facilitating the creation of systems of support for women in the workplace, including establishing multiple avenues for advocacy for women in the workplace; and (b) encouraging the development and enforcement of workplace boundaries. These suggestions are interwoven with supporting literature for how organizations can promote and sustain a more diverse workforce.

Networking Opportunities That Are Accessible for Women

Networking is essential for success in one's career, as mentors can provide advice on career development and sponsors can support, promote, and advocate for women (e.g., de Klerk & Verreynne, 2017). Unfortunately, women in general, and women with young children in particular, are not afforded as many opportunities to network with experienced colleagues in a position to become part of a system of workplace support, including finding mentorship and sponsorship. First, women often have additional obligations outside of work (e.g., Acker, 2006; de Klerk & Verreynne, 2017; Durbin & Tomlinson, 2010) that prevent them from attending official and unofficial networking events outside of work hours. Second, women report feeling a lack of confidence in participating in the stereotypically male activities that are often required for successful networking (e.g., playing or attending sporting events; de Klerk & Verreynne, 2017). Third, there is often unconscious bias against women that leads to men developing more intricate networks, resulting in higher status contacts and job success (e.g., McDonald, 2011).

Ameliorating these deficits at the institutional level will facilitate the creation of systems supporting women networking and thus supporting women. To achieve these goals, participants in the present study suggested making sure women hold visible positions of power in the organization and establishing an official mentoring program for women and minorities. These suggestions are in alignment with research-supported methods to increase networking, including developing a space that brings women together to facilitate networking (e.g., Barnes & Beaulieu, 2017), encouraging men to include women and minorities in their networking spheres, holding networking events at different times of day and location (e.g., not a bar happy hour) to accommodate the diversity of the workforce (e.g., Ozkazanc-Pan & Clark Muntean, 2018), and training women how to network effectively (de Klerk & Verreynne, 2017). Increasing one's network also increases one's support system because one has more people to call on for help, information, and opportunities (De Vita et al., 2014).

The development of a support system via networking can help women establish industry-specific boundaries to keep them safe in the workplace. For example, one young woman participant in sales discussed issues with clients overstepping boundaries by sending her inappropriate text messages and emails unrelated to their business relationship. An older woman with experience in the field can help her establish boundaries and expectations for clients to work to prevent as well as navigate these situations. Furthermore, an older mentor can be a source of support to advocate on her behalf (e.g., de Klerk & Verreynne, 2017) if, for instance, a client crosses a line in such a way that the business relationship needs to be terminated.

Institutional Policies to Counteract Gender and Age Inequity

Most importantly, organizations need to recognize that gender and age inequity exist in the workplace (e.g., Ozkazanc-Pan & Clark Muntean, 2018). Therefore, it is important for boundaries and expectations to be founded and made visible at the institutional level as well as the individual level. This is an important component of a multilevel support system because well-designed and enforced institutional policies to protect and empower women in the workplace help employees set boundaries at the individual level. One idea presented by a participant included training employees in bystander methods of intervening when they witness discriminatory workplace practices. Bystander behavior is well documented in the literature (e.g., Banyard et al., 2007; Coker et al., 2015), and making the goal to end discrimination everyone's problem rather than the problem of a few is much more likely to elicit a positive response and actually change behaviors. It is important to note that institutional policies will vary by industry, company, and role; furthermore, well-designed policies are informed by listening to the voices of experienced middle-aged and older women in the field.

Participants also described what advocacy in their workplace has looked like to them. Messages or acts of support in the workplace can come from coworkers, supervisors, mentors, and institutional policies. An older woman discussed how she worked with her male colleagues to construct methods for them to force clients to listen to her in a way that did not jeopardize their patronage. Younger male participants noted how their colleagues have spontaneously come to their defense when their competency has been questioned. Essentially, women are more likely to benefit from a colleague or supervisor who is willing to go to bat for them. As in previous studies (e.g., de Klerk & Verreynne, 2017), men noted they had been the recipient of unsolicited advocacy and support from their colleagues; however, women in this study discussed colleagues and supervisors advocating for them after a prompt either from the employee or in response to an unsubstantiated claim. The creation of a supportive work community with the addition of bystander training to prevent workplace discrimination may help promote unsolicited advocacy on behalf of women and minorities.

CONCLUSION

Studying the experiences of women and men across the lifespan also helps us better understand the uniqueness of older women in the workforce. For one, older women, particularly those in male-dominated industries and companies, too often come with a lifetime of experience navigating sexism in the workplace. When they reach older adulthood, their competence is questioned not only because of their gender but now because of their age as well. For older women working in male-dominated industries, this questioning of their competence does not necessarily change the way they are treated in a meaningful way because it is simply a continuation of the behavior they have experienced throughout their career. Participant descriptions suggest the treatment they receive is qualitatively similar (i.e., competence questioned); however, by necessity, they manage it more effectively, and the age of the perpetrators tend to be younger. Methods of coping with this treatment often revolve around establishing or reestablishing their competence, a phenomenon that, if successful, leads them to being appraised by others as "competent" at the cost of being simultaneously perceived as "cold" (Fiske et al., 2002).

For older women in female-dominated fields (e.g., teaching, nursing), sexism is not salient in their everyday work lives with their colleagues. Although they experienced competence questioning when they were new to their field, once their expertise was established the competence questioning did not reassert itself until they reached late middle age to older adulthood. In this way, women in female-dominated fields and men of all fields follow a somewhat similar trajectory. The difference in older adulthood is that although older women in female-dominated fields are questioned for their intellectual competence, older men are questioned for their physical competence—something women are assumed not to have in the first place. Thus, a better understanding of the experiences of women and men from various industries across the lifespan allowed us to make important distinctions between the experiences of older women in male-dominated industries and those of older women in female-dominated industries.

Participant responses suggest that understanding how experiences with ageism are shaped by both gender and age across the lifespan adds to our conceptualization of how women are treated in the workplace. Specifically, it is clear from the participant responses that they feel that experiences with ageism are not a phenomenon reserved for older adulthood and that gender intersects with age to create opportunities for both oppression and resistance across the lifespan. It is likely that research looking at ageism and sexism in the workplace separately misses the nuances that exist for women, particularly older women. Furthermore, the women in this study illustrated the importance of valuing the ability for older women in the workplace to pave the way for younger generations with their leadership, mentorship, support, and advocacy.

It is important to note that the approach used in this study is limited because of the exclusion of identity categories other than age and gender that impact how individuals are treated in the workplace (e.g., race, class, sexual orientation, weight). This is an important limitation considering that the largest number of complaints filed with the U.S. EEOC in 2019 were related to disability status and race (EEOC, n.d.-b).

REFERENCES

Acker, J. (2006). Inequality regimes: Gender, class, and race in organizations. *Gender & Society*, *20*(4), 441–464. https://doi.org/10.1177/0891243206289499

Banyard, V. L., Moynihan, M. M., & Plante, E. G. (2007). Sexual violence prevention through bystander education: An experimental evaluation. *Journal of Community Psychology*, *35*(4), 463–481. https://doi.org/10.1002/jcop.20159

Barnes, T. D., & Beaulieu, E. (2017). Engaging women: Addressing the gender gap in women's networking and productivity. *PS: Political Science & Politics*, *50*(2), 461–466. https://doi.org/10.1017/S1049096516003000

Barreto, M., & Ellemers, N. (2005). The burden of benevolent sexism: How it contributes to the maintenance of gender inequalities. *European Journal of Social Psychology*, *35*(5), 633–642. https://doi.org/10.1002/ejsp.270

Barreto, M., Ellemers, N., Piebinga, L., & Moya, M. (2010). How nice of us and how dumb of me: The effect of exposure to benevolent sexism on women's task and relational self-descriptions. *Sex Roles*, *62*(7–8), 532–544. https://doi.org/10.1007/s11199-009-9699-0

Becker, J. C. (2010). Why do women endorse hostile and benevolent sexism? The role of salient female subtypes and internalization of sexist contents. *Sex Roles*, *62*(7–8), 453–467. https://doi.org/10.1007/s11199-009-9707-4

Calasanti, T. (2005). Ageism, gravity, and gender: Experiences of aging bodies. *Generations*, *29*(3), 8–12.

Cary, L. A., Chasteen, A. L., & Remedios, J. (2017). The Ambivalent Ageism Scale: Developing and validating a scale to measure benevolent and hostile ageism. *The Gerontologist*, *57*(2), e27–e36.

Coker, A. L., Fisher, B. S., Bush, H. M., Swan, S. C., Williams, C. M., Clear, E. R., & DeGue, S. (2015). Evaluation of the green dot bystander intervention to reduce interpersonal violence among college students across three campuses. *Violence Against Women, 21*(12), 1507–1527. https://doi.org/10.1177/1077801214545284

de Klerk, S., & Verreynne, M. L. (2017). The networking practices of women managers in an emerging economy setting: Negotiating institutional and social barriers. *Human Resource Management Journal, 27*(3), 477–501. https://doi.org/10.1111/1748-8583.12151

De Vita, L., Mari, M., & Poggesi, S. (2014). Women entrepreneurs in and from developing countries: Evidences from the literature. *European Management Journal, 32*(3), 451–460. https://doi.org/10.1016/j.emj.2013.07.009

Duncan, C., & Loretto, W. (2004). Never the right age? Gender and age-based discrimination in employment. *Gender, Work and Organization, 11*(1), 95–115. https://doi.org/10.1111/j.1468-0432.2004.00222.x

Durbin, S., & Tomlinson, J. (2010). Female part-time managers: Networks and career mobility. *Work, Employment and Society, 24*(4), 621–640. https://doi.org/10.1177/0950017010380631

Finkelstein, L. M., Burke, M. J., & Raju, N. S. (1995). Age discrimination in simulated employment contexts: An integrative analysis. *Journal of Applied Psychology, 80*(6), 652–663. https://doi.org/10.1037/0021-9010.80.6.652

Fiske, S. T., Cuddy, A. J. C., Glick, P., & Xu, J. (2002). A model of (often mixed) stereotype content: Competence and warmth respectively follow from perceived status and competition. *Journal of Personality and Social Psychology, 82*(6), 878–902. https://doi.org/10.1037/0022-3514.82.6.878

Fowers, A. F., & Fowers, B. J. (2010). Social dominance and sexual self-schema as moderators of sexist reactions to female subtypes. *Sex Roles, 62*(7–8), 468–480. https://doi.org/10.1007/s11199-009-9607-7

Glick, P., & Fiske, S. T. (1996). The Ambivalent Sexism Inventory: Differentiating hostile and benevolent sexism. *Journal of Personality and Social Psychology, 70*(3), 491–512. https://doi.org/10.1037/0022-3514.70.3.491

Glick, P., & Fiske, S. T. (2001). An ambivalent alliance. Hostile and benevolent sexism as complementary justifications for gender inequality. *American Psychologist, 56*(2), 109–118. https://doi.org/10.1037/0003-066X.56.2.109

Glick, P., & Fiske, S. T. (2011). Ambivalent sexism revisited. *Psychology of Women Quarterly, 35*(3), 530–535. https://doi.org/10.1177/0361684311414832

Glick, P., Fiske, S. T., Mladinic, A., Saiz, J. L., Abrams, D., Masser, B., Adetoun, B., Osagie, J. E., Akande, A., Alao, A., Brunner, A., Willemsen, T. M., Chipeta, K., Dardenne, B., Dijksterhuis, A., Wigboldus, D., Eckes, T., Six-Materna, I., Expósito, F., . . . López, W. (2000). Beyond prejudice as simple antipathy: Hostile and benevolent sexism across cultures. *Journal of Personality and Social Psychology, 79*(5), 763–775. https://doi.org/10.1037/0022-3514.79.5.763

Gordon, R. A., & Arvey, R. D. (2004). Age bias in laboratory and field settings: A meta-analytic investigation. *Journal of Applied Social Psychology, 34*(3), 468–492. https://doi.org/10.1111/j.1559-1816.2004.tb02557.x

Gordon, R. A., Rozelle, R. M., & Baxter, J. C. (1988). The effect of applicant age, job level, and accountability on the evaluation of job applicants. *Organizational Behavior and Human Decision Processes, 41*(1), 20–33. https://doi.org/10.1016/0749-5978(88)90044-1

Graf, N. (2018, April 4). *Sexual harassment at work in the era of #MeToo*. Pew Research Center. https://www.pewsocialtrends.org/2018/04/04/sexual-harassment-at-work-in-the-era-of-metoo

Granleese, J., & Sayer, G. (2006). Gendered ageism and "lookism": A triple jeopardy for female academics. *Women in Management Review, 21*(6), 500–517. https://doi.org/10.1108/09649420610683480

Handy, J., & Davy, D. (2007). Gendered ageism: Older women's experiences of employment agency practices. *Asia Pacific Journal of Human Resources, 45*(1), 85–99. https://doi.org/10.1177/1038411107073606

Heilman, M. E., & Chen, J. J. (2005). Same behavior, different consequences: Reactions to men's and women's altruistic citizenship behavior. *Journal of Applied Psychology, 90*(3), 431–441. https://doi.org/10.1037/0021-9010.90.3.431

Heilman, M. E., & Okimoto, T. G. (2007). Why are women penalized for success at male tasks?: The implied communality deficit. *Journal of Applied Psychology, 92*(1), 81–92. https://doi.org/10.1037/0021-9010.92.1.81

Hurd Clarke, L., & Bundon, A. (2009). From 'the thing to do' to 'defying the ravages of age': Older women reflect on the use of lipstick. *Journal of Women & Aging, 21*(3), 198–212. https://doi.org/10.1080/08952840903054757

Hurd Clarke, L., & Griffin, M. (2008). Visible and invisible ageing: Beauty work as a response to ageism. *Ageing and Society, 28*(5), 653–674. https://doi.org/10.1017/S0144686X07007003

Hurd Clarke, L., & Korotchenko, A. (2016). 'I know it exists . . . but I haven't experienced it personally': Older Canadian men's perceptions of ageism as a distant social problem. *Ageing and Society, 36*(8), 1757–1773. https://doi.org/10.1017/S0144686X15000689

Isopahkala-Bouret, U. (2017). "It's a great benefit to have gray hair!": The intersection of gender, aging, and visibility in midlife professional women's narratives. *Journal of Women & Aging, 29*(3), 267–277. https://doi.org/10.1080/08952841.2016.1142773

Jones, K., Stewart, K., King, E., Morgan, W. B., Gilrane, V., & Hylton, K. (2014). Negative consequence of benevolent sexism on efficacy and performance. *Gender in Management, 29*(3), 171–189. https://doi.org/10.1108/GM-07-2013-0086

Jyrkinen, M., & McKie, L. (2012). Gender, age and ageism: Experiences of women managers in Finland and Scotland. *Work, Employment and Society, 26*(1), 61–77. https://doi.org/10.1177/0950017011426313

King, E. B., Botsford, W., Hebl, M. R., Kazama, S., Dawson, J. F., & Perkins, A. (2012). Benevolent sexism at work: Gender differences in the distribution of challenging developmental experiences. *Journal of Management, 38*(6), 1835–1866. https://doi.org/10.1177/0149206310365902

Koch, A. J., D'Mello, S. D., & Sackett, P. R. (2015). A meta-analysis of gender stereotypes and bias in experimental simulations of employment decision making. *Journal of Applied Psychology, 100*(1), 128–161. https://doi.org/10.1037/a0036734

Koenig, A. M. (2018). Comparing prescriptive and descriptive gender stereotypes about children, adults, and the elderly. *Frontiers in Psychology, 9*, 1086. https://doi.org/10.3389/fpsyg.2018.01086

Lee, T. L., Fiske, S. T., & Glick, P. (2010). Next gen ambivalent sexism: Converging correlates, causality in context, and converse causality, an introduction to the special issue. *Sex Roles, 62*(7–8), 395–404. https://doi.org/10.1007/s11199-010-9747-9

Lyness, K. S., & Heilman, M. E. (2006). When fit is fundamental: Performance evaluations and promotions of upper-level female and male managers. *Journal of Applied Psychology, 91*(4), 777–785. https://doi.org/10.1037/0021-9010.91.4.777

McDonald, S. (2011). What's in the "old boys" network? Accessing social capital in gendered and racialized networks. *Social Networks, 33*(4), 317–330. https://doi.org/10.1016/j.socnet.2011.10.002

McGann, M., Ong, R., Bowman, D., Duncan, A., Kimberley, H., & Biggs, S. (2016). Gendered ageism in Australia: Changing perceptions of age discrimination among older men and women. *Economic Papers, 35*(4), 375–388. https://doi.org/10.1111/1759-3441.12155

Moustakas, C. (1994). *Phenomenological research methods.* Thousand Oaks, CA: Sage.

Ng, T. W. H., & Feldman, D. C. (2008). The relationship of age to ten dimensions of job performance. *Journal of Applied Psychology, 93*(2), 392–423. https://doi.org/10.1037/0021-9010.93.2.392

Ozkazanc-Pan, B., & Clark Muntean, S. (2018). Networking towards (in) equality: Women entrepreneurs in technology. *Gender, Work and Organization, 25*(4), 379–400. https://doi.org/10.1111/gwao.12225

Parker, K. (2018, March 7). *Women in majority-male workplaces report higher rates of gender discrimination.* Pew Research Center. https://www.pewresearch.org/fact-tank/2018/03/07/women-in-majority-male-workplaces-report-higher-rates-of-gender-discrimination

Parker, K., & Funk, C. (2017, December 14). *Gender discrimination comes in many forms for today's working women.* Pew Research Center. https://www.pewresearch.org/fact-tank/2017/12/14/gender-discrimination-comes-in-many-forms-for-todays-working-women

Perron, R. (2018). *The value of experience: Age discrimination against older workers persists.* American Association of Retired Persons. https://doi.org/10.26419/res.00177.002

Rhoades, L., & Eisenberger, R. (2002). Perceived organizational support: A review of the literature. *Journal of Applied Psychology, 87*(4), 698–714. https://doi.org/10.1037/0021-9010.87.4.698

U.S. Equal Employment Opportunity Commission. (n.d.-a). *Age Discrimination in Employment Act (charges filed with EEOC) FY 1997–FY 2019).* https://www.eeoc.gov/eeoc/statistics/enforcement/adea.cfm

U.S. Equal Employment Opportunity Commission. (n.d.-b). *Charge statistics (charges filed with EEOC) FY 1997 through FY 2019.* https://www.eeoc.gov/eeoc/statistics/enforcement/charges.cfm

U.S. Equal Employment Opportunity Commission. (n.d.-c). *Title VII of the Civil Rights Act of 1964 charges (charges filed with EEOC) FY 1997–FY 2019.* https://www.eeoc.gov/eeoc/statistics/enforcement/titlevii.cfm

Walker, R. V., Zelin, A. I., Behrman, C., & Strnad, R. (2017). Qualitative analysis of student perceptions: "Some advisors care. Some don't." *NACADA Journal, 37*(2), 44–54. https://doi.org/10.12930/NACADA-15-027

Young, L. M., & Nauta, M. M. (2013). Sexism as a predictor of attitudes toward women in the military and in combat. *Military Psychology, 25*(2), 166–171. https://doi.org/10.1037/h0094958

PART **III** DIVERSITY AND
PERSONAL GRIT
IN THE WORKPLACE
AND BEYOND

INTRODUCTION

Diversity and Personal Grit in the Workplace and Beyond

Chapters 10 through 13 cover individual-difference factors affecting older women's workforce participation. The United States and other industrialized nations are becoming more diverse in terms of ethnicity, religion, and other categories (United Nations, 2015). According to Colby and Ortman (2015), the United States will show significant shifts in its racial and ethnic composition by 2044 (e.g., growing numbers of non-White Hispanic age groups), becoming a "plurality nation." The authors acknowledged that health disparities by race/ethnicity and women working longer than ever before are two trends that need to be addressed currently and in the decades to come. Abrams et al. (2014) recognized the need to better understand the dynamics and social complexity associated with the motivational needs of Black women (e.g., given the "strong Black Woman" social schema). Greater diversity of societal members necessitates social change in many levels of policies and services for a growing aging population. Furthermore, as a result of a continuing life expectancy advantage, older women of all ethnicities will predominantly outlive their male counterparts. This demographic trend by gender and age underscores the need for focus on quality-of-life concerns and needs in and outside the workplace (Whiston et al., 2015).

Older women need to be proactively engaged in planning and accomplishing work- and non–work-related activities to support their financial needs but to also go beyond and fulfill personal goals and interests ("kaleidoscope career model," August, 2011; "career flow," Niles, 2011). From a diversity perspective, there may be cultural, health, and/or cohort-related factors restricting older women's access to opportunities for workplace and/or civic engagement (Mahmood, 2008; Majeed et al., 2015). Questioning older women's roles dictated by society and reflective of potential ageist or gender stereotypes, or a combination thereof (e.g., "double jeopardy"), has direct ramifications for the quality of life in later-life role fulfillment of women across cultures and communities.

Addressing the diverse needs and understanding the diverse backgrounds associated with the growing numbers of older women who are living longer than ever before and wish to engage in self-fulfilling activities are essential for all community members, ranging from employers to community program planners. The benefits of such engagement of women in later life can both enhance their quality of life and also, importantly, enrich the communities that benefit from their skills, wisdom, and expertise (Levinson, 1996). Older women have much to offer, but they may not be seen as resources within their communities and in the workplace (Bimrose et al., 2013). Social schemas about what it means to be older and a woman need significant revision in response to the present and future cohorts of older women who may be erroneously regarded as a silent majority in society.

In addition to societal change, personal change (e.g., "self-schema") is also needed on the part of these growing numbers of older women to exercise their right to opportunities and be adaptable in the face of challenges and obstacles (Hurd, 1999; McMahon et al., 2012). This does entail utilizing personal characteristics of grit and resilience in the face of potentially blatant ageism and sexism from family members, employers, and other members of society (Moore, 2009). Social change is needed to better support and facilitate the many motivations and needs of diverse older women in communities (McMahon et al., 2013; Wiggs, 2010; Wray, 2007).

Across the chapters in Part III, emergent themes include the following:

- adaptation to late-life work engagement (Chapters 10, 11, 12, and 13),
- role of historical and economic context (Chapters 10 and 11),
- gender and situational factors in embodied journeys (Chapters 10 and 11),
- being proactive in the face of age-related challenges (Chapters 11 and 13),
- grit and resilience despite discrimination (Chapter 12), and
- culture change to overcome restrictive societal expectations (Chapters 12 and 13).

REFERENCES

Abrams, J. A., Maxwell, M., Pope, M., & Belgrave, F. Z. (2014). Carrying the world with the grace of a lady and the grit of a warrior: Deepening our understanding of the "Strong Black Woman" schema. *Psychology of Women Quarterly, 38*(4), 503–518. https://doi.org/10.1177%2F0361684314541418

August, R. A. (2011). Women's later life career development: Looking through the lens of the kaleidoscope career model. *Journal of Career Development, 38*(3), 208–236. https://doi.org/10.1177/0894845310362221

Bimrose, J., McMahon, M., & Watson, M. (2013). Career trajectories of older women: Implications for career guidance. *British Journal of Guidance & Counselling, 41*(5), 587–601. https://doi.org/10.1080/03069885.2013.779639

Colby, S. L., & Ortman, J. M. (2015). Projections of the size and composition of the U.S. population: 2014 to 2060. *Current Population Reports* (No. P25-1143). U.S. Census Bureau.

Hurd, L. C. (1999). "We're not old!": Older women's negotiation of aging and oldness. *Journal of Aging Studies, 13*(4), 419–439. https://doi.org/10.1016/S0890-4065(99)00019-5

Levinson, D. J. (1996). *The seasons of a woman's life.* Knopf.

Mahmood, S. (2008). Professional preparation for older women: A view from New Zealand. *Educational Gerontology, 34*(6), 462–476. https://doi.org/10.1080/03601270802000618

Majeed, T., Forder, P., Mishra, G., & Byles, J. (2015). Women, work, and illness: A longitudinal analysis of workforce participation patterns for women beyond middle age. *Journal of Women's Health, 24*(6), 455–465. https://doi.org/10.1089/jwh.2014.5009

McMahon, M., Watson, M., & Bimrose, J. (2012). Career adaptability: A qualitative understanding from the stories of older women. *Journal of Vocational Behavior, 80*(3), 762–768. https://doi.org/10.1016/j.jvb.2012.01.016

McMahon, M., Watson, M., & Bimrose, J. (2013). Older women's careers: Systemic perspectives. In W. Patton (Ed.), *Conceptualising women's working lives: Moving the boundaries of discourse* (pp. 119–133). Brill/Sense.

Moore, S. (2009). "No matter what I did I would still end up in the same position": Age as a factor defining older women's experience of labor market participation. *Work, Employment and Society, 23*(4), 655–671. https://doi.org/10.1177%2F0950017009344871

Niles, S. G. (2011). Career flow: A hope-centered model of career development. *Journal of Employment Counseling, 48*(4), 173–175. https://doi.org/10.1002/j.2161-1920.2011.tb01107.x

United Nations. (2015). *The world's women 2015: Trends and statistics.* https://unstats.un.org/unsd/gender/worldswomen.html

Whiston, S. C., Feldwisch, K. M., Evans, K. M., Blackman, C. S., & Gilman, L. (2015). Older professional women's views on work: A qualitative analysis. *The Career Development Quarterly, 63*(2), 98–112. https://doi.org/10.1002/cdq.12007

Wiggs, C. M. (2010). Creating the self: Exploring the life journey of late-midlife women. *Journal of Women & Aging, 22*(3), 218–233. https://doi.org/10.1080/08952841.2010.495574

Wray, S. (2007). Women making sense of midlife: Ethnic and cultural diversity. *Journal of Aging Studies, 21*(1), 31–42. https://doi.org/10.1016/j.jaging.2006.03.001

10

APPALACHIAN GRIT
Women and Work in West Virginia

JULIE HICKS PATRICK, ABIGAIL M. NEHRKORN-BAILEY,
MICHAELA S. CLARK, AND MADELINE M. MARELLO

There is never peace in West Virginia because there is never justice. Injunctions and guns, like morphia, produce a temporary quiet. Then the pain, agonizing and more severe, comes again. So it is with West Virginia. . . . When I get to the other side, I shall tell God Almighty about West Virginia!

—Mother Jones

Early sociological studies based in Appalachia—a region in the eastern United States named for the ancient Appalachian mountain range it encompasses—were guided by a framework of "double or multiple jeopardy" in which the cumulative disadvantages of aging, rurality, and gender interacted to negatively affect health and economic well-being (Patrick et al., 2017). Current investigations of aging women in Appalachia take a more nuanced view, incorporating both the historical and contextual background in which people live, work, and grow old. As in other regions, the baby boom generation has changed the landscape of aging in Appalachia. Simultaneously, however, changes in natural resource-extractive technologies

https://doi.org/10.1037/0000212-011
Older Women Who Work: Resilience, Choice, and Change, E. Cole and L. Hollis-Sawyer (Editors)

have altered the employment opportunities in the region, resulting in more female-dominated jobs but also more part-time positions and low wages (Latimer & Oberhauser, 2005). Thus, informed by lifespan developmental frameworks of cumulative disadvantage and resilience (Baltes, 1987; Smith & Hayslip, 2012), we explore in this chapter some of the historical and contextual factors influencing employment trends and unpaid labor among older West Virginian women.

Before one can understand the experience of older working Appalachian women, first it is necessary to understand Appalachia. Appalachia is a 420-county region in the United States, including all of West Virginia and portions of 12 other states. The region is large, encompassing 205,000 square miles. It extends about 1,000 miles along the Appalachian mountains, from southern New York to northeastern Mississippi (Appalachian Regional Commission [ARC], n.d.). Although older adults aging in rural contexts share many of the same challenges as do their suburban and urban counterparts, there are unique challenges to rural aging in general and to aging in Appalachia, in particular (Krout & Hash, 2015). Rural Appalachia is a region marked by place-based health disparities (Allen & Roberto, 2014; Krout & Hash, 2015; Weaver et al., 2018), where the effects of multiple influences converge in ways that challenge the economic, physical, and emotional well-being of its residents.

As the employment opportunities in the region have shifted away from coal mining, timber production, and other extractive industries, the economic well-being of its residents has also shifted. In 1960, more than 30% of the residents of Appalachia lived in poverty. By 2016, the rate was less than 17%. Similarly, the number of high-poverty counties decreased from about 70% (i.e., 295 counties) in 1960 to about 22% (i.e., 93 counties) in 2016 (ARC, n.d.).

However, Appalachia continues to face significant challenges, with its 25 million residents earning lower annual incomes and experiencing higher unemployment, higher morbidity, and shorter life expectancies than does the rest of the United States (ARC, n.d.). Because West Virginia is the only state contained entirely within Appalachia, it serves as an important reference point regarding health and other disparities for the region and the nation. Whereas 90.6% of U.S. women ages 45 to 64 have at least a high school education, only 79.4% of their female West Virginian age-peers have a high school diploma. Among women ages 65 and older, 85.9% nationally and only 54.9% in West Virginia have earned a high school degree. Similarly, although 34.3% of U.S. women ages 45 to 64 and 25.3% of those ages 65 and older have earned a bachelor's degree or higher, only 15.1% and 7.7%

of West Virginian women of the same age have earned their college degrees (U.S. Census, 2019a).

Other resources that contribute to employment are also lower among West Virginians. When compared with their rural and nonrural peers, adults in West Virginia are older, face higher morbidity, have fewer economic opportunities, and have lower educational attainment (Pollard & Jacobsen, 2011). Among working-age adults, West Virginians report higher levels of depressive symptoms (Muntaner & Barnett, 2000; Post et al., 2013) than do workers in other states. This poor health is observed in a variety of outcome measures, self-report items, and health behaviors, as shown in Table 10.1 (Givens et al., 2019).

INTERSECTIONALITY AMONG APPALACHIAN STEREOTYPES

The current inequalities between West Virginia and the rest of the United States are the result of several complex and interacting forces. Among these are an abundance of negative stereotypes and a history of exploitation. Increasing evidence shows that adults, including older adults, are often negatively affected by stereotypes (Andreoletti et al., 2015; Kang & Chasteen, 2009). Appalachians are often described as suspicious of outsiders and fatalistic about their health and future (Catte, 2018; Drew & Schoenberg, 2011; L. Jones, 1994). However, Appalachian culture is much more nuanced than these simple stereotypes would suggest. For example, Appalachians are often described pejoratively as "clannish" and resistant to the influences of outsiders. This observation is rooted in truth because of the geography of

TABLE 10.1. Health Disparity in West Virginia

Health indicator	United States	West Virginia
Premature death: Years of life lost before age 75 per 100,000	6,900	10,500
Adults reporting fair/poor health (%)	16	24
Physically unhealthy days per month	3.7	5.2
Emotionally unhealthy days per month	3.8	5.2
Insufficiently physically active (%)	22	28
Current cigarette smoker (%)	17	25

Note. From *2019 County Health Rankings Report: West Virginia* (p. 11), by M. Givens, A. Jovaag, and A. Roubal, 2019, University of Wisconsin Population Health Institute and Robert Wood Johnson Foundation (https://www.countyhealthrankings.org/sites/default/files/media/document/state/downloads/CHR2019_WV.pdf). Copyright 2019 by University of Wisconsin Population Health Institute and Robert Wood Johnson Foundation. Adapted with permission.

the region and the history of its settlement. Appalachia was settled in waves by various ethnic groups, many of whom chose to settle in the region with an express desire to be segregated. A prime example is the town of Helvetia, located in Randolph County in central West Virginia. Whereas most German immigrants settled in the eastern panhandle of the state, the isolated Helvetia was first settled in 1869 by Swiss and German immigrants. With its 2010 population listed at 59, Helvetia has remained an isolated Swiss colony, with a language dialect that is essentially unchanged over the past 150 years.

Similarly, with the influx of Irish and Scottish immigrants settled in the southern hills and valleys ("hollers") of West Virginia, reliance on family ("clan") was appropriate, as the difficulties of travel made self-sufficient living a necessity. Large groups of Italian immigrants and, later, immigrants from Eastern Europe settled in north-central West Virginia. Thus, in addition to the geographic barriers, differences in language and native customs also contributed to the isolation of different ethnic groups.

That out-of-state business owners encouraged such separation is also evident in the history of coal camps and other boom towns in the region (Shogan, 2006). Keeping workers segregated by ethnicity and nativity helped to decrease the rise of unions and other workers' rights movements. The exploitation of Appalachians by outsiders persists and extends beyond the coal fields. Although the term *rednecks* is meant as a slur by outsiders, Appalachians know that it refers to the 1921 labor uprising known as the Battle of Blair Mountain, in which red bandanas and neckerchiefs distinguished the workers from those who opposed them (Shogan, 2006). West Virginians remain proud that they stood together against the threat of bombs being dropped from private planes. When the mostly White miners were confronted with Black and Italian men willing to cross the picket line, they invited these workers to join the union and stand with them against the unfair labor practices. Thus, at Blair Mountain, "as the 10,000-strong integrated army marched towards a showdown with the coal owners' private army, the strikers desegregated whites-only public spaces at gunpoint" (Luce, 2019).

Finally, many Appalachians are viewed as holding a fatalistic view of their health and well-being (L. Jones, 1994). Perhaps a more accurate interpretation is that many Appalachian residents embrace humility and espouse a philosophical view that God is in control of their fate. Thus, a belief in the will of God, not fatalism, per se, guides behavior.

Other stereotypes intersect with these views of Appalachian culture. Appalachians have a complex relationship with race, and that is true in West Virginia as well. For example, West Virginia is the only state formed by presidential proclamation, becoming the 35th state as a function of Abraham Lincoln's Emancipation Proclamation (ARC, n.d.). West Virginians recall the

Civil War–era abolitionist John Brown and his famous raid on the federal arsenal at Harper's Ferry. Brown and 21 others had hoped that local slaves would join the rebellion. The rebellion ended when soldiers, led by General Robert E. Lee, killed Brown's sons and arrested and hanged him for treason. Northerners hail Brown as a martyred hero; Southerners regard him as a traitor. Opinions are divided in West Virginia (Catte, 2018).

West Virginians also proudly claim the legacy of John Henry, that steel-driving Black man who beat the steam-powered drill (Hauser, 2019). Yet, in addition to the five recognized hate groups that operate freely in the Mountain State, each of the five states with which West Virginia shares a border has between 13 and 39 such groups (Southern Poverty Law Center, 2019). West Virginia, a state in which 93% of the residents are White (U.S. Census, 2019b), is quite literally surrounded by hate groups.

HISTORY OF WOMEN AND WORK IN APPALACHIA

As complex as the intersections with race are, Appalachian gender stereo-types are even more complicated. Specifically, women are often over-sexualized and marginalized while simultaneously lauded as the backbone of the family and active contributors to the welfare of their families and communities. Women in Appalachia have always contributed to the economic well-being of their families. In the storytelling tradition of the region, William Blizzard (2010) shared a tale of life in the coal towns in the 1920s. Some wives, whose husbands were injured and unable to work in the mines, would exchange sexual favors with the supervisors and others to maintain their homes and accounts at the company stores. Others in the coal towns knew that "accounts were being settled" when the window shades in the upper rooms of the company store were lowered. Other wives and mothers provided for the economic well-being of their families by working off the books in the coal mines. When workers were paid piece-rate, children and wives would often work alongside the male householder to increase the amount of coal obtained. When mine disasters occurred, the number of women and children who also perished often outnumbered that of the workers on the books (Blizzard, 2010).

In addition to supporting the well-being of their own households by curtailing eviction and working in the mines, Appalachian women have lobbied to improve working conditions for others. Perhaps the best-known activist is Mary Harris "Mother" Jones. Mary Harris immigrated to North America from County Cork, Ireland, at age 5. When she was 24 years old, she left a teaching position in Michigan for a similar position in Tennessee, where she met and married her husband. At age 30, Mary Harris Jones survived the outbreak of yellow fever, which claimed the lives of her husband and four children. As a young widow in Civil War–era Appalachia, she witnessed strong anti-Black and anti-Irish nativism. Moving to Chicago, she began work as a seamstress, until the building in which she worked was destroyed in the Great Chicago Fire of 1871. With the fire leaving more than 100,000 people homeless and unemployed, Mary Harris Jones began advocating for the rights of workers. In 1877, she was a leader in the Great Railroad Strike in Pittsburgh (Michals, 2015). As she turned her attention to coal miners in West Virginia, she was briefly employed by the United Mine Workers. She worked on behalf of miners in Colorado and then returned to West Virginia, which had the nation's highest mortality rate among miners (Gorn, 2002). During the especially violent Paint Creek–Cabin Creek strike in West Virginia in 1912 and 1913, she was convicted of conspiracy to commit murder and sentenced to 20 years in prison. The governor of West Virginia commuted her sentence, and she continued to advocate for workers' rights into her 90s (Gorn, 2002; Michals, 2015).

One might think that with such strong advocates as Mother Jones, working conditions would have improved markedly in Appalachia. But unsafe conditions continued through the period of the Monongah mining disaster in 1907, which killed at least 360 miners and an untold number of their sons. Fewer than 2 weeks later, the Darr Mine explosion in southwestern Pennsylvania claimed the lives of another 239 men and boys. It was wives and daughters who supported and organized the rescue efforts (Hammond, 2016). This same commitment to better working conditions was seen again on a national stage during the teachers' walkout in February 2018 and February 2019. It is notable that the teachers, who are predominantly women, ensured that the children who needed the school-based nutrition program resources continued to receive access to breakfast and lunch during the work stoppage (Balingit, 2019).

WEST VIRGINIAN WOMEN IN THE LABOR FORCE

Although a staunch supporter of the 8-hour work day, decent wages, and basic safety for workers, Mary Harris Jones did not support the women's suffrage movement and viewed a woman's higher calling to be firmly rooted in the home (Michals, 2015). Thus, she advocated for better working conditions for men so that women would be able to remain at home and care for family. This notion persists today in many areas of Appalachia: Strong Appalachian women build and nurture families. This phenomenon prompted

Bolgiano (2011) to claim that "Appalachian women are the ones who hold all of . . . 'the paradoxes of Appalachian identity' together" (p. 165).

Currently, about 40% of Americans ages 55 and older are active in the labor force. However, substantial increases in the numbers of workers ages 65 to 74 and those ages 75 and older are expected through the year 2024 (Toossi & Torpey, 2017). Increases in the number of adults working in late life relate to many factors, including higher education levels, better health, and longer life expectancies. Other reasons include delayed access to Social Security benefits, inadequate pensions and retirement plans, insufficient savings, and the rising cost of living (Toossi & Torpey, 2017). These factors operate differently for different groups of people. Thus, it is not surprising that the number and proportion of older workers differ by age, gender, geography, and industry.

West Virginia has the lowest total labor force participation rate in the nation. Moreover, only 32.7% of men ages 55 and older and 26.5% of women ages 55 and older are in the labor force (Toossi & Torpey, 2017). As shown in Table 10.2, it is largely late middle-aged workers who contribute to this percentage, with relatively few adults over age 65 remaining in the civilian labor force.

With lower educational attainment and limited job opportunities, aging women in West Virginia face unique employment challenges. Employment histories of women in West Virginia differ from those in other regions, perhaps because more women have acted out traditional gender roles of women as homemakers. Labor force participation among older women in West Virginia includes lower participation rates, in general, and more part-time employment (Latimer & Oberhauser, 2005). As the number of jobs in extractive industries has declined in recent decades, jobs that often excluded racial minorities and women (Bell & York, 2010; Latimer & Oberhauser, 2005), there is competition for the limited number of jobs that remain, an increase in female-dominated jobs, more part-time employment, and a

TABLE 10.2. West Virginia Employment by Age

Age	% Men	% Women
55–59	61.43	55.70
60–61	50.20	44.60
62–64	39.50	33.10
65–69	23.28	20.80
70–74	14.24	11.70
75 and older	6.56	3.60
Overall	32.68	26.50

Note. Data from the U.S. Bureau of Labor Statistics (2020).

preponderance of low-wage positions. Although about half of working-age West Virginian women are employed, only 27% are employed in professional fields, with a significant percentage employed in the service industry (25%) and office and administrative positions (21.5%; Institute for Women's Policy Research [IWPR], 2019).

Wages for both men and women in West Virginia are lower than in other parts of the country. As in other areas, however, a significant gender wage gap is evident. In a state in which the poverty rate is at 19.1% (U.S. Census, 2019a), the gender gap in pay may have especially profound effects. Women with more education earn higher wages than do their less well-educated sisters. However, the wage gap is exacerbated by race. In West Virginia, Asian women earn nearly 92% of men's pay, whereas White and multiracial women earn about 70% of men's pay. In West Virginia, Black and Hispanic women experience an even wider gender gap in pay (IWPR, 2019), earning 65.2% and 61.5% of men's pay, respectively. Across racial and ethnic groups, women in West Virginia earn about $1,000 a month less than men do. The IWPR (2019) predicted that at the current rate, pay equity between men and women in West Virginia will not be reached for another 80 years.

Self-Owned Businesses

Nationally, older adults are more likely than any other age group to work for themselves (Toossi & Torpey, 2017). Additionally, there has been significant growth in women-owned businesses during the past 4 decades. This growth is evident in the number of businesses launched, the number of jobs created, and the revenues earned (American Express, 2018). National trends show that nearly two thirds of women-owned businesses are owned by women over the age of 45. About half of all women-owned businesses in the United States are clustered in three areas: (a) health and social assistance; (b) professional, technical, and scientific services; and (c) other services (American Express, 2018). The growth and influence of these women-owned businesses vary across geography.

With respect to percentage of women-owned businesses, West Virginia is ranked 24th among the states; about one third (34.1%) of West Virginian businesses are women-owned, an increase from 28% a decade earlier (IWPR, 2019). These 39,000 women-owned businesses are not distributed equally across West Virginia. A lack of opportunity characterizes the southern part of the state, whereas Morgantown, located in north-central West Virginia, is ranked in the top 6% of places in the United States to launch a woman-owned business (Hub, 2016). Of note, two other West Virginia cities also ranked highly, with Beckley in the top 8% and Wheeling in the top 20% of places to launch a woman-owned business (Hub, 2016). However, despite growth in numbers, women-owned businesses in West Virginia lack the economic clout that other such businesses exert across the United States. In fact, women-owned businesses in West Virginia rank among the lowest in terms of job creation and increased wages (American Express, 2018).

One possible reason for the low economic clout of women-owned businesses in West Virginia may relate to the kinds of opportunities available. For example, with strong gender norms, low health resources, and low educational resources, West Virginia women often engage in informal and home-based livelihood strategies (Oberhauser, 2005). These efforts often include such activities as working community gardens for both personal sustenance and retail, sewing and knitting enterprises, and selling other artisanal crafts.

Unpaid Labor

West Virginia women also engage in a high volume of unpaid labor. For example, nearly 21% of West Virginia women live with a person with a disability (IWPR, 2019). Nearly 25% of West Virginians are family caregivers, providing regular care or assistance to a family member or friend (Centers for Disease Control and Prevention [CDC], 2018). About half of these caregivers have provided care for 2 or more years, and about 58% are women. Moreover, about 18% are age 65 or older (CDC, 2018). A large portion, 40%, are providing care to a parent or parent-in law, and 11% are providing care to a person with dementia.

West Virginians also provide a high level of caregiving to young grandchildren. Of the 70 million American grandparents, about 10% live with their young grandchildren. In more than 40% of these coresident dyads, the grandparent has primary responsibility for the grandchild's basic needs (Wu, 2018). Compared with noncustodial grandparents, those responsible for raising grandchildren report more chronic health problems and more psychological distress (Hayslip & Patrick, 2006; Patrick & Tomczewski, 2008). Despite data showing that custodial grandparents reside in a variety of urban, suburban, and rural locations, research has focused on large metropolitan areas (Kohn & Smith, 2006). Yet, significant differences exist across geographies.

Grandparents in rural areas may encounter a variety of unmet needs and geographic isolation (Cohen & Pyle, 2000). West Virginians also provide a disproportionately high level of assistance to young grandchildren. Nearly 11% of West Virginian children younger than age 18 live with a nonparent relative, the majority of which are grandparents (GrandFamilies, 2017). These custodial grandparents number more than 21,000. In about 42% of these households, the parent is not coresident, with the grandparent providing the bulk of daily care for the child. As in other locations, the factors influencing custodial grandparenting in West Virginia are complex (Dolbin-MacNab & Yancura, 2018; Jang & Tang, 2016). Custodial grandparenting has many challenges (Hayslip & Patrick, 2006), but providing such care may be especially difficult in West Virginia.

RECENT INTERSECTIONS THAT THREATEN OLDER WOMEN'S EMPLOYMENT

We started this chapter with a quote from Mother Jones, words that she spoke in 1925, in relation to the fight for workers' rights. Indeed, West Virginia is again fighting a fierce and painful battle. This time, the battle is with "morphia." Among the chief reasons for custodial and caregiving grandparenting in West Virginia is the dramatic increase in opioid abuse and addiction. Contrary to stereotypes about illegal drugs, the CDC has stated that the driving factor for the increase in opioid-related mortality is prescription abuse and misuse. Relative to the rest of the United States, West Virginia has the highest drug-overdose death rate and the highest prescription rate for opioids and is in the top 10 states for rates of prescriptions for high-dose opioids and extended-release opioids. In 2017, there were 833 opioid overdose deaths in West Virginia, bringing the rate to nearly 50 deaths per 100,000 people. That is twice the rate just 7 years prior and three times higher than the national average (fewer than 15 deaths per 100,000; CDC, 2018).

Although several factors contribute to this phenomenon, West Virginia fares especially poorly regarding opioid dependence. Chief among these reasons are the high number of work-related injuries, a medical focus on treating pain with pharmaceuticals, its status as a medically underserved area, high rates of unemployment, and lower education levels (Jacobs, 2016).

In addition to death, opioid addiction poses other threats as well. Among infants whose mothers are opioid-dependent, risks include preterm birth, hepatitis C, and neonatal abstinence syndrome (NAS; Mactier, 2013). NAS is a constellation of problems in neonates that result from exposure to opioids during gestation. Nationwide, about six out of every 1,000 births involve NAS. West Virginia has seen a dramatic increase from about eight per 1,000 in 2007 to more than 31 per 1,000 in 2013. In general, babies born with NAS remain in the hospital for about 2 weeks longer than do neonates without NAS, putting a strain on mothers, the family, and the health care system. In addition to the vulnerable physical state at birth, infants born with NAS may experience persistent learning and developmental challenges throughout childhood (Stabler et al., 2017). The increase in NAS is a direct link to the increase in opioid addictions, and West Virginia women are again stepping up to care for the health and well-being of their families. Families often step in to assist with infants born with NAS; clearly, the opioid epidemic is a lifespan, family problem.

However, custodial grandparenting is further complicated by the employment situation of the grandmother. In West Virginia, about 46.5% of custodial grandparents are in the workforce, about 21% have incomes below the poverty line, and 24.5% have a disability (GrandFamilies, 2017). The research shows that when grandparents are both raising grandchildren and active in the labor force, they often face interacting challenges to their own health and well-being (Pruchno & McKenney, 2006). When asked about the effects of custodial grandparenting on their employment, a large study of custodial grandmothers ($N = 506$) reported several areas in which caregiving interfered with their paid employment. Approximately 17% reported having quit a job because of grandparenting demands, 50% reported arriving late to work, 60% reported having missed work, 64% reported leaving work early, and 46% reported having to leave work suddenly (Pruchno & McKenney, 2006). For those older women who are both raising grandchildren and in the paid labor force, the demands of caregiving increase their need for financial resources and jeopardize their ability to continue working.

MOVING OLDER WEST VIRGINIAN WOMEN FORWARD

"There is never peace in West Virginia" (M. Jones, 1925), and the work for justice continues. Service providers, advocates, and others cannot adequately perform in the new battles ahead without at least three resources. To better support older working women (and men) of West Virginia, the field needs (a) more high-quality data, (b) theoretically driven research questions, and (c) more sophisticated analytical tools.

The existing data related to aging women in work are relatively local, small in scope, or derived from the U.S. Census. Although these data sets offer important insights, researchers must move beyond small descriptive studies and those that examine easily measured variables. With regard to data related to aging women who work in rural areas, Helton and Keller (2010) noted that there are few empirical examinations of resilience of Appalachian women. This is especially true for aging women. Although Helton and Keller attributed this lack of attention to the historical and cultural patriarchy of Appalachian culture, one that has obscured the unique roles and experiences of women, they also noted the distinct cultural values of

Appalachia. To wit, Helton and Keller echoed L. Jones (1994) in noting that Appalachian adults value family (clan), independence, love of nature and place, and humility ("fatalism"). As shown by Oberhauser (2005), these values interact in ways which make the work–life roles of Appalachian women highly nuanced and complex. Moreover, Oberhauser noted that these values are enacted within the context of the unique political and capitalistic movements. To more fully understand the work life of older Appalachian women, researchers must incorporate these kinds of constructs.

Thus, in addition to gathering richer data, researchers must begin to ask and examine theoretically derived research questions. Cumulative disadvantage theories (e.g., Patrick et al., 2017) and a lifespan focus of development (Baltes, 1987) and resilience (Smith & Hayslip, 2012) may allow the field to answer questions about which aspects of late-life work are similar across contexts and which are unique to Appalachia and other rural areas. This is the kind of information that is needed to develop better policies and programs that support older women who work.

Finally, with better quality data and theoretically derived research questions, the field will need to use more sophisticated analyses. Bohlmann et al. (2018) highlighted the need to include moderators in the examination of aging and work. Moreover, they called for an examination of construct that might mediate the moderating effect of age. We echo their recommendation but advocate for these sophisticated moderation models to be examined within the context of lifespan theory, work behavior theory, or gender theory. An example of applying these models could include examining possible mechanisms through which age influences a work outcome. Such a model could be tested in a standard mediation approach whereby the researcher examines the reduction in the effect of age on some work-related outcome when the mediator is included in the model (Hayes, 2018). Such a model would take the form shown in Figure 10.1. Note that age is not the mediator; rather, this model attempts to explain why age differences might exist.

FIGURE 10.1. Explaining Age Effects With a Mediator

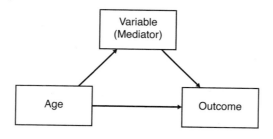

FIGURE 10.2. Age Moderates the Effect of the Predictor on the Outcome

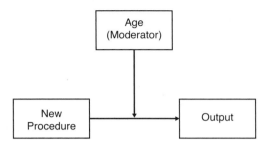

Although the four-step approach highlighted by Baron and Kenny (1986) was once the standard for examining such models, more recent tools include Hayes's (2018) PROCESS macro, which examines indirect and conditional effects even in the case in which age does not directly influence the outcome.

Other analytic models can also be used to examine how age might interact with a predictor variable to result in different outcomes. For example, one might examine whether new procedures (the moderator) alter productive output differently for younger, middle-aged, and older workers. Perhaps the older workers flourish with the new procedures, whereas younger workers' output remains stable. This kind of question can readily be examined in a moderation model, as shown in Figure 10.2.

Increasingly sophisticated questions can be posed and examined using models like the one shown in Figure 10.3. It is with these types of models that the effects of gender, rurality, and other constructs in relation to aging and work can be examined.

FIGURE 10.3. The Moderating Effect of Age Is Moderated by Another Variable

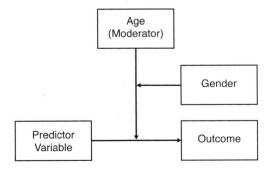

CONCLUSION

Thus, a rejection of Appalachian stereotypes, an appreciation for Appalachian history and cultural values, and rigorous methodology are needed to improve the quality of data about older Appalachian women who work. For older Appalachian women who work, whether in the paid labor force, the unpaid labor force, or both, such examinations may be key to developing supportive programs and policies.

Appalachian West Virginia and other rural areas provide a challenging context in which to age and work (Krout & Hash, 2015). Relative to other regions, adults aging in West Virginia have poorer physical health, poorer emotional health, lower economic resources, and more caregiving demands (U.S. Census, 2019a). Moreover, they live within a context of negative social stereotypes that may further influence their health and well-being. When marginalized adults internalize negative stereotypes, health and emotional challenges often result (Andreoletti et al., 2015; Kang & Chasteen, 2009). Researchers interested in maximizing the healthy work span of older women in Appalachia may need to examine the interactions of age, gender, and rural stereotypes of these women's well-being.

Because many adults in Appalachia value independence, humility, and privacy (Catte, 2018; Drew & Schoenberg, 2011; L. Jones, 1994), employment interventions must respect these values. Most current older women in Appalachia were raised in the era in which extractive industries provided many jobs with high wages. Advanced education was often not required. Coal mining and other such jobs were often closed to women, which further reinforced gendered work. Moreover, many women were content to support their families by being full-time homemakers or working part-time. These approaches color their opportunities in mid- and late life. Outsiders who wish to improve the lot of aging workers in Appalachia must be mindful of these cultural and historical trends.

The key to improved policies and programs to support older West Virginian women who work likely rests in improved data quality obtained via rigorous research. Rural aging experts must collaborate with experts in industrial–organizational scholarship to design studies and analyze data that speak to the many barriers of late-life employment and unpaid labor in West Virginia. In addition to a more sophisticated use of mediation and moderation, researchers need to examine work–life balance issues and how these constructs change over time for older women in West Virginia and other rural areas. Then, the older working women and all of West Virginia might achieve both the peace and the justice of which Mother Jones spoke.

REFERENCES

Allen, K. R., & Roberto, K. A. (2014). Older women in Appalachia: Experiences with gynecological cancer. *The Gerontologist, 54*(6), 1024–1034. https://doi.org/10.1093/geront/gnt095

American Express. (2018). *State of women-owned businesses report.* https://about.americanexpress.com/files/doc_library/file/2018-state-of-women-owned-businesses-report.pdf

Andreoletti, C., Leszczynski, J. P., & Disch, W. B. (2015). Gender, race, and age: The content of compound stereotypes across the life span. *International Journal of Aging & Human Development, 81*(1–2), 27–53. https://doi.org/10.1177/0091415015616395

Appalachian Regional Commission. (n.d.). *The Appalachian region.* https://www.arc.gov

Balingit, M. (2019, February 18). West Virginia teachers, whose protests sparked a nationwide movement, prepare to walk out again. *The Washington Post.* https://www.washingtonpost.com/education/2019/02/19/west-virginia-teachers-whose-protests-sparked-nationwide-movement-prepare-walk-out-again/?noredirect=on&utm_term=.60429a6ed7eb

Baltes, P. B. (1987). Theoretical propositions of life-span developmental psychology: On the dynamics between growth and decline. *Developmental Psychology, 23*(5), 611–626. https://doi.org/10.1037/0012-1649.23.5.611

Baron, R. M., & Kenny, D. A. (1986). The moderator–mediator variable distinction in social psychological research: Conceptual, strategic, and statistical considerations. *Journal of Personality and Social Psychology, 51*(6), 1173–1182. https://doi.org/10.1037/0022-3514.51.6.1173

Bell, S. E., & York, R. (2010). Community economic identity: The coal industry and ideology construction in West Virginia. *Rural Sociology, 75*(1), 111–143. https://doi.org/10.1111/j.1549-0831.2009.00004.x

Blizzard, W. C. (2010). *When miners march.* PM Press.

Bohlmann, C., Rudolph, C. W., & Zacher, H. (2018). Methodological recommendations to move research on work and aging forward. *Work, Aging and Retirement, 4*(3), 225–237. https://doi.org/10.1093/workar/wax023

Bolgiano, C. (2011). On becoming Appalachian. *Appalachian Journal, 38*(2–3), 164–168.

Catte, E. (2018). *What you are getting wrong about Appalachia.* Belt Publishing.

Centers for Disease Control and Prevention. (2018). *West Virginia Caregiving: 2015 Behavioral Risk Factor Surveillance System (BRFSS) Data.* https://www.cdc.gov/aging/data/infographic/2015/west-virginia-caregiving.html

Cohen, C. S., & Pyle, R. (2000). Support groups in the lives of grandmothers raising grandchildren. In C. B. Cox (Ed.), *To grandmother's house we go and stay: Perspectives on custodial grandparents* (pp. 235–267). Springer.

Dolbin-MacNab, M. L., & Yancura, L. A. (2018). International perspectives on grandparents raising grandchildren: Contextual considerations for advancing global discourse. *International Journal of Aging & Human Development, 86*(1), 3–33. https://doi.org/10.1177/0091415016689565

Drew, E. M., & Schoenberg, N. E. (2011). Deconstructing fatalism: Ethnographic perspectives on women's decision making about cancer prevention and treatment. *Medical Anthropology Quarterly, 25*(2), 164–182. https://doi.org/10.1111/j.1548-1387.2010.01136.x

Givens, M., Jovaag, A., & Roubal, A. (2019). *2019 County Health Rankings Report: West Virginia*. University of Wisconsin Population Health Institute and Robert Wood Johnson Foundation. https://www.countyhealthrankings.org/sites/default/files/media/document/state/downloads/CHR2019_WV.pdf

Gorn, E. J. (2002). *Mother Jones: The most dangerous woman in America*. Hill and Wang.

GrandFamilies. (2017). *GrandFacts: State fact sheets for grandfamilies—West Virginia* [Fact sheet]. http://www.grandfamilies.org/Portals/0/State%20Fact%20Sheets/Grandfamilies-Fact-Sheet-West-Virginia2.pdf

Hammond, T. (2016, December 7). U.S. coal mining's deadliest month: December 1907 [Blog post]. *Fishwrap*. https://blog.newspapers.com/u-s-coal-minings-deadliest-month-december-1907

Hauser, J. (2019). *John Henry: The rebel versions*. https://sites.google.com/site/johnhenrytherebelversions/home

Hayes, A. F. (2018). *Introduction to mediation, moderation, and conditional process analysis: A regression-based approach* (2nd ed.). Guilford Press.

Hayslip, B., Jr., & Patrick, J. H. (Eds.). (2006). *Custodial grandparenting: Individual, cultural, and ethnic diversity*. Springer Publishing.

Helton, L. R., & Keller, S. M. (2010). Appalachian women: A study of resiliency assets and cultural values. *Journal of Social Service Research, 36*(2), 151–161. https://doi.org/10.1080/01488370903578124

Hub, W. V. (2016, October 13). *Women's business center to launch in West Virginia*. http://wvhub.org/?s=women+owned+businesses

Institute for Women's Policy Research. (2019). *Status of women in the States: State data*. https://statusofwomendata.org/state-data

Jacobs, H. (2016, May 1). Here's why the opioid epidemic is so bad in West Virginia— the state with the highest overdose rate in the US. *Business Insider*. https://www.businessinsider.com/why-the-opioid-epidemic-is-so-bad-in-west-virginia-2016-4

Jang, H., & Tang, F. (2016). Effects of social support and volunteering on depression among grandparents raising grandchildren. *International Journal of Aging & Human Development, 83*(4), 491–507. https://doi.org/10.1177/0091415016657561

Jones, L. (1994). *Appalachian values*. Jesse Stuart Foundation.

Jones, M. (1925). *The autobiography of Mother Jones*. Charles H. Kerr & Company. https://digital.library.upenn.edu/women/jones/autobiography/autobiography.html

Kang, S. K., & Chasteen, A. L. (2009). The moderating role of age-group identification and perceived threat on stereotype threat among older adults. *International Journal of Aging & Human Development, 69*(3), 201–220. https://doi.org/10.2190/AG.69.3.c

Kohn, S. J., & Smith, G. C. (2006). Social support among custodial grandparents within a diversity of contexts. In B. Hayslip & J. H. Patrick (Eds.), *Custodial grandparenting: Individual, cultural, and ethnic diversity* (pp. 199–223). Springer.

Krout, J. A., & Hash, K. M. (2015). What is rural? Introduction to aging in rural areas. *Aging in rural places. Policies, programs, and profession practices*. Springer.

Latimer, M., & Oberhauser, A. M. (2005). Exploring gender and economic development in Appalachia. *Journal of Appalachian Studies, 10*(3), 269–291.

Luce, E. (2019, June 26). America's new redneck rebellion. *Financial Times*. https://www.ft.com/content/327a9c4a-9799-11e9-9573-ee5cbb98ed36?fbclid=IwAR1-nw89VXXKMYOsjuft3SKn7Nlg5SfHzahCDBoni5djfqbFLWQjsqAd1RU

Mactier, H. (2013). Neonatal and longer term management following substance misuse in pregnancy. *Early Human Development, 89*(11), 887–892. https://doi.org/10.1016/j.earlhumdev.2013.08.024

Michals, D. (Ed.). (2015). *Mary Harris Jones (1837–1930), National Women's History Museum.* https://www.womenshistory.org/education-resources/biographies/mary-harris-jones

Muntaner, C., & Barnett, E. (2000). Depressive symptoms in rural West Virginia: Labor market and health services correlates. *Journal of Health Care for the Poor and Underserved, 11*(3), 284–300. https://doi.org/10.1353/hpu.2010.0788

Oberhauser, A. M. (2005). Scaling gender and diverse economies: Perspectives from Appalachia and South Africa. *Antipode, 37*(5), 863–874. https://doi.org/10.1111/j.0066-4812.2005.00536.x

Patrick, J. H., Knepple Carney, A., & Nehrkorn, A. M. (2017). Aging in the context of life events. *International Journal of Aging & Human Development, 84*(3), 209–212. https://doi.org/10.1177/0091415017690275

Patrick, J. H., & Tomczewski, D. K. (2008). Grandparents raising grandchildren: Benefits and drawbacks? Custodial grandfathers. *Journal of Intergenerational Relationships, 5*(4), 113–116. https://doi.org/10.1300/J194v05n04_11

Pollard, K., & Jacobsen, L. A. (2011). *The Appalachian region in 2010: A census data overview chartbook.* Population Reference Bureau. https://www.arc.gov/assets/research_reports/AppalachianRegion2010CensusReport1.pdf

Post, D. M., Gehlert, S., Hade, E. M., Reiter, P. L., Ruffin, M., & Paskett, E. D. (2013). Depression and SES in women from Appalachia. *Rural Mental Health, 37*(1), 2–15. https://doi.org/10.1037/rmh0000001

Pruchno, R., & McKenney, D. (2006). Grandmothers raising grandchildren: The effects of work disruptions on current work hours and income. In B. Hayslip, Jr., & J. H. Patrick (Eds.), *Custodial grandparenting: Individual, cultural, and ethnic diversity* (pp. 3–20). Springer.

Shogan, R. (2006). *The battle of Blair Mountain: The story of America's largest labor uprising.* Basic Books.

Smith, G. C., & Hayslip, B., Jr. (2012). Resilience in adulthood and later life: What does it mean and where are we heading? *Annual Review of Gerontology & Geriatrics, 32*(1), 1–28. https://doi.org/10.1891/0198-8794.32.3

Southern Poverty Law Center. (2019). *Groups in West Virginia.* https://www.splcenter.org/states/west-virginia

Stabler, M. E., Long, D. L., Chertok, I. R., Giacobbi, P. R., Jr., Pilkerton, C., & Lander, L. R. (2017). Neonatal abstinence syndrome in West Virginia substate regions, 2007–2013. *The Journal of Rural Health, 33*(1), 92–101. https://doi.org/10.1111/jrh.12174

Toossi, M., & Torpey, E. (2017, May). Older workers: Labor force trends and career options. *Career Outlook.* U.S. Bureau of Labor Statistics. https://www.bls.gov/careeroutlook/2017/article/older-workers.htm#later-in-life-career-options

U.S. Bureau of Labor Statistics. (2020). *Economy at a glance: West Virginia.* https://www.bls.gov/eag/eag.wv.htm

U.S. Census. (2019a, February 21). *Educational attainment in the United States: 2018.* https://www.census.gov/data/tables/2018/demo/education-attainment/cps-detailed-tables.html

U.S. Census. (2019b). *Quick facts: United States [Fact sheet].* https://www.census.gov/quickfacts/fact/table/US/PST045218

Weaver, R. H., Roberto, K. A., & Blieszner, R. (2018). Older adults in rural Appalachia: Preference and expectations for future care. *International Journal of Aging & Human Development, 86*(4), 364–381. https://doi.org/10.1177/0091415017720891

Wu, H. (2018). *Prevalence of grandparenthood in the U.S.* Bowling Green State University. https://doi.org/10.25035/ncfmr/fp-18-03

11

MISSIONS CONTINUED

Contextualizing Older Women's Work Pursuits and Passions in Lifelong Journeys

NIVA PIRAN

I remember [at age 5] sitting in the swing at home and singing my heart out and nobody heard me. I was singing into emptiness. To this day, singing and my work it's the same thing. It's hard to have talents in small, isolated communities. I want to develop my own talents and get better at what I do and I want to inspire and be able to identify the talents of the people I work with. I see the clock ticking, I don't have ten years. I feel all the things that I want to do and not being able to do them. . . . I feel like I am in a cocoon that is tight and I can't yet break the shell to become the butterfly. . . .

—Sarah

In the narrative above, Sarah, a White woman in her mid-50s, described the intense passion she was experiencing in relation to a work mission she had identified during her recently completed university degree in business administration. Self-reflections during these studies led Sarah to first link her childhood experiences of "singing into emptiness" to the lack of validation of her talents and work-related passions in her social and occupational

https://doi.org/10.1037/0000212-012
Older Women Who Work: Resilience, Choice, and Change, E. Cole and L. Hollis-Sawyer (Editors)

environment, and, second, to crystallize her work–life mission of not solely finding validation for her own talents but also validating the talents of coworkers. Sarah's narrative brings to the fore challenges at the intersection of work-related passions and conditions that can nurture and sustain such passions. It also exemplifies continued reflections and shifts in work–life missions in which women in midlife and older adulthood engage that can enhance their continued work-related passions, the focus of this chapter.

Sarah (research name), together with another 30 cisgender women, ages 50 to 70, participated in a qualitative study about older women's embodied journeys (Piran, 2017). Participants were of diverse backgrounds in terms of ethnocultural heritage, social class, sexual orientation, residence in rural and urban communities, and health and disability (see Piran, 2017, for a more detailed description of participants). Participants chose their research names and identifying information has been changed to protect confidentiality. All participants described themselves as cisgender women during the time of the study; one of the participants identified as transgender while a younger adult. Most of the 31 women participated in two research interviews, and the rest participated in only one (for a total of 54 interviews). The qualitative study utilized a life history approach, which aims to examine the intersection between individuals' experiences and their social contexts, throughout the lifespan, with a special focus on points of transition (Cole & Knowles, 2001).

The study with older women was part of a research program on the embodied lives of girls, younger women, and older women that led to the emergence of the developmental theory of embodiment (DTE), an integrated critical social theory about processes that shape embodied agency, passion, desire, body connection, and attuned self-care. In line with the DTE, social processes that shape embodiment take place in three core domains: the social power and relational connections domain, the social discourses domain, and the physical domain. The theory further describes the aggregation of social barriers, named "corsets," during adolescence and the loosening of some of these corsets during older age. In particular, middle adulthood to older age often represents a time of change in most women's lives, associated with factors such as the end of the inequitably distributed task of child rearing, changes in partnership relationships (e.g., divorce, partner's retirement, changes in sexual orientation), adult children becoming a source of relational support, health-related changes, and a greater recognition of the finality of life (Piran, 2017). These changes can open opportunities for women to engage differently in varied aspects of their lives, including work.

Work emerged as one of the key areas of these women's experiences of engaging with the world around them. Consistent with findings across a broad body of literature (e.g., Organisation for Economic Co-operation and Development, 2018), the women engaged in multiple forms of labor, of which only a segment was remunerated. The constructivist grounded theory analysis (Charmaz, 2006), utilized in the embodiment project, included work-related narratives. In this chapter, I delineate findings of the research program in relation to remunerated work, with an emphasis on constructive changes in which women engaged in what I term "continued missions" that enhanced their work–life balance. The chapter starts with a discussion of these women's financial challenges, as financial pursuits were central to women's work–life missions. Following that is a description of work-related constructive shifts older women undertook in the three domains of the social environment outlined by the DTE. The chapter ends with a brief conclusion.

FINANCIAL MISSION

Financial strains were present in most women's lives. Whereas 16 women were working (two lost their jobs between the first and second interviews), six others were in search of employment. Most of the women who were working or seeking employment could not afford retirement during their mid- to late 60s or beyond because they did not have access to a living income from a pension plan or other investments. Women typically described interrupted work histories (related to the care of children or aging parents, immigration, etc.) and employment in settings with no traditional pension plans (especially no defined benefit pension plans). About half had no professional or vocational training, which led to them working in low-paying jobs and holding multiple part-time jobs. Of the seven who described themselves as retired, four lived off modest pensions that allowed them to be self-reliant, two relied heavily on their partners' income, and one lived off an old-age pension. One woman lived on disability payments, and one woman was prohibited by her husband from working throughout her adult life. Eight women (25.8%), all nonpartnered, were living below the poverty line.

These financial challenges of study participants reflect the aggregated impact of inequitable access to resources, such as education and equitable pay, across the lifespan. Indeed, during the past 5 years, poverty rates among older women have increased significantly (Institute for Research on Poverty at the University of Wisconsin–Madison, n.d.). Twice as many older women as men live in poverty, with rates of poverty higher among African American women than among White women. Similarly, a recent report by the National Institute on Retirement Security (Brown et al., 2016) has highlighted that women are much more likely to face financial difficulties in retirement compared with men. A woman's retirement nest egg is substantially smaller than a man's because of the gender gap in income, time out of careers for caregiving, patterns of part-time employment, and other factors, necessitating continued employment into older age.

The following discussion of varied constructive work–life shifts at an older age needs to be considered within the context of financial constraints in the life of women. Addressing enhanced poverty at an older age requires multiple systemic changes, such as closing the gender gap in salaries and increasing defined contribution plan eligibility for part-time workers (Brown et al., 2016).

MISSIONS CONTINUED: TARGETING SOCIAL POWER AND SOCIAL JUSTICE

Inhabiting female bodies and being socially labeled *girls* and *women*, girls and women face, at the intersection of gender with other dimensions of social locations, prejudicial treatment such as inequitable access to resources (e.g., education, equitable pay for labor) and varied expressions of harassment. The aggregated impact of such inequity becomes particularly poignant during older age, reflected, for example, by women's higher rates of poverty at that phase. Concurrently, the exposure to prejudicial treatment may lead to the internalization of such inequitable treatment, adversely affecting self- and body concept and relational patterns, as well as reducing embodied agency and passion in acting in the world (Piran, 2017).

For several participants, continued missions during mid- to older adulthood involved addressing challenges related to equity, steps that helped sustain their passions at work. I exemplify such processes by describing the stories of Sarah and Gwen, who tackled inequity by upgrading their work-related skills; Grace and Alice, who changed their self-experience at work through pursuing out-of-work activities; and Viviane, who chose to work with people who have been socially disenfranchised.

Upgrading Skills

Growing up in a working-class family and in a rural town, Sarah was consistently at the top of her elementary and high school classes and found to be gifted in music, even supporting her family income by giving piano lessons. However, she experienced the absence of nurturing and validation of her talents and work ambitions, in contrast to her friends and her brothers who attended university. "My brothers went away to school. My parents had a little bit of a life insurance for my brothers." No money was allotted for her education: "Education was not an option for me." The absence of validation and support continued throughout her early adulthood. Keen on working, even leaving her community for a short time to hold a job in a major corporation in a large city, she submitted to pressures to return home, get married, and followed the dictate of "taking care of my husband and having children." Repeated moves between rural communities for her husband's career and restrictions related to childrearing limited the jobs she could take on to "bottom jobs with no responsibilities." Even teaching piano at home was deemed a disturbance and not supported. Nonetheless, she secretly completed a correspondence business certificate.

As her children became young adults, while she was in her early 50s, Sarah decided to shift her work-related experiences and registered in a business administration university program, this time resisting the familiar strong opposition by her husband and parents (even clarifying she would be ready to put her marriage at risk). The educational program comprised a deeply meaningful experience for her as she was invited to reflect about her life and work, leading to the crystallization of her work mission of validating both her own and colleagues' talents within a job context. It is there that she linked her childhood experiences of "singing into emptiness" with her work history, an insight that again fueled her work-related passions. After completing her degree, in her mid-50s, Sarah was hired for an administrative job in a rural setting. Connected to her passions, she was clear that if her job did not provide a nurturing setting, she would follow her work mission through conducting workshops or writing a book about her work journey.

Gwen, a White woman in her late 60s who grew up in a working-class family, developed a heightened awareness of issues related to social justice in her early childhood through a close relationship with her grandmother. "My rebelliousness comes from Granny. She had an incredibly strong character and she fought for justice." Gwen was encouraged by her parents not to study but rather to marry early and raise children. For over a generation she was in a "sort of heterosexist and patriarchal" marriage, where she held a "deferent" role and where her interest in social justice was ridiculed. "When I had an opinion about injustices, his line was, 'Oh there she goes again, that's just your mom, boys, women are *hysterical*.'" A government-subsidized community-based course for stay-at-home mothers started a passionate process of university education, including graduate degrees, with a focus on antioppressive education and community-based activism. It is within this context that Gwen reconnected with her childhood passion for social justice, shaping her successful career in her late 50s and throughout her 60s as a professional within the field of education.

Enhancing Work Experience Through Outside Pursuits

At times, heightened awareness at mid- to older adulthood to issues of equity could lead not to new meaningful work opportunities but rather to actions that enhanced women's ongoing work experiences. Grace, a Black woman in her mid-50s, suffered hunger and unemployment after immigrating with her children from a country in East Africa to Canada. Having obtained vocational training in Africa and securing, after multiple years, a job in her vocation in Canada, she was keen on holding that job despite suffering daily racism. With her children grown, Grace's reflections about the adverse impact of racism at work ("I always think, am I in perfect order? Do I speak clearly enough?") guided her to initiate community-based educational sessions about her heritage, reinforcing a sense of pride. "I like people to know about our culture, history, the food we eat, the plants, trees, and everything that is unique to this place. It makes my life's journey more pleasant. I feel differently about myself."

Alice, a White woman in her late 60s, was not supported in pursuing education, which affected her self-concept. "I always remember my father saying that it was more important for boys to go to university. It made me feel less smart as my brothers, less special." As a young adult, she consequently pursued a course in a community college and ended up working as a low-paid educational assistant for most of her working life, always feeling "less smart." In her early 60s, as a mother of adult children, Alice took the Mensa test, became a Mensa member, and pursued undergraduate education. Although it was too late for her to change her low-paying job, her self-experience at, and outside of, work had shifted constructively.

Choosing a Social Justice Work Field

Viviane, a woman in her mid-50s, escaped from Vietnam in her early 20s and endured both homelessness and stays in several refugee camps in China before arriving in Canada. Although she had held several jobs in Canada, she described in her interviews that in that older phase of her life, she felt most connected to her mission of attending to people, especially women, who were homeless or under other forms of distress. She had therefore chosen to work at a community center. As she described, "I feel so bad when I see a homeless woman because of her needs. She is so much more vulnerable. . . . I enjoy helping people out, giving referrals to services."

Work–life missions related to countering inequity and resisting its internalization comprised important processes in which several older women engaged that sustained their passions toward their activities. These women pursued education in mid- to older adulthood, sometimes against all odds, at times needing to overcome long-held internalized negative self-beliefs about their talents or their worth. They further chose to pursue work and other activities that nurtured passions anchored in their life experiences, including those that took place during childhood. In pursuing these actions, the women used critical reflections about the impact of social experiences throughout their lives on their work–life and self-concept.

MISSIONS CONTINUED: TARGETING SOCIAL SCRIPTS AND STEREOTYPES

Learned, internalized social discourses shape women's engagement with the world around them, including in the domain of work (e.g., Fredrickson & Roberts, 1997; Ibarra et al., 2013; Piran, 2017). The study with older women revealed that during older adulthood, related to changed partnership relationships, new life experiences, and, at times, less ongoing scrutiny regarding appearance and other constraining social norms (Piran, 2017), women are mobilized to counter constraining social expectations. Work comprised one life domain where older women engaged in countering adverse social discourses.

Countering Social Expectations of Women's Bodies

The expectation that women live in their bodies as gazed-at and deficient objects is one femininity-related discourse internalized by women (Fredrickson & Roberts, 1997; Piran, 2017). This discourse disempowers women, reduces their agency in the world, and leads to an ongoing engagement in body repair. Several women, such as Nina and Gwen, found work in older adulthood to be a domain where their resistance to objectifying discourses was expressed and solidified, enhancing their connection to their work.

Nina, a White woman in her mid-60s, felt devastated in her late 50s when her husband asked her to "lose a bit of weight before we go to the conference." Initially, she was complicit with the objectification discourse. "I felt self-critical that I let him down, I felt bad about myself. . . . I went out and bought new, modern clothes, but I couldn't starve myself." Yet, gradually, she started to protest this injurious objectifying comment. "Am I an accessory? I don't want to fit your body image of what a woman should look like." The rift in the relationship at that time led to a divorce, and, like other women who went through a marital separation, Nina had to take on remunerated work outside of the home. Nina had not had the opportunity to pursue university education because her parents allocated their savings to educating her brothers and she married and had children early, while also moving a lot. Consequently, following the divorce, Nina took a job as a receptionist in a community center for women with negative body image and disordered eating patterns. This job has had a profound effect in supporting Nina with her passionate resistance to objectifying pressures. Reflecting about her own and other women's experiences, Nina has become a vocal resistor of the objectification of girls and women and has shifted to live in her body comfortably, accept the aging of the body, and engage in attuned self-care. Of this experience she commented,

> I think [the community center] helped me more than I gave to them. Being there made me aware of my body more than ever before because a comfort level with your body is essential to working with people who have such strong body image issues. I learned to see how sad it is that there are women who have given up so much to be what other people wanted them to be or to fit that image. All related to my experience with my husband. I have also become very aware of the diet food industry. How dangerous some foods and laxatives they sell in the pharmacy can be for you. . . . I think my body is a body of a woman in her 60s, I appreciate it. I'd never have plastic surgery, because I want to grow old gracefully.

Gwen similarly felt that work was one factor that supported her in living in her body, free of self-objectification. Other supportive factors included her social justice education, membership in lesbian communities, and age. She found herself keen to transmit to younger colleagues at work the value of freedom from appearance-related expectations. "I don't want my mentees to think that you need to wear make-up. Lots of time I don't wear it."

Countering Expectations That Women Prioritize Others Above Themselves

Similarly to combating objectification, several women countered, through work, other femininity-related social discourses, particularly discourses that I describe as belonging to the "woman as docile" cluster (Piran, 2017). Discourses in this cluster include, among others, social expectations that women be other- (rather than self-) attuned; subvert their own needs, wishes, and meaningful pursuits to those of boys and men; and act submissive or demure, attenuating their own power and passions. As with objectification, these discourses reduce women's agency in the world and compromise their self-concept.

Sonia's work-related story exemplifies the cost of another social discourse, namely the expectation that women (and sometimes girls) practice other-focused care, subverting their own wishes, pursuits, desires, and passions for the sake of the other; importantly, as the embodiment research reveals, this expectation is not buffered by a concurrent protective discourse of care of self (Piran, 2017). Sonia, a woman in her late 60s of South Asian heritage, immigrated as a young adult to Canada from a country in Africa. Sonia retired from a clerical job she had held for 20 years a short time before the research interviews; she subsisted on a small pension and on income from cooking for her neighbors. Sonia's work mission, prior to her retirement, had been to support others: her sick mother, her addicted husband, and additional family members. She described her typical workday: "After work, I'd get groceries, go to my mother's, cook and feed her, then go to my apartment, cook for my husband, return to mom, do the dishes and sit with her, then clean my own home." Sonia was consistently "stressed, tired, and depressed" at work and at home. Sonia complied with her cultural norms, whereby she was prohibited from cooking for her mother in the kitchen she and her husband shared; she therefore cooked two sets of meals daily, one in her own kitchen and one in her mother's kitchen.

Sonia retired from her office job after her mother, husband, and other family members of whom she took care died. Following her retirement, Sonia's work as a cook served a new mission, supporting attuned self-care and joy:

> Now it's me, me, me. Now I live alone by myself, and I can do whatever I want. If I don't want to cook, I don't cook. But I do cook these days for order from my neighbors to pay the bills. I sometimes go for a walk and use the sauna and steam room. When I'm tired, I go to bed. I watch TV in the bedroom. I go with friends for lunch or for shows or movies. During Christmas I worked really hard and so I made some money and I am going to visit my friend in [a state in the U.S.]. It's great. I feel, God you are great. Good things are working out for me.

Like Sonia, other women countered at an older age the exclusive care-of-others discourse and problematized the absence of a concurrent care-of-self discourse. This enabled them to continue working while maintaining a positive connection to their work and a sense of well-being.

Countering the Submissiveness Script

Countering the submissive/demure discourse comprised another continued journey for several older women, resulting in enhanced work experience. For example, May, a woman in her mid-50s, who arrived in Canada in her early adulthood as a refugee of the Vietnam War, described the long process of countering her early socialization as a girl in an upper-class home in Vietnam prior to the war. She described her compliance with learned expectations, noting, "I was a nice, shy girl," and later, as a wife to her ex-husband,

> You have to stay home and cook and give him his slippers, shut up, and be grateful and good for him; but I was tired, and, I am sorry, you have to share some jobs with me, because I was also working.

After her husband left her, May, who did not have a good command of the English language and was supporting young adult daughters in school, was forced by financial circumstances to hold three low-paying jobs for a total of 70 hours a week. May highlighted positive changes she saw in herself as a working woman following her divorce that differed strikingly from her early socialization. "I am not so shy, I talk to the customers, and I am very independent and very strong. I am not scared to talk even to my boss, I have my own right to say something." She felt that these shifts in the way she engaged with others at work gave her the opportunity to model strength to her daughters and to be protective of them when needed.

Countering Age and Scripts Related to Socioeconomic Status

Social scripts exist in relation to all dimensions of social location. Older women described having to counter age-related scripts to stay connected positively to work they chose to do. For example, Marie, a White woman in her 60s, described her process of countering the prejudicial "you are what you do" discourse that privileges younger, able-bodied people at the top of the professional field and deprecates people of lower socioeconomic and professional standing. After years of working in the health field, Marie retired, opting to live in a small farming community. Since her retirement, a short time prior to the research interviews, she felt that she had worked hard to counter the "you are what you do" discourse so that she could feel comfortable in her daily life on the farm and cherish her new chosen work. "A big part of society says, 'you are what you do,' and I'm cleaning the barn, so what am I? I am coming to the realization that I am not what I do. It's *what I am!*"

Countering constraining social discourses allowed these women in older adulthood to act more comfortably, passionately, and powerfully at work and comprised important continued missions. Being able to counter internalized social discourses at an older age, commonly discourses with which the women lived for most of their lives, is inspiring. Similar to countering inequity, the women's critical reflections at older adulthood about their life journeys facilitated such important shifts.

MISSIONS CONTINUED: TARGETING PHYSICAL CONSTRAINTS

Physical constrictions in women's lives, such as compromised safety, restricted freedom of movement in the public sphere, and opportunities to practice attuned care of the body, reduce women's experiences of agency and well-being (Piran, 2017). For several women, work-related goals and passions formed at mid- to older adulthood directly addressed these constraints.

Geographical Freedom

One area of physical constraint women talked about in relation to their work journeys involved the freedom to choose their geographical site of residence. Women were often under pressure by family members (parents, husbands) not to move away (or uproot their families) to cities or areas that held work opportunities for them and, instead, prioritize loyalty to family members' wishes or pursuits. In a similar vein, married women in heterosexual relationships were often expected to comply with repeated moves propelled by their husbands' work opportunities, disrupting their own education, professional development, or even support of family members in childrearing that could enable them to work.

Constraints related to geographical sites of residence were central to the work journeys of Sarah, Gwen, and Nina, as described previously. Louise's work-related story exemplifies the search for freedom in choosing sites of residence and in seeking freedom of movement in the public sphere. Louise, a woman in her mid-50s of mainly European as well as Aboriginal heritage, grew up in a rural site to a working-class family. She described that the most cherished aspects of her childhood were her physical freedom and an active immersion in her physical environment. "I was very active. Outside 24/7, playing, exploring. My mother did not care, we would come home at night, and she was already sleeping. This freedom in my body is still here, like a wild horse that lives outside."

Louise was so keen on maintaining her freedom that, following high school, she left her community; her family did not support vocational education for women and even made it difficult for her to get her own driver's license. Louise had been cut off from and considered the black sheep of the family for moving away and pursuing vocational education. "I am reprimanded for leaving. 'You move out, you are on your own. You go wherever the grass is greener. A woman stays home.'" Louise pursued an education as a lab technician during her early adulthood. Yet, she found the following 20 years, working as a technician and rearing children as a divorced woman, very confining to her. "When the children were small, I had to pay for a babysitter to do what I wanted." To respond to the "wild horse" in her and her joy of physical activities, once the children left for university, during her early 50s, she trained and became a passionate yoga instructor, a practitioner of holistic health, a marathon runner, and a traveler. To support her new passions, Louise changed her work to involve multiple part-time jobs. "I have multiple small contracts to teach. . . . I am grateful for every day."

Rest and Care of Self

Another physical constraint in relation to work that women at mid- to older adulthood addressed and that enhanced a positive connection to their work related to incorporating physical care of their bodies into their working lives. Prioritizing attuned care of the body often related to ending intense caregiving relationships, being confronted with different medical issues in self or others, assessing the costs of body neglect, and maintaining a stronger appreciation of the aging body. Gwen, for example, highlighted how much she appreciated the well-remunerated job she held only during her older adulthood for its focus on social justice and for allowing her and her partner to balance self-care with work. "It's the best time in my life, to have a job that I love, to have money enough to travel, to have time with family, to have down time, to have this balance." Reflecting about the demeaning objectification of her body by her husband, Nina developed a deep appreciation of maintaining a positive connection to her body while working with individuals with negative body image. "From my work I see how important it is to feel comfortable in your body. In yoga I feel comfortable, like an embrace, it's nurturing, not the gym where you strive to achieve something."

Sonia and May both worked as cooks. As described earlier, Sonia maintained a positive connection to her work by cooking to order in her own kitchen and by being able to tailor her workload to her need for rest. "Sometimes I have these orders and by the time I fill them I'm tired. So I just take a shower and go to bed. It is good now." May, who was employed out of the house, felt good about her cooking when she could balance it with proper rest at home, especially once her husband had moved out after a period of marital discord. When rested, she sometimes went to the library and read about cooking. "When I have free time, and I can rest, and I don't have to cook, I just go to the library. I enjoy reading cookbooks. I am a good cook."

Continued missions of older women, therefore, included valuing and pursuing opportunities to work in ways that responded to their physical needs and wishes. This allowed for maintaining a positive connection to work.

CONCLUSION

The financial challenges experienced by the women who participated in the research are in line with findings of large-scale studies with older women. The women faced multiple barriers to education and vocational training, inequitable pay and distribution of responsibilities related to the care of others, breakdown of relationships, immigration, and other challenges. The wide recognition of the financial plight of older women has propelled a call for systemic changes in the life of working women (e.g., Brown et al., 2016).

Within the context of these challenges, this study found that many of the women engaged in meaningful work-related journeys at an older age that helped them surpass barriers to meaningful work engagement—hence the opening phrase of the chapter title: "missions continued." These journeys should not be invisible. Rather, these ongoing missions are important because, first, many women continue to work past their mid-60s; second, they relate to women's well-being; and third, they are laden with information about processes that need to be validated and nurtured in women's ongoing work journeys. This chapter, which highlighted positive movement within the context of documented barriers, invites further dialogue and studies on these important phenomena, considering the inherent partial and situated nature of all constructed knowledge (Collins, 2000; Gannon & Davies, 2012).

The period of older adulthood is unique in that shifts in several constrictive systems in women's lives, coupled with a heightened awareness of health and longevity, lead women to reflect about their journeys, connecting with not only barriers but also with lifelong (including childhood) passions. In turn, these reflections guide the pursuit of uncompleted missions. In this chapter, I use the frame of the DTE (Piran, 2017), which is a lifelong theory, to describe domains of continued missions.

In terms of targeting social power and social justice, several older women sought to reverse lifelong barriers to education and to accessing relational, educational, and professional forums that could validate their talents and work–life passions. These continued missions clarified not only the value of access to education and skills training but also the critical value of communities of support and validation in sustaining work-related passions, success, and well-being. Furthermore, these journeys revealed that, as older women accessed such resources, they offered their workplaces unique knowledge anchored in rich life experiences.

Targeting social scripts by older women was another type of mission toward liberating agency, power, and self-attunement while at work. Countering long-held social scripts by older women is an inspiring process. Older women described enhanced awareness of losses accrued through adherence to these constraining discourses as well as insight about the ways in which these social scripts served to maintain the social status quo. It is of note that as women resisted learned scripts, they often highlighted the value of modeling such resistance to younger women.

Experiences in the physical domain were just as important to career paths. Indeed, older women described in great detail the way in which factors such as the physical freedom to choose their sites of residence and the ability to integrate attuned care of their bodies while working affected work–life achievements and well-being. Accordingly, several women prioritized continued missions in this domain by countering physical constraints. Indeed, recent publications have highlighted the value of addressing physical aspects of older women at work (e.g., Hardy et al., 2018).

Altogether, the chapter aims to make visible inspiring work–life missions in which older women engage, informed by their lifelong experiences. Although barriers to older women's work are often highlighted, continued, constructive work-related missions need to validate and inform both scholarly research and interventions in the domain of work.

REFERENCES

Brown, J. E., Rhee, N., Saad-Lessler, J., & Oakley, D. (2016, March). *Shortchanged in retirement: Continuing challenges to women's financial future.* National Institute on Retirement Security. http://laborcenter.berkeley.edu/pdf/2016/NIRS-Women-In-Retirement.pdf

Charmaz, K. (2006). *Constructing grounded theory: A practical guide through qualitative analysis.* Sage.

Cole, A. L., & Knowles, J. G. (2001). *Lives in context: The art of life history research.* Altamira.

Collins, P. H. (2000). *Black feminist thought: Knowledge, consciousness, and the politics of empowerment* (2nd ed.). Routledge.

Fredrickson, B. L., & Roberts, T. (1997). Objectification theory: Toward understanding women's lived experiences and mental health risks. *Psychology of Women Quarterly, 21*(2), 173–206. https://doi.org/10.1111/j.1471-6402.1997.tb00108.x

Gannon, S., & Davies, B. (2012). Postmodern, poststructural, and critical theories. In S. N. Hesse-Biber (Ed.), *Handbook of feminist research: Theory and praxis* (pp. 65–90). Sage.

Hardy, C., Hunter, M. S., & Griffiths, A. (2018). Menopause and work: An overview of UK guidance. *Occupational Medicine, 68*(9), 580–586. https://doi.org/10.1093/occmed/kqy134

Ibarra, H., Ely, R. J., & Kolb, D. M. (2013, September). Women rising: The unseen barriers. *Harvard Business Review.* https://hbr.org/2013/09/women-rising-the-unseen-barriers

Institute for Research on Poverty at the University of Wisconsin–Madison. (n.d.). *Who is poor?* https://www.irp.wisc.edu/resources/who-is-poor

Organisation for Economic Co-operation and Development. (2018). *Employment: Time spent in paid and unpaid work, by sex.* https://stats.oecd.org/index.aspx?queryid=54757

Piran, N. (2017). *Journeys of embodiment at the intersection of body and culture: The developmental theory of embodiment.* Elsevier Press.

12

OLDER IMMIGRANT WOMEN WHO WORK

Building Resilience, Changing Perceptions and Policies

JASMIN TAHMASEB MCCONATHA AND
FRAUKE SCHNELL

These days, it feels to me like you make a devil's pact when you walk into this country. You hand over your passport at the check-in, you get stamped, you want to make a little money, get yourself started . . . but you mean to go back! Who would want to stay? Cold, wet, miserable; terrible food, dreadful newspapers—who would want to stay? In a place where you are never welcomed, only tolerated. Just tolerated. Like you are an animal finally house-trained.

–Zadie Smith (2001, p. 407)

In a time when social tolerance is being challenged, discrimination against older immigrant workers is on the rise. In this troubling social climate, people migrate from place to place in search of refuge, safety, economic opportunity, and employment. In 21st-century America, immigration, both documented and undocumented, is a highly controversial topic. In 2017, there were more than 44.5 million immigrants in the United States, which means that one in seven U.S. residents is foreign-born (Camarota & Zeigler, 2018).

https://doi.org/10.1037/0000212-013
Older Women Who Work: Resilience, Choice, and Change, E. Cole and L. Hollis-Sawyer (Editors)

There are four main ways to enter the United States legally: through a family relationship, employment sponsorship, humanitarian protection (refugees or asylum seekers), and the diversity visa (DV) lottery. In contrast to popular belief, most immigrants are in the United States legally. Of the 45.6 million people that compose the United States' foreign-born population, 77% are lawful immigrants (Passel, 2019). Although immigrants come to the United States from around the globe, many come from Latin American countries where there are ongoing struggles with widespread poverty, corruption, gang violence, and social inequality. In addition to the legal foreign-born U.S. population, 10.5 million undocumented immigrants live within America (Passel, 2019). Roughly 67% of unauthorized immigrants came from Mexico and Central America; 16% from Asia; 6% from South America; 5% from Europe, Canada, or Oceania; and 3% from the Caribbean and Africa. Most unauthorized immigrants came from Mexico (53%), El Salvador (6%), Guatemala (5%), and China and Honduras (3% each; Batalova et al., 2020).

As the world is aging, people are living longer, including immigrants who are both legal and undocumented. In the past 20 years, the population of older immigrants in the United States has increased by 70% or from 2.7 million to 4.6 million (Population Reference Bureau [PRB], 2013). Older Latinos account for one of the largest increases in the older immigrant population (PRB, 2013). In 2030, they will constitute 22% of the population over the age of 65, compared with 8% of today's older adults (PRB, 2013). To understand the personal and economic needs of aging immigrant workers, it is important to explore the challenges and supports that enable older working immigrants to maintain their well-being, particularly when they age in homes far away from their home countries, their extended families, and their support systems.

In this chapter, we explore the concerns, stressors, and resilience of older Latina workers. Even in the best of circumstances, immigration and acculturation are stressful processes. When older immigrants are faced with discrimination compounded with possible health concerns associated with aging, the stressors are magnified. For older Latina immigrants, the difficulties may be compounded further as they face these difficult challenges while aging in a cultural framework that is very different from where they expected to age, in a social and cultural environment that may be alien and hostile to them. For this chapter, we rely on a broad definition of age; our analysis is not limited to retirees but focuses on older immigrant women, many of them still working, who are in their 50s and beyond.

Although some immigrants, mainly from East Asia and the Indian subcontinent, can be described as "the American success story," the majority of recent immigrants are people of color who left their homes seeking economic opportunities for themselves and their families. Many of these immigrants hope to eventually return "home" so they might become elders in their own communities and villages. This hope is one that is not often realized. Frequently immigrants must confront the social, physical, and existential issues of aging and dying in a culturally alien environment.

Numerous factors determine the adaptive success of new immigrants. The intersecting factors of language competence, cultural familiarity, education, economic conditions, health status and access to health care, and the presence (or absence) of social and emotional support all shape the immigrant experience at any age. Older Latina workers are particularly vulnerable; they often toil at low-paying jobs with little security or economic protection. Like many other immigrants of all ages, these working immigrant women must also confront increased anti-immigrant discrimination. Their day-to-day lives are filled with stress and anxiety. They are fearful of being victimized, which, in turn, has a negative impact on their well-being. As is discussed later, there is a dearth of social policies that support older workers, particularly older women immigrant workers. Their stories need to be told.

Well-being across adulthood, particularly in later adulthood, is shaped by the intersecting influences of personal, spiritual, social, environmental, and cultural circumstances. In the following pages, we discuss how these factors shape the life of Marta, an older immigrant woman from Ecuador. As this composite case illustrates, personal and social factors shape the stories of immigrants to the United States and elsewhere.

MARTA'S STORY

Marta is 61 years old. She comes from a large farming family in rural Ecuador. In her youth, she aspired to be a nurse, but her family fell on difficult times. She and two of her brothers needed to leave home to find work to support the family. She first arrived in the United States with a J-1 Exchange Visitor visa when she was in her early 20s. She worked briefly as a nanny for a well-to-do family who supported her desire to learn English. They helped her find free English classes in the evening at a local church. After 1 year in residence, Marta returned to Ecuador and applied for a visa to return to the United States. She was determined to make the move to the United States. When her visa was granted, she returned to America and moved in with a cousin. She found work as a housecleaner, working long hours, many of them of on her hands and knees cleaning house after house. The ongoing physical labor made her ache with pain. The cleaning chemicals she had to use bothered her sinuses. Even so, she persevered.

Her dream was to start her own cleaning business. She continued to live with her cousin to save money. As she accumulated savings, family members asked her to help pay their way into the United States. On one occasion, she gave a family member $5,000, on another occasion $10,000. These costs depleted her finances, but she did not resent aiding her family. In addition, she also regularly sent money to her aging parents and aunt. Eventually, Marta met a Mexican man. In Mexico, he had been a teacher. In America, he painted houses. Luckily, Marta was able to obtain permanent residency status through this gentleman because he was a green card holder. They married and had two children. In time and with much persistence, Marta started her cleaning business and hired teams of house cleaners. Several of her employees are undocumented workers who have been in the United States since early adulthood. Marta has struggled to pay her employees decent wages. For many years, Marta did not have health insurance, which meant that neither she nor her husband scheduled regular checkups. Eventually they purchased health insurance so that their children would have benefits. The additional expense created considerable family stress. Now in her 60s, Marta is still reasonably healthy. Her husband suffers from Type 2 diabetes and is no longer able to work regularly. Marta's business continues to generate enough income to support the family.

Not all is well, however. Years of manual labor have left her with chronic back pain and knee problems. How will she and her husband, she wonders, manage in their old age when they are no longer able to work? Although they paid Social Security, neither Marta or her husband will receive enough retirement income to provide for their own needs and those of their extended family in Ecuador and Mexico. They have also not been able to save sufficiently for retirement. Marta has no current plans to slow down, but she hopes that her children who are now working and going to community college will be able to help support her as well as two of her siblings who still live in rural Ecuador and need regular help.

Marta's life story illuminates the dynamic social and cultural tensions that are often at work in transnational families. She represents an example of someone who has relied on personal strength and resilience to survive and thrive. Marta has demonstrated the ability to cope with stressful life experiences (Tugade & Fredrickson, 2004). She has managed to confront the numerous obstacles that life placed on her path with reasonable optimism, and now as she approaches later life, she is still optimistic and views life positively.

Social science research has linked resiliency to a predisposition to ward off illness—even in adverse and stressful environments (Bonanno, 2005). For psychologists, resilience devolves from the notion of hardiness, which includes personality aspects of commitment, control, and challenge (Bartone, 2007; Kobasa et al., 1982). Resilient individuals such as Marta tend to use adaptive strategies to cope with difficult life circumstances. People like Marta also are less likely to become depressed or anxious and as such they are also less likely to experience burnout (Shatté et al., 2017).

Marta and women like her have had to confront a set of difficult choices between personal concerns and individual freedom and between individual desires and family obligation. Marta has successfully managed to cope with the demands of her family because she loves them and appreciates the support she receives in return. Mutual social support is helpful to people of all ages, but it becomes particularly important with older adults. The limited research that considers the well-being of aging Hispanic immigrant women suggests that they struggle with difficult work conditions, the absence of benefits and health insurance, and considerable fear and anxiety over their immigration status (Park et al., 2018). Even legal immigrants such as Marta have become fearful. Despite these very real problems, we have not heard their stories in the social science literature. As the case of Marta illustrates, older immigrant women all too often find themselves among the most vulnerable and disadvantaged segments of American society.

Like Marta, many Latin American women immigrated to the United States to escape poverty and provide a better life for themselves and their families. Many older immigrant workers arrived in the United States and, like Marta, struggled with language ability, lack of education, and a lack of cultural competence. Most of them worked hard year after year in various low-paying and insecure jobs. Generally, Latina immigrants tend to arrive in the United States during young adulthood and, although some have successful careers and adequate health care, many do not (National Academies of Sciences, Engineering, and Medicine, 2015).

It is important to note that although working immigrant women overall have a diverse socioeconomic profile in the workforce, most of them struggle at the bottom of the ladder. A lifetime of discriminatory treatment tends to block their upward mobility. As a disadvantaged group, older working immigrant women also become victims of the intersecting prejudices of age, gender, and immigration status (Friedman, 2012). With age, the cumulative stressful effects of low-paying and physically challenging jobs begin to have detrimental effects on their health and well-being. Historically, immigrants to the United States live longer and tend to be healthier than do native-born Americans (Markides & Rote, 2019; Riosmena et al., 2018). This trend, however, is changing, as the "healthy immigrant effect" appears to be dissipating. Years of difficult labor conditions, discrimination, and lack of access to health care has resulted in an aging population that is struggling with acute and chronic health conditions. In later life these conditions may also lead them to isolation, loneliness, and increased caregiving responsibilities for other family members (Treas & Mazumdar, 2002).

WELL-BEING, RESILIENCE, AND CONTROL

Throughout her struggles, Marta has maintained a degree of control over her life circumstances. Now as she is adapting to age-related changes, she also struggles to adapt to physiological, social, and environmental changes. One of the most important factors that determines individual reaction to the social environment is a person's perception of resilience, competence, and control (Troy & Mauss, 2011). The attempt to maintain a sense of competence and control in one's life is an important challenge for people of all ages, but older immigrant women may be more at risk for loss of resilience, competence, and control, especially as they face the possibility of poor health, economic challenges, and discrimination (Guruge et al., 2015).

One threat to the well-being of aging immigrant working women is social isolation (McConatha & Volkwein-Caplan, 2011; Steptoe et al., 2013). Social isolation is characterized by feelings of exclusion from the sociocultural environment. The risk of social isolation increases with age, especially if accompanied by discriminatory treatment and powerlessness. Feeling socially isolated can result in further physical deterioration, mental illness, and even premature death. The key defense against social isolation seems to be networks of social support and resources, a network that has helped Marta. Many immigrants have left their families behind and lack the support they need during difficult and stressful times. Personal and social resources develop and maintain feelings of integration. Support from family and friends and access to services such as health care, transportation, and language classes serve as buffers against the negative effects of stressful life events (Treas & Mazumdar, 2002). As Marta's case illustrates, close family relationships can serve as a buffer in difficult times (Rook & Charles, 2017).

Hobfoll and colleagues' (1990) social support resource theory considers how people obtain and protect their personal and social resources. In times of stress, these resources are perceived as buffers because they provide a person with a sense of control in a chaotic situation and help manage feelings of pain and anxiety. Friends and family can be very helpful with everyday stressors. Having access to such support can help older working women feel more resilient and competent in coping with aging-related changes (Vassilev et al., 2011). Many working immigrant women who do not have access to the personal, familial, and economic resources that Marta worked hard to develop and maintain may find themselves feeling helpless and socially isolated.

THE INTERPLAY OF INEQUALITIES

As shown throughout this chapter, older immigrant women's experiences are influenced by a confluence of factors, including race, class, immigration status, age, and gender. Most immigrant working women in the United States today are likely to come from ethnic minority groups and lower socioeconomic backgrounds (Radford & Noe-Bustamante, 2019). They are likely to have less formal education and not be proficient in English. These conditions exacerbate their disadvantaged status and leave them vulnerable. Race, class, and gender are typically the three factors highlighted in intersectionality studies (e.g., Calasanti & Giles, 2018; Crenshaw, 1991). In addition to these variables, widespread ageism leads to further exclusions in the political, social, cultural, and economic realms. As Calasanti (2003) argued, to be old is to be socially excluded from full citizenship. Being an immigrant adds a myriad of additional structural barriers, including, but not limited to, the constant threat of deportation, disadvantages in the labor market, and lack of access to health care.

In addition to these barriers, older Latina immigrants such as Marta are likely to experience discriminatory hostility. Many immigrants, especially those from Central and South America, are often cast as aliens who are unable or unwilling to assimilate (García, 2017). García's study of Mexican American women shows that they are often assumed to be undocumented, regardless of their immigration status. Even documented immigrants are often likely to be seen as illegal because the public overestimates the number of illegal immigrants. Those who look and speak differently are likely to be identified as being in the country illegally. In reality, lawful immigrants account for about three quarters of the foreign-born population. Fewer than half of Americans, however, know that most immigrants in the United States are here legally (Cohn, 2017).

This popular perception of illegality is closely linked to the public discourse of immigrants from Latin American presenting a threat to national identity (Chavez, 2013). According to this popular narrative, immigrants from Latin

American, unlike previous generations of mostly European immigrants, prefer to be linguistically and socially isolated (e.g., Huntington, 2004).

This rhetoric contributes to shaping people's views about immigrants and also has implications for how immigrants and U.S.-born Mexican and Latin Americans feel about their own social position and sense of belonging (Massey & Sánchez, 2010). For example, a 2018 Pew Research Center survey (Lopez et al., 2018) indicated that 51% of Latino and Latina immigrants have serious concerns about their place in America. This is also reflected in the reality of their lived experiences. The same Pew Research Center study revealed that nearly four in 10 Latina and Latino immigrants say that they have experienced discrimination, such as being victimized and criticized for speaking Spanish or being told to go back to their own country.

How can the impact of these multiple barriers to economic success and well-being be reduced? In terms of successful aging practices, the factors that are typically discussed focus on the importance of maintaining physical and mental health, strong social relationships, and civic and community engagement. These important factors are addressed in this book. In the remainder of this chapter, we highlight the importance of public policies tailored toward the needs of older adults, women, and immigrants, as well as the significant role public discourse plays in shaping how others perceive immigrants and how this shapes their self-perception and feelings of resilience and vulnerability.

IMMIGRATION POLICY PRESCRIPTIONS FOR AGING IMMIGRANT WORKERS

Ageism in the workplace is widespread. Despite the Age Discrimination in Employment Act (2012) prohibiting employers from making employment decisions based on age, age discrimination remains a pervasive force in the workplace. Although the most blatant forms of discrimination such as mandatory retirement and maximum hiring ages are distant memories, more subtle forms still exist. These subtler forms of age discrimination suggest that although employers may overtly attempt to comply with the law, stereotypes about aging continue to taint their practices.

The most common misconceptions about older workers like Marta are that they are less productive, more expensive, less adaptable, and more rigid and that they do not really want to work but would rather retire as soon as possible. This cultural climate of ageism in America is so firmly entrenched that it is virtually impossible to avoid the social and profession pitfalls of this kind of widely acceptable discrimination. Although civil rights protections such as the Age Discrimination in Employment Act offer some very limited safeguards to older working adults, they offer little to no recourse to immigrant women who are more likely to work in jobs that are physically very demanding and where age may well affect their ability to perform. In a similar vein, Title VII protections against discrimination based on race, sex, national origin, or religion often do not offer protections to immigrant women. Currently, this legislation applies only to employers with more than 15 employees; thus, it does not cover many workers employed by small farms, businesses, or households. Employers can also circumvent this legislation by classifying their workers as independent contractors.

None of these policies apply to legal and illegal immigrants who work in the informal economy where exploitative and illegal practices abound. Such hiring practices allow employers to ignore prohibitions on hiring illegal workers and avoid minimum wage laws and insurance requirements. Domestic and care work is one of the employment sectors most affected by this practice. Moreover, even if documented immigrants perform this type of work, the 1935 National Labor Relations Act does not cover them. Thus, many domestic workers face slave-like working conditions; they are not protected from racial discrimination and sexual harassment and have no right to days off, overtime, or paid leave.

Forty-five percent of private household workers are immigrants, with lawful immigrants slightly outnumbering unauthorized immigrants (DeSilver, 2017). Ninety-five percent of these workers are female. A federal domestic workers bill of rights would go a long way in addressing the concerns of these workers (Domestic Workers Bill of Rights Act, 2019–2020). At the time of this writing, similar legislation has already been passed by eight states, addressing the right to overtime pay, breaks, and sick leave. It guarantees the protections mandated by the Occupational Safety and Health Administration and the right to form unions, and it contains recourse against harassment and discrimination. In addition, it increases access to retirement benefits, thus greatly expanding immigrant women's economic safety net.

CHANGING THE NARRATIVE ABOUT IMMIGRANTS

Any attempt to address the system of oppression faced by older immigrant women like Marta also requires the reframing of the immigration debate. There is much research attesting to the fact that the public often holds conflicting and fragmented attitudes on many issues and that public opinion can greatly vary depending on how the issue is defined and interpreted (e.g., Callaghan & Schnell, 2005; Chong & Druckman, 2007; Ryan & Gamson,

2006). Research on framing effects first analyzes the dominant frames created by the media and other political elites. This is typically followed up with an experimental approach that examines the impact different frames have on how the public perceives the issue.

Haynes et al.'s (2016) comprehensive analysis of media coverage of the immigration issue from 2007 to 2016 documents that frames differ starkly between news organizations in ways that reveal their political leaning. Mainstream and liberal media outlets were slightly more likely to avoid the term *illegal* in favor of *undocumented*. The term *illegal* was the language of choice for more conservative media outlets. In terms of coverage of the issue, mainstream and liberal media generally focused mostly on human-interest stories, many of them involving children. On the other hand, conservative media sources such as Fox News prioritized statistics about illegal immigration and often used the amnesty frame, invoking the image of immigrants breaking the nation's laws.

The body of research on the framing of immigration politics suggests that policy frames can have a profound impact on public opinion (Haynes et al., 2016; Lecheler et al., 2015). Exposure to language portraying immigrants as lawbreakers seeking amnesty led to more support for deportation and other strict immigration measures than did immigration coverage based on human-interest type of stories. On the other hand, research participants who were exposed to stories highlighting the plight or contributions of individual immigrants displayed more support for legalization. Frames that described the DREAM (Development, Relief and Education for Alien Minors) Act by referring to immigrants who came over as young children were particularly effective in decreasing support for strict immigration measures (Merolla et al., 2013).

This research suggests significant evidence that the framing of the immigration debate matters. Nevertheless, it also shows that the success of framing to change the hearts and minds of Americans is limited because it requires exposure to varying frames. Ample evidence suggests that citizens have migrated to the ends of the liberal–conservative scale and that people select the media environment that is most supportive of their political views (e.g., Iyengar & Hahn, 2009). Conservative media are the dominant choice of conservative citizens; more liberal-leaning members of the public are more likely to be attracted to media sources such as CNN or MSNBC. This selective exposure to different media influences the types of frames consumers receive and reinforces already existing attitudes. This effect is only likely to strengthen as consumers are increasingly able to customize their news content.

Similarly, negative perceptions of older adults in the media are pervasive (Adams-Price & Morse, 2009; McConatha et al., 1999), and attitudes about aging are also impacted by framing (Busso et al., 2019). This means that exposure to examples of frames that include counterstereotypic descriptions of aging and older adults can lead to reductions in negative stereotypes and age bias. This suggests that there are significant opportunities for communicators and advocates to shape the public's perceptions of the aging process and older adults.

CONCLUSION

This chapter has illustrated the plight of older immigrant women and detailed the intersectional prejudices of age, class, gender, and immigration status on their well-being. These factors often result in their economic, social, and cultural marginalization. The case of Marta, a Latina immigrant from Ecuador, demonstrates that social support systems can alleviate much of the stress associated with marginalized status. We also argue that if barriers to the economic success of immigrant women are to be successfully lowered, there needs to be increased advocacy for public policies that are friendly to the aging immigrant population. Last, cultural change requires a symbolic reframing of the immigration issue that not only underscores the resiliency of immigrants but also highlights their contributions and sacrifices.

REFERENCES

Adams-Price, C. E., & Morse, L. W. (2009). Dependency stereotypes and aging: The implications for getting and giving help in later life. *Journal of Applied Social Psychology, 39*(12), 2967–2984. https://doi.org/10.1111/j.1559-1816.2009.00557.x

Age Discrimination in Employment Act, 29 U.S.C. § 629 *et seq.* (2012), as amended by P. L. 102-166.

Bartone, P. T. (2007). Test-retest reliability of the dispositional resilience scale-15, a brief hardiness scale. *Psychological Reports, 101*(3), 943–944. https://doi.org/10.2466/pr0.101.3.943-944

Batalova, J., Blizzard, B., & Bolter, J. (2020, February 14). *Frequently requested statistics on immigrants and immigration in the United States.* https://www.migrationpolicy.org/article/frequently-requested-statistics-immigrants-and-immigration-united-states

Bonanno, G. A. (2005). Resilience in the face of potential trauma. *Current Directions in Psychological Science, 14*(3), 135–138. https://doi.org/10.1111%2Fj.0963-7214.2005.00347.x

Busso, D. S., Volmert, A., & Kendall-Taylor, N. (2019). Reframing aging: Effect of a short-term framing intervention on implicit measures of age bias. *The Journals of Gerontology: Series B, 74*(4), 559–564. https://doi.org/10.1093/geronb/gby080

Calasanti, T. (2003). Theorizing age relations. In S. Biggs, A. Lowenstein, & J. Hendricks (Eds.), *The need for theory: Critical approaches to social gerontology for the 21st Century* (pp. 199–218). Baywood.

Calasanti, T., & Giles, S. (2018). The challenges of intersectionality. *Generations, 41*(4), 69–74.

Callaghan, K., & Schnell, F. (2005). *Framing American politics*. University of Pittsburgh. https://doi.org/10.2307/j.ctt6wrbqk

Camarota, S., & Zeigler, K. (2018, September 15). Record 44.5 million immigrants in 2017: Non-Mexico Latin American, Asian, and African populations grew the most. Center for Immigration Studies. https://cis.org/Report/Record-445-Million-Immigrants-2017

Chavez, L. (2013). *The Latino threat: Constructing immigrants, citizens, and the nation*. Stanford University Press.

Chong, D., & Druckman, J. N. (2007). Framing public opinion in competitive democracies. *The American Political Science Review, 101*(4), 637–655. https://doi.org/10.1017/S0003055407070554

Cohn, D. (2017, August 3). *5 key facts about U.S. lawful immigrants*. Pew Research Center. https://www.pewresearch.org/fact-tank/2017/08/03/5-key-facts-about-u-s-lawful-immigrants

Crenshaw, K. (1991). Mapping the margins: Intersectionality, identity politics, and violence against women of color. *Stanford Law Review, 43*(6), 1241–1299. https://doi.org/10.2307/1229039

DeSilver, D. (2017, March 16). *Immigrants don't make up a majority of workers in any U.S. industry*. Pew Research Center. https://www.pewresearch.org/fact-tank/2017/03/16/immigrants-dont-make-up-a-majority-of-workers-in-any-u-s-industry

Domestic Workers Bill of Rights Act, S.2112, 116th Congress (2019–2020). https://www.congress.gov/bill/116th-congress/senate-bill/2112/text

Friedman, S. H. (2012). Loneliness. In S. Louse & M. Sakatovic (Eds.), *Encyclopedia of immigrant health*. Springer. https://doi.org/10.1007/978-1-4419-5659-0_470

García, S. J. (2017). Racializing "illegality": An intersectional approach to understanding how Mexican-origin women navigate an anti-immigrant climate. *Sociology of Race and Ethnicity (Thousand Oaks, Calif.), 3*(4), 474–490. https://doi.org/10.1177/2332649217713315

Guruge, S., Birpreet, B., & Samuels-Dennis, J. A. (2015). Health status and health determinants of older immigrant women in Canada: A scoping review. https://doi.org/10.1155/2015/393761

Haynes, C., Merolla, J., & Ramakrishnan, S. K. (2016). *Framing immigrants: News coverage, public opinion, and policy*. Russell Sage.

Hobfoll, S. E., Freedy, C. L., & Geller, P. (1990). Conservation of social resources: Social support resource theory. *Journal of Social and Personal Relationships, 7*(4), 465–478. https://doi.org/10.1177%2F0265407590074004

Huntington, S. P. (2004). The Hispanic challenge. *Foreign Policy, 141*, 30–45. https://doi.org/10.2307/4147547

Iyengar, S., & Hahn, K. (2009). Red media, blue media: Evidence of ideological selectivity in media use. *Journal of Communication, 59*(1), 19–39. https://doi.org/10.1111/j.1460-2466.2008.01402.x

Kobasa, S. C., Maddi, S. R., & Kahn, S. (1982). Hardiness and health: A prospective study. *Journal of Behavioral Medicine, 6*, 41–51. https://doi.org/10.1037/0022-3514.42.1.168

Lecheler, S., Bos, L., & Vliegenthart, R. (2015). The mediating role of emotions: News framing effects on opinions about immigration. *Journalism & Mass Communication Quarterly, 92*(4), 812–838. https://doi.org/10.1177%2F1077699015596338

Lopez, M. H., Gonzalez-Barrera, A., & Krogstad, J. M. (2018, October 25). *More Latinos have serious concerns about their place in America under Trump.* Pew Research Center. https://www.pewhispanic.org/2018/10/25/more-latinos-have-serious-concerns-about-their-place-in-america-under-trump

Markides, K. S., & Rote, S. (2019). The healthy immigrant effect and aging in the United States and other western countries. *The Gerontologist, 59*(2), 205–214. https://doi.org/10.1093/geront/gny136

Massey, D. S., & Sánchez, M. R. (2010). *Brokered boundaries: Creating immigrant identity in anti-immigrant times.* Russell Sage.

McConatha, J. T., Schnell, F., & McKenna, A. (1999). Description of older adults as depicted in magazine advertisements. *Psychological Reports, 85*(3), 1051–1056. https://doi.org/10.2466/pr0.1999.85.3.1051

McConatha, J. T., & Volkwein-Caplan, K. (2011). Community and well-being among older women in the Russia diaspora. *Making connections: Interdisciplinary approaches to cultural diversity.* Pennsylvania State System of Higher Education and the Frederick Douglass Institute Collaborative.

Merolla, J., Ramakrishnan, S. K., & Haynes, C. (2013). "Illegal," "undocumented," or "unauthorized": Equivalency frames, issue frames, and public opinion on immigration. *Perspectives on Politics, 11*(3), 789–807. https://doi.org/10.1017/S1537592713002077

National Academies of Sciences, Engineering, and Medicine. (2015). *The integration of immigrants into American society.* The National Academies Press.

National Labor Relations Act, 29 U.S.C. §§ 151–169 (1935).

Park, H., Choi, E., & Wenzel, J. A. (2018). Racial/ethnic differences in correlates of psychological distress among five Asian-American subgroups and non-Hispanic Whites. *Ethnicity & Health, 1*–17. https://doi.org/10.1080/13557858.2018.1481495

Passel, J. (2019). *Measuring illegal immigration: How Pew Research Center counts unauthorized immigrants in the U.S. Pew Research Center.* Pew Research Center. https://www.pewresearch.org/fact-tank/2019/07/12/how-pew-research-center-counts-unauthorized-immigrants-in-us

Population Reference Bureau. (2013, October 31). *Elderly immigrants in the United States.* https://www.prb.org/us-elderly-immigrants

Radford, J., & Noe-Bustamante, L. (2019, June 3). *Facts on U.S. Immigrants, 2017: Statistical portrait of the foreign-born population in the United States.* Pew Research Center. https://www.pewhispanic.org/2019/06/03/facts-on-u-s-immigrants-trend-data

Riosmena, F., Kuhn, R., & Jochem, W. C. (2018). Explaining the immigrant health advantage: Self-selection and protection in health-related factors among five major national-origin immigrant groups in the united states. *Demography, 54*(1), 175–200. https://doi.org/10.1007/s13524-016-0542-2

Rook, K. S., & Charles, S. T. (2017). Close social ties and health in later life: Strengths and vulnerabilities. *American Psychologist, 72*(6), 567–577. https://doi.org/10.1037/amp0000104

Ryan, C., & Gamson, W. (2006). The art of reframing political debates. *Contexts, 5*(1), 13–18. https://doi.org/10.1525/ctx.2006.5.1.13

Shatté, A., Perlman, A., Smith, B., & Lynch, W. D. (2017). The positive effect of resilience on stress and business outcomes in difficult work environments. *Journal of Occupational and Environmental Medicine, 59*(2), 135–140. https://doi.org/10.1097/JOM.0000000000000914

Smith, Z. (2001). *White teeth*. Penguin Books.

Steptoe, A., Shankar, A., Demakakos, P., & Wardle, J. (2013). Social isolation, loneliness, and all-cause mortality in older men and women. *Proceedings of the National Academy of Sciences of the United States of America, 110*(15), 5797–5801. https://doi.org/10.1073/pnas.1219686110

Treas, J., & Mazumdar, S. (2002). Older people in America's immigrant families: Dilemmas of dependence, integration, and isolation. *Journal of Aging Studies, 16*(3), 243–258. https://doi.org/10.1016/S0890-4065(02)00048-8

Troy, A. S., & Mauss, I. B. (2011). Resilience in the face of stress: Emotion regulation as a protective factor. In S. M. Southwick, B. T. Litz, D. Charney, & M. J. Friedman (Eds.), *Resilience and mental health: Challenges across the lifespan* (pp. 30–44). Cambridge University Press. https://doi.org/10.1017/CBO9780511994791.004

Tugade, M. M., & Fredrickson, B. L. (2004). Resilient individuals use positive emotions to bounce back from negative emotional experiences. *Journal of Personality and Social Psychology, 86*(2), 320–333. https://doi.org/10.1037/0022-3514.86.2.320

Vassilev, I., Rogers, A., Sanders, C., Kennedy, A., Blickem, C., Protheroe, J., Bower, P., Kirk, S., Chew-Graham, C., & Morris, R. (2011). Social networks, social capital and chronic illness self-management: A realist review. *Chronic Illness, 7*(1), 60–86. https://doi.org/10.1177/1742395310383338

13

USE IT OR LOSE IT

Older Women and Civic Engagement

LISA HOLLIS-SAWYER

What exactly do we mean by civic engagement? It can mean stepping forward to participate in our communities, providing leadership to solve problems, set priorities, and get things done. Granted, not every woman is in a position to run for office, but there are lots of ways—such as writing letters to the Editor or joining in social media discussions—to make our voices heard, and it's important that we are informed and engaged citizens.

—Lynn Yeakel, *Is Civic Engagement an On-Ramp to the Women's Equality Expressway?*

According to the U.S. Bureau of Labor Statistics (2016), older adults make up approximately 23.5% of all volunteers, and women continue to volunteer at a higher rate than do men. Because a lower percentage of older adults are employed in work for pay compared with younger adults, it would seem to follow that aging adults should be more engaged than younger generations through volunteerism and other civic engagement activities (Scharf et al.,

https://doi.org/10.1037/0000212-014
Older Women Who Work: Resilience, Choice, and Change, E. Cole and L. Hollis-Sawyer (Editors)

2016; Warburton et al., 2013). However, the numbers suggest otherwise. Giving a voice to a segment of the population who may feel ignored and invisible is critical for the growth and development of the graying world population. Demographic trends of the baby boom generation succeeded by the baby bust generation have resulted in an imbalance in financial support ratios (e.g., the support ratio of active workers to the number of retirees in the Social Security system) and other support ratios (e.g., the number of available caregivers to care for the number of aging care recipients). In view of these trends, volunteerism among baby boomers is an important and relatively untapped resource that benefits the social, emotional, and physical health needs of this large aging population (Harvard School of Public Health–MetLife Foundation Initiative on Retirement and Civic Engagement, 2004).

Increased community engagement among older women can help address their financial and/or social support needs because they can gain opportunities toward continued employment and/or social networks (e.g., social capital through community engagement; Son et al., 2010). For example, involvement in religious organizations may be one of those important social contexts for such civic and social engagement for aging women (and men) in many different cultures and communities (Hendricks & Cutler, 2001). Increased civic engagement and community political involvement can also bring positive attention to the social issues of aging women in many industrialized nations. For example, the Older Women's League's political message is "Don't agonize—Organize!" (Martinson & Minkler, 2006). Becoming civically engaged may assist in women's processes of aging adaptation and associated self-exploration beginning as early as midlife (Rubin, 1979). The holistic outcomes of being mentally, socially, and psychologically engaged within one's social environment through civic engagement activities are discussed in the remainder of this chapter.

OLDER WOMEN'S CIVIC ENGAGEMENT AND THE "USE IT OR LOSE IT" PRINCIPLE

Civic engagement, defined as the active involvement of individuals within the functioning of society, is an evolving concept, and it has interesting implications for the role of individuals in the broader society (Evers & von Essen, 2019; Minkler & Holstein, 2008; Wray-Lake et al., 2019). Civic engagement for older women can take many forms, ranging from internet use (Bo, 2008) to physical activities (e.g., swimming, running) and face-to-face neighborhood participation (Cagney & Cornwell, 2010). Hinterlong

(2008) emphasized the social issue of "productive engagement" among older Americans, suggesting that societal support among aging adults is important for both the functioning of society and public policy processes. Another way to think of productive engagement is by likening it to the "use it or lose it" principle behind physical activity and rehabilitation. It is important for older adults, as well as anyone across the lifespan, to engage in activities that stimulate their mental and physical functioning on a daily basis. In a review of related studies, Hogan (2005) discussed the mind–body connection that can be supported through exercise activities designed around aging adults' needs and capabilities. This mind–body connection is a key component for positive aging and later-life health outcomes (Bashore, 1990; Kramer et al., 2000). The use it or lose it concept can be applied to civic engagement and community involvement for older women, providing both physical and mental health outcomes (Ackerman et al., 2010) as well as the benefits of older adults' engagement for the broader community (Hinterlong & Williamson, 2006).

Volunteerism and civic engagement are powerful conduits to older women's daily physical, mental, and social well-being (Bowen et al., 2000; Dowling, 1997). Although the motivation to become involved in community activities and causes can be lifelong, beginning in childhood and adolescence (e.g., high school volunteerism; Greenfield & Moorman, 2018), for many this motivation begins in later life. In fact, new learning of activities is a significant aspect of healthy aging (Park & Reuter-Lorenz, 2009). Engaging in community-involved volunteerism and civic activities has been associated with lowered cardiovascular disease incidence (Burr et al., 2018), decreased issues of physical disability over time (Carr, Kail, & Rowe, 2018), better cognitive functioning (Guiney & Machado, 2018; Proulx et al., 2018), and increased positive coping and social engagement (Carr, 2018; Carr, Kail, Matz-Costa, & Shavit, 2018). See Appendix 13.1 for famous quotes by older women about civic engagement.

SELF-REGULATION AND CIVIC ENGAGEMENT

One theory associated with the concept of continual cognitive engagement is self-regulation theory (Kuyper et al., 2000). Self-regulation theory purports that individuals undergo a systematic process of anchoring and adjusting while learning and conducting performance tasks in response to corrective feedback within their social and physical environment that impacts both adaptation and feelings of personal self-efficacy (Cervone & Peake, 1986; Tversky & Kahneman, 1974). Application of this theory to the successful aging trajectory of older women, the processes of enhanced self-awareness of one's current performance, and an understanding of ways to perform better considering aging-related changes is important to explore within the context of lifelong learning (Clark et al., 2000; Lightfoot & Brady, 2005).

A real-world application of this self-regulation concept would be community-based programs that teach older women how best to improve their quality of life through civic engagement to achieve prolonged independence, expanded social networks, and a desired level of mental and physical activity (e.g., see "individual thriving" outcomes in Lerner et al., 2014). For program development and intervention purposes, it is critical to understand longitudinal factors predicting the degree to which older women are actively engaged in social activities (e.g., community participation at age 80 in Holahan & Chapman, 2002). To ensure that their voice is heard regarding needs and motivations, aging women need to be socially and civically engaged in community activities and processes (e.g., see "voting in politics" in Turner et al., 2001).

PERSONAL AND SOCIAL BENEFITS OF OLDER WOMEN'S ACTIVE ENGAGEMENT

Ongoing daily physical activity has multiple positive impacts on aging women's cognitive functioning across many different performance domains, such as decision making (Netz et al., 2011), as well as feelings and psychological well-being (Netz et al., 2005). A lack of ongoing daily activities that engage one's body and mind can exacerbate cognitive and attentional declines into later life. Pesce et al. (2011), for example, wrote about older athletes' declines in attentional capacity. The same idea of maintaining physical and cognitive functioning capabilities can be applied to the rate of physical and mental decline within a continuing care facility (see exercise program usage, as described in Baum et al., 2003), which emphasizes again the importance of the use it or lose it principle. The degree to which older women can and do engage in mentally and physically challenging activities on a regular basis is a quality-of-life issue that communities and broader societies across the world should address through programs and policies supporting such activities (Resnick, 2001). Older women's civic engagement can have many social benefits for all aspects of society (Tan et al., 2010; Tang et al., 2010), which suggests the importance, if not urgency, of public policy initiatives to help create and maintain age-friendly communities and broader societies (Bushway et al., 2011).

Public policies and institutions within communities should better encourage and support the civic engagement activities of aging women because of the quality-of-life outcomes for women (Cutler & Hendricks, 2000; Enguidanos et al., 2010; Gonzales & Morrow-Howell, 2009; Mukherjee, 2011; Rozanova et al., 2012). Women's lives and their adjustment to later-life transitions can be improved through volunteerism activities (Parkinson et al., 2010; Rawsthorne et al., 2017). Additionally, one might argue that older women's civic engagement creates a higher social valuation of their role(s) in society (e.g., Martinez et al., 2011; Morrow-Howell, 2010) as well as helps them in their transitioning in later life from a work role to a retirement role (Kaskie et al., 2008; Lancee & Radl, 2012). The following subsections review the benefits of active aging through civic engagement.

Intergenerational Learning and Mentoring

One very important outcome of social engagement is increased exposure to other age groups and cohorts. This mutual learning and intergenerational sharing of ideas can be beneficial to both younger and older generations (Kleiber & Nimrod, 2008). Interacting with others and communicating ideas can be a productive form of cognitive stimulation that can help older women maintain cognitive competency over time, barring of course any non-normative or genetic issues (Anderson & Dabelko-Schoeny, 2010; Chappell, 2005), and can enhance relationships within many different contexts, including their own family (Davey et al., 2004).

Sharing of ideas, activities, and interests enhances the quality of life of all age groups involved, demystifying the aging process while increasing gerocompetencies for younger women (see Dauenhauer et al., 2010) and adding meaning to later life for older women through engaging in meaningful activities (Eakman et al., 2010). Insights from such exposure to different cultures and people through service-learning activities may benefit younger women in becoming more culturally sensitive when interacting with aging generations (Hegeman et al., 2010; Horowitz et al., 2010; Jones et al., 2010; Zucchero, 2011) as well as possibly their own aging trajectories. For example, the physical health of younger generations can be positively impacted through a close, positive mentoring relationship with experienced older women health professionals (Simson et al., 2008).

Extended Social Support Resources

Being civically engaged in the community and broader cultural contexts benefits lower income older women because they can become empowered to access and maintain social support and other resources when they may otherwise lack such resources because of economic conditions (McBride et al., 2006; Ziegler, 2012). For example, involvement in religious activities through a church, synagogue, or mosque can be a wonderful opportunity for older women's active civic engagement and exposure to different social support contacts that have the potential to positively impact their longevity (e.g., Hill et al., 2005, described this benefit for Mexican American adults).

Through volunteering, older women can better maintain social connections with different community groups. These groups will benefit from the experience and knowledge of this large aging subpopulation of women. In turn, these different community groups may share information and resources benefiting older women (Meier & Stutzer, 2008; Wilson & Musick, 1999). Social exchange theory (Emerson, 1976) suggests that it is advantageous to establish and maintain social relationships that offer benefits to us. The civic engagement and community involvement of older women would assist in optimizing the social exchange process for positive aging outcomes.

Active Social Participation

Active involvement of older women in society is beneficial to all, but it is important to tailor social activities to best motivate and match the interests and attitudes of those involved to ensure that the positive benefits and usefulness of the activities are apparent (Leedahl et al., 2011; Morrow-Howell et al., 2009; Okamoto & Tanaka, 2004). Older women who participate as "Polar Bear" swimmers every cold winter in Martha's Vineyard do so because they perceive an inherent, meaningful benefit to engaging in this physical activity that may not appeal to other groups of older women (Peters, 2012). It is critical for aging women to "know thyself" during the aging process and choose civic activities that have a meaning to their lives to assist in achieving personal successful aging outcomes.

It has been argued from an activity theory perspective (Kelly, 1993) that older women would benefit from the social civic engagement on the psychological, social, physical, and emotional levels (Duke et al., 2002; Gottlieb & Gillespie, 2008). Successful physical, cognitive, and psychological aging of women can be optimized through active engagement in daily tasks (Menec, 2003; Piercy et al., 2011; Pillemer et al., 2010; Wahrendorf et al., 2010; Walter-Ginzburg et al., 2002). For example, Zunzunegui et al. (2003) stated that active civic engagement and associated maintenance of social support networks could assist with cognitive competency in later life. Involvement of older women in society has the advantage of disseminating their wisdom and expertise to their community and broader society. Bukov et al. (2002) applied this concept to social participation of the "oldest old."

Having a Voice in Politics and Community Activities

As stated previously, active civic engagement of older women creates a voice for them through their community and/or political activities that benefits many different constituents. This can be an empowering outcome for an aging subpopulation that may be isolated or ignored within communities, but the intervention needs to be effective to create positive change (Findlay, 2003), including effectively improving quality of life and possibly reducing risk toward increased mortality (Steptoe et al., 2013). Creating a voice, however, necessitates older women becoming active in their roles and providing input, such as in their local or national voting activity (Binstock, 2000). In many different cultures, this may be a shift in cultural role expectations for women, especially older women, in society (e.g., see Brody et al., 1983, regarding eldercare role expectations). The very idea of what it means to be an older woman can be reevaluated through these kinds of empowerment experiences (Hurd, 1999).

Positive Role Models of Aging

One significant benefit of increased visibility of older women through increased civic engagement is that they are likely to become positive role models for younger women in society. Girls and younger women can be exposed to within-gender examples who can demonstrate positive aging outcomes as a woman in the community (Rhodes, 1994; Rhodes et al., 1992). Civic engagement across a woman's lifespan into later life can produce positive psychosocial growth for both the aging woman and the lives that she touches through her efforts (Peters, 2012). This cultural exposure to civically engaged aging women can help guide the aging trajectory of younger generations of women. Bandura (1977) suggested in social learning theory that role models that we deem to be significant in our lives can significantly influence our learning and associated development. Positive role models of aging women who are actively engaged in community and broader national activities can significantly and positively transform society and meaningfully influence future cohorts of women (Webster-Wright, 2019).

Mentoring From Experienced Older Adults

Mentoring of younger generations by older generations is a valuable social process. Through women's continued civic engagement into later life, women of different age levels can learn from each other about ways to optimize their development and achieve successful developmental outcomes over time (Chrisler et al., 2015). Older women in many different cultures across the world can be inspirational mentors for younger women and girls needing guidance in finding who they are and, possibly more important, who they can be in later life (Block & Tietjen-Smith, 2016). Mentoring activities within the context of community involvement may focus on attaining and/or maintaining social support resources, establishing financial security, and other adjustment issues. The concept of "womentoring" (Hetherington & Barcelo, 1985) is an organizational idea regarding the formal and/or informal communication and assistance that can occur between experienced and novice female employees in an organization (Denmark et al., 2015). Applying this concept of womentoring to a broader context outside of the workplace, older women can certainly actively guide and shape the aging trajectories of younger women from diverse backgrounds and needs (Rayburn et al., 2010).

Older women, as contributing members to community activities, share their invaluable resources related to decades of accumulated knowledge and expertise in communities (Miles, 2005) and the workplace (Netting & Thibault, 2012; Resnick et al., 2013). The underutilization of older women as valuable social resources in communities and organizations can negatively affect the social and economic functioning of society (Stallmann et al., 1999).

OLDER WOMEN'S POWER AS SOCIAL CHANGE AGENTS

In different cultures across the world, many women do not have the social power and resources that they need for successful aging, and they need to create social equity through community engagement efforts (Abu-Lughod, 1990; Stephen, 2010). Older women's social resources and attitudes toward social involvement may be influenced by race (Barnes et al., 2004); functional capability (Dabelko-Schoeny et al., 2010); sexual orientation (Davis et al., 2012; Hostetler, 2012); work/retirement status (Nesteruk & Price, 2011); marital status, including widowhood (Isherwood et al., 2012; Utz et al., 2002); and cohort membership (e.g., pre–baby boomers and baby boomers; Hudson, 2008; MaloneBeach & Langeland, 2011). Understanding these societal issues can assist in helping create more opportunities for women's empowerment through activism (Ackelsberg, 1998; Wray, 2004).

Older women become social change agents through civic involvement and volunteerism in the community (Lips & Hastings, 2012; McHugh, 2012). To gain and/or maintain social status within a society, women must vote, volunteer, and otherwise engage in community programs and local government. This also helps to eradicate aging stereotypes and raise awareness regarding a growing aging population's social, psychological, physical, and emotional needs and capabilities (Denmark & Klara, 2007). Cullinane (2008) argued that active social engagement assists in creating a purposeful life in later adulthood among diverse populations and cultures. The Raging Grannies are an international activist organization of older women focused on eradicating aging stereotypes and furthering social causes such as environmental reforms. They exemplify the social power potential of older women in society (Roy, 2004) and, more broadly, they embody the Hebrew phrase *tikkun olam*, "repair the world."

CONCLUSION

Encouraging older women to be a civically engaged, active part of communities can assist in their mental health outcomes, such as lower susceptibility to possible social isolation and depression in later life. Their exposure to and utilization of social resources through their community involvement will create heightened social power and independence, which can empower older women and their cultures. Older women's impact on the cultures they live within, for their own benefit and the benefit of future generations of aging women, will have positive ramifications for societies across the world. As discussed previously, there are many mutual benefits to the empowerment and encouraged civic engagement of older women. As with other issues, this paradigm shift in valuing the contributions of women in later life must occur and grow in response to the proportional growth of the world's population. This shift in perspective about the value of older women to society must occur through the implementation of community-based education in many different parts of the world. Both society and older women need to recognize their inherent value to each other to promote positive aging outcomes.

As the number of older women increases in many countries across the world in the coming decades, it behooves societies to engage the knowledge, skills, and abilities of these older women with lifetimes of experience and wisdom. This active engagement will be of benefit to all involved, creating opportunities for both multigenerational learning and increased activity levels of this aging subpopulation within many diverse cultures and communities. Greater social and civic engagement for women will mean that they will be more physically and mentally engaged daily, which will assist in their positive aging over time. From an interventionist perspective, understanding the cultural contexts in which older women can engage in such activities is important because it affects the design of community-based programs and supportive educational activities. The valuation of older women's contributions to many aspects of social functioning (e.g., political discourse) will help create moral, ethical societies and optimize positive aging outcomes across their lifespans.

APPENDIX 13.1

FAMOUS QUOTES BY OLDER WOMEN ABOUT CIVIC ENGAGEMENT

"We have a shared destiny, a shared responsibility to save the world from those who attempt to destroy it."—Winnie Madikizela-Mandela (1936–2018), activist

"Fight for the things that you care about but do it in a way that will lead others to join you."—Ruth Bader Ginsburg (1933–present), associate justice of the Supreme Court of the United States

"Never doubt that a small group of thoughtful, committed citizens can change the world; indeed, it's the only thing that ever has."—Margaret Mead (1901–1978), anthropologist

"The greatness of a community is most accurately measured by the compassionate actions of its members."—Coretta Scott King (1927–2006), civil rights leader and activist

"Women are the real architects of society."—Harriet Beecher Stowe (1811–1896), author

"A woman is like a tea bag—you never know how strong she is until she gets in hot water."—Eleanor Roosevelt (1884–1962), diplomat and activist

"Being the Queen is not all about singing, and being a diva is not all about singing. It has much to do with your service to people. And your social contributions to your community and your civic contributions as well."—Aretha Franklin (1942–2018), musician

"I can honestly say that I was never affected by the question of the success of an undertaking. If I felt it was the right thing to do, I was for it regardless of the possible outcome."—Golda Meir (1898–1978), political leader

"Who knows what women can be when they are finally free to be themselves."—Betty Friedan (1921–2006), author and human rights activist

REFERENCES

Abu-Lughod, L. (1990). The romance of resistance: Tracing transformations of power through Bedouin women. *American Ethnologist, 17*(1), 41–55. https://doi.org/10.1525/ae.1990.17.1.02a00030

Ackelsberg, M. A. (1998). Communities, resistance, and women's activism: Some implications for a democratic policy. In A. Bookman & S. Morgan (Eds.), *Women and the politics of empowerment* (pp. 297–309). Temple University Press.

Ackerman, P. L., Kanfer, R., & Calderwood, C. (2010). Use it or lose it? Wii brain exercise practice and reading for domain knowledge. *Psychology and Aging, 25*(4), 753–766. https://doi.org/10.1037/a0019277

Anderson, K. A., & Dabelko-Schoeny, H. I. (2010). Civic engagement for nursing home residents: A call for social work action. *Journal of Gerontological Social Work, 53*(3), 270–282. https://doi.org/10.1080/01634371003648323

Bandura, A. (1977). *Social learning theory*. Prentice Hall.

Barnes, L. L., Mendes de Leon, C. F., Bienias, J. L., & Evans, D. A. (2004). A longitudinal study of Black–White differences in social resources. *The Journals of Gerontology: Series B, 59*(3), S146–S153. https://doi.org/10.1093/geronb/59.3.S146

Bashore, T. R. (1990). Age, physical fitness, and mental processing speed. In M. P. Lawton (Ed.), *Annual Review of Gerontology and Geriatrics* (pp. 120–144). Springer. https://doi.org/10.1007/978-3-662-40455-3_4

Baum, E. E., Jarjoura, D., Polen, A. E., Faur, D., & Rutecki, G. (2003). Effectiveness of a group exercise program in a long-term care facility: A randomized pilot trial. *Journal of the American Medical Directors Association, 4*(2), 74–80. https://doi.org/10.1016/S1525-8610(04)70279-0

Binstock, R. H. (2000). Older people and voting participation: Past and future. *The Gerontologist, 40*(1), 18–31. https://doi.org/10.1093/geront/40.1.18

Block, B. A., & Tietjen-Smith, T. (2016). The case for women mentoring women. *Quest, 68*(3), 306–315. https://doi.org/10.1080/00336297.2016.1190285

Bo, X. (2008). Civic engagement among older Chinese internet users. *Journal of Applied Gerontology, 27*(4), 424–445. https://doi.org/10.1177%2F0733464808315292

Bowen, D. J., Andersen, M. R., & Urban, N. (2000). Volunteerism in a community-based sample of women aged 50 to 80 years. *Journal of Applied Social Psychology, 30*(9), 1829–1842. https://doi.org/10.1111/j.1559-1816.2000.tb02470.x

Brody, E. M., Johnsen, P. T., Fulcomer, M. C., & Lang, A. M. (1983). Women's changing roles and help to elderly parents: Attitudes of three generations of women. *Journal of Gerontology, 38*(5), 597–607. https://doi.org/10.1093/geronj/38.5.597

Bukov, A., Maas, I., & Lampert, T. (2002). Social participation in very old age: Cross-sectional and longitudinal findings from BASE. *The Journals of Gerontology: Series B, 57*(6), 510–517. https://doi.org/10.1093/geronb/57.6.P510

Burr, J. A., Han, S., Lee, H. J., Tavares, J. L., & Mutchler, J. E. (2018). Health benefits associated with three helping behaviors: Evidence for incident cardiovascular disease. *The Journals of Gerontology: Series B, 73*(3), 492–500. https://doi.org/10.1093/geronb/gbx082

Bushway, L. J., Dickinson, J. L., Stedman, R. C., Wagenet, L. P., & Weinstein, D. A. (2011). Benefits, motivations, and barriers related to environmental volunteerism for older adults: Developing a research agenda. *International Journal of Aging & Human Development, 72*(3), 189–206. https://doi.org/10.2190/AG.72.3.b

Cagney, K. A., & Cornwell, E. Y. (2010). Neighborhoods and health in later life: The intersection of biology and community. *Annual Review of Gerontology & Geriatrics*, *30*(1), 323–348. https://doi.org/10.1891/0198-8794.30.323

Carr, D. (2018). Volunteering among older adults: Life course correlates and consequences. *The Journals of Gerontology: Series B*, *73*(3), 479–481. https://doi.org/10.1093/geronb/gbx179

Carr, D. C., Kail, B. L., Matz-Costa, C., & Shavit, Y. Z. (2018). Does becoming a volunteer attenuate loneliness among recently widowed older adults? *The Journals of Gerontology: Series B*, *73*(3), 501–510. https://doi.org/10.1093/geronb/gbx092

Carr, D. C., Kail, B. L., & Rowe, J. W. (2018). The relation of volunteering and subsequent changes in physical disability in older adults. *The Journals of Gerontology: Series B*, *73*(3), 511–521. https://doi.org/10.1093/geronb/gbx102

Cervone, D., & Peake, P. K. (1986). Anchoring, efficacy, and action: The influence of judgmental heuristics on self-efficacy judgments and behavior. *Journal of Personality and Social Psychology*, *50*(3), 492–501. https://doi.org/10.1037/0022-3514.50.3.492

Chappell, N. L. (2005). Perceived change in quality of life among Chinese Canadian seniors: The role of involvement in Chinese culture. *Journal of Happiness Studies*, *6*, 69–91. https://doi.org/10.1007/s10902-004-1754-5

Chrisler, J. C., Rossini, M., & Newton, J. R. (2015). Older women, power, and the body. In V. Muhlbauer, J. C. Chrisler, & F. L. Denmark (Eds.), *Women and aging* (pp. 9–30). Springer, Cham. https://doi.org/10.1007/978-3-319-09306-2_2

Clark, N. M., Janz, N. K., Dodge, J. A., Schork, M. A., Fingerlin, T. E., Wheeler, J. R., Liang, J., Keteyian, S. J., & Santinga, J. T. (2000). Changes in functional health status of older women with heart disease: Evaluation of a program based on self-regulation. *The Journals of Gerontology: Series B*, *55*(2), S117–S126. https://doi.org/10.1093/geronb/55.2.S117

Cullinane, P. (2008). Purposeful lives, civic engagement, and Tikkun Olam. *Generations*, *32*(2), 57–59.

Cutler, S. J., & Hendricks, J. (2000). Age differences in voluntary association memberships: Fact or artifact. *The Journals of Gerontology: Series B*, *55*(2), S98–S107. https://doi.org/10.1093/geronb/55.2.S98

Dabelko-Schoeny, H., Anderson, K. A., & Spinks, K. (2010). Civic engagement for older adults with functional limitations: Piloting an intervention for adult day health participants. *The Gerontologist*, *50*(5), 694–701. https://doi.org/10.1093/geront/gnq019

Dauenhauer, J. A., Steitz, D. W., Aponte, C. I., & Fromm Faria, D. (2010). Enhancing student gerocompetencies: Evaluation of an intergenerational service learning course. *Journal of Gerontological Social Work*, *53*(4), 319–335. https://doi.org/10.1080/01634371003715577

Davey, A., Janke, M., & Savla, J. (2004). Antecedents of intergenerational support: Families in context and families as context. *Annual Review of Gerontology & Geriatrics*, *24*, 29–54.

Davis, S., Crothers, N., Grant, J., Young, S., & Smith, K. (2012). Being involved in the country: Productive ageing in different types of rural communities. *Journal of Rural Studies*, *28*(4), 338–346. https://doi.org/10.1016/j.jrurstud.2012.01.008

Denmark, F. L., Goldstein, H., Thies, K., & Tworecke, A. (2015). Older women, leadership, and encore careers. In V. Muhlbauer, J. C. Chrisler, & F. L. Denmark

(Eds.), *Women and Aging* (pp. 71–88). Springer, Cham. https://doi.org/10.1007/978-3-319-09306-2_5

Denmark, F. L., & Klara, M. (2007). Empowerment: A prime time for women over 50. In V. Muhlbauer & J. C. Chrisler (Eds.), *Women over 50: Psychological perspectives* (pp. 182–203). Springer. https://doi.org/10.1007/978-0-387-46341-4

Dowling, W. (1997). Volunteerism among older women. In J. Coyle (Ed.), *Handbook on women and aging* (pp. 242–250). Greenwood Press.

Duke, J., Leventhal, H., Brownlee, S., & Leventhal, E. A. (2002). Giving up and replacing activities in response to illness. *The Journals of Gerontology: Series B, 57*, 367–376. https://doi.org/10.1093/geronb/57.4.P367

Eakman, A. M., Carlson, M. E., & Clark, F. A. (2010). The Meaningful Activity Participation Assessment: A measure of engagement in personally valued activities. *International Journal of Aging & Human Development, 70*(4), 299–317. https://doi.org/10.2190%2FAG.70.4.b

Emerson, R. M. (1976). Social exchange theory. *Annual Review of Sociology, 2*(1), 335–362. https://doi.org/10.1146/annurev.so.02.080176.002003

Enguidanos, S., Pynoos, J., Denton, A., Alexman, S., & Diepenbrock, L. (2010). Comparison of barriers and facilitators in developing NORC programs: A tale of two communities. *Journal of Housing for the Older Adults, 24*(3/4), 291–303. https://doi.org/10.1080/02763893.2010.522445

Evers, A., & von Essen, J. (2019). Volunteering and civic action: Boundaries blurring, boundaries redrawn. *Voluntas, 30*(1), 1–14. https://doi.org/10.1007/s11266-018-00086-0

Findlay, R. A. (2003). Interventions to reduce social isolation amongst older people: Where is the evidence? *Ageing and Society, 23*(5), 647–658. https://doi.org/10.1017/S0144686X03001296

Gonzales, E., & Morrow-Howell, N. (2009). Productive engagement in aging friendly communities. *Generations, 33*(2), 51–58.

Gottlieb, B. H., & Gillespie, A. A. (2008). Volunteerism, health, and civic engagement among older adults. *Canadian Journal on Aging, 27*(4), 399–406. https://doi.org/10.3138/cja.27.4.399

Greenfield, E. A., & Moorman, S. M. (2018). Extracurricular involvement in high school and later-life participation in voluntary associations. *The Journals of Gerontology: Series B, 73*, 482–491. https://doi.org/10.1093/geronb/gbw168

Guiney, H., & Machado, L. (2018). Volunteering in the community: Potential benefits for cognitive aging. *The Journals of Gerontology: Series B, 73*(3), 399–408. https://doi.org/10.1093/geronb/gbx134

Harvard School of Public Health—MetLife Foundation Initiative on Retirement and Civic Engagement. (2004). *Reinventing aging: Baby boomers and civic engagement.* https://assets.aarp.org/rgcenter/general/boomers_engagement.pdf

Hegeman, C. R., Roodin, P., Gilliland, K. A., & Ó'Flathabháin, K. B. (2010). Intergenerational service learning: Linking three generations: Concept, history, and outcome assessment. *Gerontology & Geriatrics Education, 31*(1), 37–54. https://doi.org/10.1080/02701960903584418

Hendricks, J., & Cutler, S. J. (2001). The effects of membership in church-related associations and labor unions on age differences in voluntary association affiliations. *The Gerontologist, 41*(2), 250–256. https://doi.org/10.1093/geront/41.2.250

Hetherington, C., & Barcelo, R. (1985). Womentoring: A cross-cultural perspective. *Journal of the National Association of Women Deans, Administrators, and Counselors, 49*(1), 12–15.

Hill, T. D., Angel, J. L., Ellison, C. G., & Angel, R. J. (2005). Religious attendance and mortality: An 8-year follow-up of older Mexican Americans. *The Journals of Gerontology: Series B, 60*(2), S102–S109. https://doi.org/10.1093/geronb/60.2.S102

Hinterlong, J. E. (2008). Productive engagement among older Americans: Prevalence, patterns, and implications for public policy. *Journal of Aging & Social Policy, 20*(2), 141–164. https://doi.org/10.1080/08959420801977491

Hinterlong, J. E., & Williamson, A. (2006). The effects of civic engagement of current and future cohorts of older adults. *Generations, 30*(4), 10–17.

Hogan, M. (2005). Physical and cognitive activity and exercise for older adults: A review. *International Journal of Aging & Human Development, 60*(2), 95–126. https://doi.org/10.2190/PTG9-XDVM-YETA-MKXA

Holahan, C. K., & Chapman, J. R. (2002). Longitudinal predictors of proactive goals and activity participation at age 80. *The Journals of Gerontology: Series B, 57*(5), 418–425. https://doi.org/10.1093/geronb/57.5.P418

Horowitz, B. P., Wong, S. D., & Dechello, K. (2010). Intergenerational service learning: To promote active aging, and occupational therapy gerontology practice. *Gerontology & Geriatrics Education, 31*(1), 75–91. https://doi.org/10.1080/02701960903578345

Hostetler, A. J. (2012). Community involvement, perceived control, and attitudes toward aging among lesbians and gay men. *International Journal of Aging & Human Development, 75*(2), 141–167. https://doi.org/10.2190%2FAG.75.2.c

Hudson, R. B. (2008). Engaging boomers: Hope or hype? *The Gerontologist, 48*(1), 124–126. https://doi.org/10.1093/geront/48.1.124

Hurd, L. C. (1999). "We're not old!": Older women's negotiation of aging and oldness. *Journal of Aging Studies, 13*(4), 419–439. https://doi.org/10.1016/S0890-4065(99)00019-5

Isherwood, L. M., King, D. S., & Luszcz, M. A. (2012). A longitudinal analysis of social engagement in late-life widowhood. *International Journal of Aging & Human Development, 74*(3), 211–229. https://doi.org/10.2190%2FAG.74.3.c

Jones, E. D., Ivanov, L. L., Wallace, D., & VonCannon, L. (2010). Global service learning project influences culturally sensitive care. *Home Health Care Management & Practice, 22*(7), 464–469. https://doi.org/10.1177/1084822310368657

Kaskie, B., Imhof, S., Cavanaugh, J., & Culp, K. (2008). Civic engagement as a retirement role for aging Americans. *The Gerontologist, 48*(3), 368–377. https://doi.org/10.1093/geront/48.3.368

Kelly, J. R. (1993). *Activity and aging: Staying involved in later life.* Sage.

Kleiber, D., & Nimrod, G. (2008). Expressions of generativity and civic engagement in a 'learning in retirement' group. *Journal of Adult Development, 15*(2), 76–86. https://doi.org/10.1007/s10804-008-9038-7

Kramer, A. F., Hahn, S., & McAuley, E. (2000). Influence of aerobic fitness on the neurocognitive function of older adults. *Journal of Aging and Physical Activity, 8*(4), 379–385. https://doi.org/10.1123/japa.8.4.379

Kuyper, H., Van der Werf, M. P. C., & Lubbers, M. J. (2000). Motivation, metacognition and self-regulation as predictors of long-term educational attainment.

Educational Research and Evaluation, 6(3), 181–205. https://doi.org/10.1076/1380-3611(200009)6:3;1-A;FT181

Lancee, B., & Radl, J. (2012). Social connectedness and the transition from work to retirement. *The Journals of Gerontology: Series B, 67*(4), 481–490. https://doi.org/10.1093/geronb/gbs049

Leedahl, S. N., Koenig, T. L., & Ekerdt, D. J. (2011). Perceived benefits of VFW post participation for older adults. *Journal of Gerontological Social Work, 54*(7), 712–730. https://doi.org/10.1080/01634372.2011.594149

Lerner, R. M., Wang, J., Champine, R. B., Warren, D. J., & Erickson, K. (2014). Development of civic engagement: Theoretical and methodological issues. *International Journal of Developmental Science, 8*(3–4), 69–79. https://doi.org/10.3233/DEV-14130

Lightfoot, K., & Brady, E. M. (2005). Transformations through teaching and learning: The story of Maine's Osher Lifelong Learning Institute. *Journal of Transformative Education, 3*(3), 221–235. https://doi.org/10.1177%2F1541344605276667

Lips, H. M., & Hastings, S. L. (2012). Competing discourses for older women: Agency/leadership vs. disengagement/retirement. *Women & Therapy, 35*(3–4), 145–164. https://doi.org/10.1080/02703149.2012.684533

MaloneBeach, E. E., & Langeland, K. L. (2011). Boomers' prospective needs for senior centers and related services: A survey of persons 50–59. *Journal of Gerontological Social Work, 54*(1), 116–130. https://doi.org/10.1080/01634372.2010.524283

Martinez, I. L., Crooks, D., Kim, K. S., & Tanner, E. (2011). Invisible civic engagement among older adults: Valuing the contributions of informal volunteering. *Journal of Cross-Cultural Gerontology, 26*(1), 23–37. https://doi.org/10.1007/s10823-011-9137-y

Martinson, M., & Minkler, M. (2006). Civic engagement and older adults: A critical perspective. *The Gerontologist, 46*(3), 318–324. https://doi.org/10.1093/geront/46.3.318

McBride, A. M., Sherraden, M. S., & Pritzker, S. (2006). Civic engagement among low-income and low-wealth families: In their words. *Family Relations, 55*(2), 152–162. https://www.jstor.org/stable/40005326

McHugh, M. C. (2012). Aging, agency, and activism: Older women as social change agents. *Women & Therapy, 35*(3–4), 279–295. https://doi.org/10.1080/02703149.2012.684544

Meier, S., & Stutzer, A. (2008). Is volunteering rewarding in itself? *Economica, 75*(297), 39–59.

Menec, V. H. (2003). The relation between everyday activities and successful aging: A 6-year longitudinal study. *The Journals of Gerontology: Series B, 58*(2), S74–S82. https://doi.org/10.1093/geronb/58.2.S74

Miles, T. P. (2005). Think globally, act locally. *Annual Review of Gerontology & Geriatrics, 25*, R19–R29.

Minkler, M., & Holstein, M. B. (2008). From civil rights to . . . civic engagement? Concerns of two older critical gerontologists about a "new social movement" and what it portends. *Journal of Aging Studies, 22*(2), 196–204. https://doi.org/10.1016/j.jaging.2007.12.003

Morrow-Howell, N. (2010). Volunteering in later life: Research frontiers. *The Journals of Gerontology: Series B, 65B*(4), 461–469. https://doi.org/10.1093/geronb/gbq024

Morrow-Howell, N., Hong, S., & Tang, F. (2009). Who benefits from volunteering? Variations in perceived benefits. *The Gerontologist, 49*(1), 91–102. https://doi.org/10.1093/geront/gnp007

Mukherjee, D. (2011). Participation of older adults in virtual volunteering: A qualitative analysis. *Ageing International, 36*(2), 253–266. https://doi.org/10.1007/s12126-010-9088-6

Nesteruk, O., & Price, C. A. (2011). Retired women and volunteering: The good, the bad, and the unrecognized. *Journal of Women & Aging, 23*(2), 99–112. https://doi.org/10.1080/08952841.2011.561138

Netting, F., & Thibault, J. M. (2012). Challenges faced by staff in faith-related agencies when dedicated volunteers age in place. *Journal of Religion, Spirituality and Aging, 24*(3), 202–212. https://doi.org/10.1080/15528030.2012.648846

Netz, Y., Dwolatzky, T., Zinker, Y., Argov, E., & Agmon, R. (2011). Aerobic fitness and multidomain cognitive function in advanced age. *International Psychogeriatrics, 23*(1), 114–124. https://doi.org/10.1017/S1041610210000797

Netz, Y., Wu, M. J., Becker, B. J., & Tenenbaum, G. (2005). Physical activity and psychological well-being in advanced age: A meta-analysis of intervention studies. *Psychology and Aging, 20*(2), 272–284. https://doi.org/10.1037/0882-7974.20.2.272

Okamoto, K., & Tanaka, Y. (2004). Subjective usefulness and 6-year mortality risks among elderly persons in Japan. *The Journals of Gerontology: Series B, 59*(5), P246–P249. https://doi.org/10.1093/geronb/59.5.P246

Park, D. C., & Reuter-Lorenz, P. (2009). The adaptive brain: Aging and neurocognitive scaffolding. *Annual Review of Psychology, 60*, 173–196. https://doi.org/10.1146/annurev.psych.59.103006.093656

Parkinson, L., Warburton, J., Sibbritt, D., & Byles, J. (2010). Volunteering and older women: Psychosocial and health predictors of participation. *Aging & Mental Health, 14*(8), 917–927. https://doi.org/10.1080/13607861003801045

Pesce, C., Cereatti, L., Forte, R., Crova, C., & Casella, R. (2011). Acute and chronic exercise effects on attentional control in older road cyclists. *Gerontology, 57*(2), 121–128. https://doi.org/10.1159/000314685

Peters, D. M. (2012). "Take me to the water"—community and renewal among aging women: A case study of social interaction and exercise among the "Polar Bears" of Martha's Vineyard. *Journal of Women & Aging, 24*(3), 216–226. https://doi.org/10.1080/08952841.2012.639668

Piercy, K. W., Cheek, C., & Teemant, B. (2011). Challenges and psychosocial growth for older volunteers giving intensive humanitarian service. *The Gerontologist, 51*(4), 550–560. https://doi.org/10.1093/geront/gnr013

Pillemer, K., Fuller-Rowell, T. E., Reid, M. C., & Wells, N. M. (2010). Environmental volunteering and health outcomes over a 20-year period. *The Gerontologist, 50*(5), 594–602. https://doi.org/10.1093/geront/gnq007

Proulx, C. M., Curl, A. L., & Ermer, A. E. (2018). Longitudinal associations between formal volunteering and cognitive functioning. *The Journals of Gerontology: Series B, 73*(3), 522–531. https://doi.org/10.1093/geronb/gbx110

Rawsthorne, M., Ellis, K., & de Pree, A. (2017). "Working with COW": Social work supporting older women living in the community. *Journal of Gerontological Social Work, 60*(1), 32–47. https://doi.org/10.1080/01634372.2016.1267671

Rayburn, C. A., Denmark, F. L., & Reuder, M. E. (2010). *A handbook for women mentors: Transcending barriers of stereotype, race, and ethnicity.* ABC-CLIO.

Resnick, B. (2001). Testing a model of overall activity in older adults. *Journal of Aging and Physical Activity, 9*(2), 142–160. https://doi.org/10.1123/japa.9.2.142

Resnick, B., Klinedinst, J., Dorsey, S., Holtzman, L., & Abuelhiga, L. S. (2013). Volunteer behavior and factors that influence volunteering among residents in continuing care retirement communities. *Journal of Housing for the Elderly, 27*(1–2), 161–176. https://doi.org/10.1080/02763893.2012.754820

Rhodes, J. E. (1994). Older and wiser: Mentoring relationships in childhood and adolescence. *The Journal of Primary Prevention, 14*(3), 187–196. https://doi.org/10.1007/BF01324592

Rhodes, J. E., Ebert, L., & Fischer, K. (1992). Natural mentors: An overlooked resource in the social networks of young, African American mothers. *American Journal of Community Psychology, 20*(4), 445–461. https://doi.org/10.1007/BF00937754

Roy, C. (2004). *The Raging Grannies: Wild hats, cheeky songs, and witty actions for a better world*. Black Rose Books.

Rozanova, J., Keating, N., & Eales, J. (2012). Unequal social engagement for older adults: Constraints on choice. *Canadian Journal on Aging, 31*(1), 25–36. https://doi.org/10.1017/S0714980811000675

Rubin, L. B. (1979). *Women of a certain age: The midlife search for self*. Harper & Row.

Scharf, T., McDonald, B., & Atkins, A. M. (2016). *Promoting civic engagement in later life through the Touchstone Programme: A resource and research guide*. Irish Centre for Social Gerontology.

Simson, S. P., Wilson, L. B., Ruben, K. A., & Thompson, L. M. (2008). Humor your way to good health: An intergenerational program to address a critical public health issue: The epidemic of overweight and obesity among children. *Journal of Intergenerational Relationships, 6*(1), 83–100. https://doi.org/10.1300/J194v06n01_06

Son, J., Yarnal, C., & Kerstetter, D. (2010). Engendering social capital through a leisure club for middle-aged and older women: Implications for individual and community health and well-being. *Leisure Studies, 29*(1), 67–83. https://doi.org/10.1080/02614360903242578

Stallmann, J. I., Deller, S. C., & Shields, M. (1999). The economic and fiscal impact of aging retirees on a small rural region. *The Gerontologist, 39*(5), 599–610. https://doi.org/10.1093/geront/39.5.599

Stephen, L. (2010). *Women and social movements in Latin America: Power from below*. University of Texas Press.

Steptoe, A., Shankar, A., Demakakos, P., & Wardle, J. (2013). Social isolation, loneliness, and all-cause mortality in older men and women. *Proceedings of the National Academy of Sciences of the United States of America, 110*(15), 5797–5801. https://doi.org/10.1073/pnas.1219686110

Tan, E. J., Tanner, E. K., Seeman, T. E., Xue, Q. L., Rebok, G. W., Frick, K. D., Carlson, M. C., Wang, T., Piferi, R. L., McGill, S., Whitfield, K. E., & Fried, L. P. (2010). Marketing public health through older adult volunteering: Experience Corps as a social marketing intervention. *American Journal of Public Health, 100*(4), 727–734. https://doi.org/10.2105/AJPH.2009.169151

Tang, F., Choi, E., & Morrow-Howell, N. (2010). Organizational support and volunteering benefits for older adults. *The Gerontologist, 50*(5), 603–612. https://doi.org/10.1093/geront/gnq020

Turner, M. J., Shields, T. G., & Sharp, D. (2001). Changes and continuities in the determinants of older adults' voter turnout 1952–1996. *The Gerontologist, 41*(6), 805–818. https://doi.org/10.1093/geront/41.6.805

Tversky, A., & Kahneman, D. (1974). Judgment under uncertainty: Heuristics and biases. *Science, 185*(4157), 1124–1131. https://doi.org/10.1126/science.185.4157.1124

U.S. Bureau of Labor Statistics. (2016). *Volunteering in the United States, 2015*. U.S. Department of Labor.

Utz, R. L., Carr, D., Nesse, R., & Wortman, C. B. (2002). The effect of widowhood on older adults' social participation: An evaluation of activity, disengagement, and continuity theories. *The Gerontologist, 42*(4), 522–533. https://doi.org/10.1093/geront/42.4.522

Wahrendorf, M., Ribet, C., Zins, M., Goldberg, M., & Siegrist, J. (2010). Perceived reciprocity in social exchange and health functioning in early old age: Prospective findings from the GAZEL study. *Aging & Mental Health, 14*(4), 425–432. https://doi.org/10.1080/13607860903483102

Walter-Ginzburg, A., Blumstein, T., Chetrit, A., & Modan, B. (2002). Social factors and mortality in the old-old in Israel: The CALAS study. *The Journals of Gerontology: Series B, 57*, S308–S318. https://doi.org/10.1093/geronb/57.5.S308

Warburton, J., Ng, S. H., & Shardlow, S. M. (2013). Social inclusion in an ageing world: Introduction to the special issue. *Ageing and Society, 33*(1), 1–15. https://doi.org/10.1017/S0144686X12000980

Webster-Wright, A. (2019). Grace and grit: The politics, poetics and performance of ageing as a woman. *Life Writing, 16*(1), 97–111. https://doi.org/10.1080/14484528.2019.1521261

Wilson, J., & Musick, M. (1999). The effects of volunteering on the volunteer. *Law and Contemporary Problems, 62*(4), 141–168. https://doi.org/10.2307/1192270

Wray, S. (2004). What constitutes agency and empowerment for women in later life? *The Sociological Review, 52*(1), 22–38. https://doi.org/10.1111%2Fj.1467-954X.2004.00440.x

Wray-Lake, L., DeHaan, C. R., Shubert, J., & Ryan, R. M. (2019). Examining links from civic engagement to daily well-being from a self-determination theory perspective. *The Journal of Positive Psychology, 14*(2), 166–177. https://doi.org/10.1080/17439760.2017.1388432

Ziegler, F. (2012). "You have to engage with life, or life will go away": An intersectional life course analysis of older women's social participation in a disadvantaged urban area. *Geoforum, 43*(6), 1296–1305. https://doi.org/10.1016/j.geoforum.2012.03.013

Zucchero, R. A. (2011). A co-mentoring project: An intergenerational service-learning experience. *Educational Gerontology, 37*(8), 687–702. https://doi.org/10.1080/03601271003723487

Zunzunegui, M. V., Alvarado, B. E., Del Ser, T., & Otero, A. (2003). Social networks, social integration, and social engagement determine cognitive decline in community-dwelling Spanish older adults. *The Journals of Gerontology: Series B, 58*(2), S93–S100. https://doi.org/10.1093/geronb/58.2.S93

Appendix

EMPLOYMENT RESOURCES FOR OLDER WOMEN

The following are some informational resources for older women to support their efforts in maintaining their employment or reentering the workforce.

BUSINESS AND WORKFORCE INVOLVEMENT RESOURCES

Advancing Women
Website: https://www.advancingwomen.com
Description: Advancing Women is a recruiting website that connects companies with women jobseekers in the fields of engineering, manufacturing, construction, technology, biotech, medical, financial, government, and defense/security.

SCORE (Service Corps of Retired Executives)
Washington, DC, Chapter (different locations by state)
409 3rd Street SW, Suite 100A
Washington, DC 20024
Phone: (202) 619-1000
Website: https://www.score.org
Description: This is a great social resource for aging professional women who are looking for ways to be more active in their communities, benefiting their own positive aging and those of others that they come in contact with through their mentoring efforts.

Senior Job Bank
Phone: (866) 562-2627
Website: http://www.seniorjobbank.org

Description: This information would be helpful for aging women looking for employment opportunities near their location.

Urban Institute: Older Workers
2100 M Street NW
Washington, DC 20037
Phone: (202) 833-7200
Website: https://www.urban.org/research-area/older-workers
Description: This information would be helpful for aging women across the world who are dealing with different issues related to staying in or reentering the workforce in later life.

Women's Business Development Center
8 S. Michigan Ave., 4th Floor
Chicago, IL 60603
Phone: (312) 853-3477
Email: wbdc@wbdc.org
Website: https://www.wbdc.org
Description: Women's Business Development Center offers guidance and courses to women starting a new business or women who are currently in business.

CAREER TRAINING RESOURCES FOR OLDER WOMEN

AARP Foundation: Back To Work 50+ Program
601 E Street NW, 4th Floor
Washington, DC 20049
Phone: (855) 850-2525
Website: https://www.aarp.org/aarp-foundation/our-work/income/back-to-work-50-plus/
Description: This program from AARP offers training, mentoring, and job search resources that would support older working women's intentions to sustain or reenter the workforce.

Older Worker Program Finder
Phone: 1-877-US2-JOBS (1-877-872-5627)
Email: info@careeronestop.org
Website: https://www.careeronestop.org/LocalHelp/EmploymentandTraining/find-older-worker-programs.aspx

Description: Older women wishing to find local older worker training programs and community resources would benefit from reviewing this employment program.

Senior Community Service Employment Program
U.S. Department of Labor
200 Constitution Ave. NW
Washington, DC 20210
Phone: 1-877-US-2JOBS (1-877-872-5627)
Website: https://www.doleta.gov/seniors
Description: This is a great national training program to support the efforts of older women to stay in or reenter the workforce.

CAREER AND CAREER TRANSITION MENTORING RESOURCES

Aspire Mentoring Network
Website: http://www.mentoringwomensnetwork.com
Description: The Mentoring Women's Network is focused on developing women through mentoring relationships so that each woman can reach her full potential professionally.

Supportive Older Women's Network (SOWN)
4100 Main Street, Suite 403
Philadelphia, PA 19127
Phone: (215) 487-3000
Email: info@sown.org
Website: https://www.sown.org
Description: The mission of SOWN is to strengthen the quality of life in older women's lives through various networking opportunities.

Women's Institute for a Secure Retirement (WISER)
1001 Connecticut Ave. NW, Suite 730
Washington, DC 20036
Phone: (202) 393-5452
Email: info@wiserwomen.org
Website: https://www.wiserwomen.org
Description: The WISER organization and associated website is focused on assisting women achieving and maintaining financial security into later life through workshops, resources, and networking opportunities.

PUBLIC POLICY RESOURCES

Mayor's Office on Women's Policy and Initiatives
1350 Pennsylvania Ave. NW, Suite 332
Washington, DC 20004
Phone: (202) 442-8150
Email: women@dc.gov
Website: https://www.owpi.dc.gov
Description: The website offers resources in domestic violence, financial literacy, wellness and health, workforce development and preparedness, and resources for women.

Urban Institute: Retirement Policy
2100 M Street NW
Washington, DC 20037
Phone: (202) 833-7200
Website: https://www.urban.org/research-area/retirementpensions
Description: This information would be very helpful for aging women who are preparing to make the transition or are currently in retirement and who need to optimize the retirement experience.

Index

A

AARP (American Association of Retired Persons), 162, 260
Abrams, J. A., 191
Academic career, 89, 99–100
Acceptance, 127
Acceptant phase, 38
Access
  to leadership, 26
  to networking opportunities, 181–182
Accomplishment, 127
Acculturation, 228
Achievement, 171–172
Active social participation, 246–247
Activism, 249
Activity theory perspective, 246
Adaptive aging, 21–22
Adjustment, psychosocial, 16
Adolescence
  in developmental theory of
    embodiment, 214
  gender-based stereotypes in, 166
  identity development in, 74
  stages of life, 36
Adult children, support or financial help
  for, 117–118, 123, 127, 140
Adulthood, young. See Young adulthood
Advancing Women, 259
Adversity, resilience and, 20
Advocacy, 177–179, 182–183
Affective infrastructure, 101
Affect optimization, 37
Africa, 106, 228
African American women. See Black
  women

Age, workplace expectations and, 163,
  166–169
Age Discrimination in Employment Act
  (2012), 234, 235
Ageism (age-based discrimination)
  assertiveness to manage, 177–178
  benevolent, 172–173
  defined, 16, 20
  in ego development theory, 40
  and gender, 162–163, 184
  for immigrant women, 233
  for older working women, 19–20
  over lifespan, 162–163
  against people of color, 162
  in resiliency model, 23
  and role of older women in society, 192
  in United States, 34, 234–235
  and work–life balance, 139
  in workplace, 161–162
Agency, 166, 222
Age-related social scripts, 222
Aggression, 167
Aging
  adaptive, 21–22
  awareness of, 38
  healthy, 21, 243
  of Latino immigrant population, 228
  meanings of, 134
  metaphors for, 63
  positive, 15–16
  positive role models of, 247
  productive, 21
  successful, 21
Aging well, 21

Agronick, G. S., 74
Alice (pseudonym), 54, 57–58, 60, 216, 218
Altschuler, J., 74, 111–112
American Association of Retired Persons (AARP), 162, 260
American Association of University Women, 111
American Catholic Church, 6
American Psychological Association (APA), 4
Amnesty frame, for immigration, 236
Analytical autoethnography, 88
Angelou, Maya, 19
Anne (pseudonym), 55, 59
Anti-immigrant discrimination, 229, 231, 233–235
APA (American Psychological Association), 4
Appalachia, 9, 195–196
Appalachian women, 195–208
    history of work by, 199–200
    intersectionality among stereotypes for, 197–199
    labor force participation by, 200–204
    opioid addiction and grandparenting by, 204–205
    support for older working women, 205–207
Appearance, 173, 220
Ascendant phase, 37
Asia, immigrants from, 228
Aspire Mentoring Network, 261
Assertiveness, 177–178
Atchley, R. C., 71
Athletes, former, 7
Autobiographical writing, 87
Autoethnography method, 87–88
Autonomous ego stage, 39–40
Autonomy, 24, 73
Autonomy stage, 36
Availability, work-related choice and, 157
Avoidance, 175–176

B

Baby boom generation
    aging metaphors used by, 63
    in Appalachia, 195
    identity formation for, 74
    sociohistorical context for retirement, 70
    volunteerism by, 242

work beyond retirement age, 4, 50, 135
work identities for women in, 83
working women in, 50
work–life balance for, 134, 144–145
Baby bust generation, 242
Back To Work 50+ Program, 260
Bandura, A., 247
Barbara (pseudonym), 56–57, 59
Barbie (pseudonym), 122–124
Baron, R. M., 207
Beckley, W.Va., 202
Belonging, sense of, 234
Bendien, E., 141
Benevolent ageism, 172–173
Benevolent sexism, 170, 172–173
Biggs, S., 137
Big-picture perspective, 46
Birkett, H., 50
Black women
    motivational needs of, 191
    poverty and wage gap for, 110, 111
    poverty rate for, 215
    resiliency for, 24–25
Blair Mountain, Battle of, 198
Blizzard, William, 199
Body image, 219–220, 224
Bohlmann, C., 206
Bolgiano, C., 201
Borden, K., 51, 65–66
Boundary setting, 178–179, 182
Brandwene, Leona, 7
Bridge employment, 71, 142, 143
British Rail, 91
Brontë, Emily, 49
Brown, John, 199
Bukov, A., 247
Business owners, 61, 202–203, 230
Business resources, 259–260
Bystander behavior, 182

C

Calasanti, T., 161, 233
Canada
    immigrants from, 228
    work–life balance in, 9, 140–144, 148
Capabilities framework, for work–life balance, 138–139
Cardiovascular disease, 243
Career
    changing, 66, 261
    defining success in, 89

in encore stage, 50, 137
generativity and building of, 36, 37
investment in, 139
as part of women's lives, 98–100
personal perspectives on, 64–66
women's choice of, 90
Career identity, 15–16
Career paths, 71, 90–98
Career training resources, 260–261
Caregiving
by Appalachian women, 203, 205
flexible work and, 147
and labor force participation, 111
by secret poor, 129
Care work
by immigrant women, 235
by older adults, 137
by women, 89, 126
and work–life balance, 136, 139–141,
146
Caribbean, immigrants from, 228
Carol (pseudonym), 55–56, 59–60
Carstensen, Laura, 11, 35
CDC (Centers for Disease Control and
Prevention), 204
Celestina (pseudonym), 113–114
Centers for Disease Control and
Prevention (CDC), 204
Central America, 228, 233
Change
in adulthood, 62–63
career, 66, 261
grit required for, 192
life structure, 42–44
older women as agents of, 248–249
relationship, 154
Chicago, Ill., Great Fire of, 200
Child care. *See also* Grandparenting
generativity and, 36, 37, 46
by secret poor, 111
and work–life balance, 137
Childhood, 36, 41
Children
adult, financial help or support for,
117–118, 123, 127, 140
and continued life–work missions, 217
delaying career for benefit of, 58
dependent, retirement age for women
with, 142
letting go of, 42
Chile, 105
China, 228

Chmitorz, A., 25–26
Choosing to work, 76–79. *See also*
Work-related choice
Cindy (pseudonym), 54, 55, 60
Civic engagement, 241–250
defined, 242
and older women as social change
agents, 248–249
personal and social benefits of,
244–248
quotes about, 250
self-regulation and, 243–244
"use it or lose it" principle for,
242–243
Civil rights movement, 70
Clannishness, in Appalachian culture,
197–198
Clinicians, resiliency assessments by, 25
CNN, 236
Coaches, 7
Coal mining, 199, 200, 208
Cognitive functioning, 243, 244
Colby, S. L., 191
Cole, E., 154
Colleagues, age/gender of, 169
Collective goals, 36
Commodification, of time, 137, 138
Communalism, 166
Communication, about diversity, 26
Community engagement, 242, 246, 247
Competence, resilience and, 232
Competency challenges
managing, 176–178
for older women, 183
workplace discrimination in form of,
169–173
Compulsory (mandatory) retirement, 70,
141
Confidence, 37
Conformist ego stage, 39
Connection, 59, 156
Conscientious stage, 39
Continued work–life missions, 213–226
financial challenges for older working
women, 215–216
physical constraints on, 222–224
for social power and social justice,
216–219
social scripts and stereotypes in,
219–222
Continuing care facilities, 244
Continuity, 134, 144

Contribution
 as employment pull factor, 144
 in gendered model of workforce
  participation, 99
 in generative phase, 7, 36, 37, 45–47
 by immigrants, 236, 237
 of older women who work, 98, 154, 157
 as reason to work, 54
 valuing of, 106
Control, sense of, 73, 80, 232–233
Convenience sample, 112, 119
Cooper, May, 73
Coping, 175–176, 243
"Corsets," in developmental theory of
  embodiment, 214
Courtney (pseudonym), 120–121
Credibility, 171
Cullinane, P., 249
Cultural-level factors, in work–life balance,
  139, 145–146
Culture
 Appalachian, 197–198, 205–206, 208
 on role of women in late adulthood,
  33–34
Cumulative disadvantage theories, 206
Custodial grandparents, 203–205
Customers, sexual harassment by,
  174–175

D

Daily routines, continuity of, 144
Daisy (pseudonym), 121–122
Daphne (pseudonym), 114–115
D'Araújo, Maria Alexandra, 10
Darr Mine explosion, 200
Deangelis, T., 53
Death of spouse, need to work after,
  113–114
Debbie (pseudonym), 54, 56, 57, 59
Denial, 175
Denmark, F. L., 137
Depression, 123–124
Desexualization, of women, 169,
  174–175
Development, Relief and Education for
  Alien Minors (DREAM) Act, 236
Developmental theory of embodiment
  (DTE), 214–215, 225–226
Development of care, theory of, 40–41
De Wind, A., 145
DiCello, D., 64

Discrimination. *See also* Ageism (age-
  based discrimination); Workplace
  discrimination study
 anti-immigrant, 229, 231, 233–235
 experiences of, 169–175
 hostile, 170, 233
 management of, 175–180
 against Mexican American women, 233
 against older immigrant workers, 227
 and poverty, 110
 and resiliency, 27
 against women of color, 20, 162
Disengaged engagement, 44
Diversionary nature of work, 80
Diversity
 and personal grit, 191–193
 and resiliency, 15, 26–27
 and societal roles of older women,
  105–107
Divorce
 financial need to work after, 115–116,
  123–126
 as reason for working, 219–220, 222
 retirement age for women after, 142
Docility, 220–221
Domestic work, 235
Domestic Workers Bill of Rights Act, 235
Dominance, 166
Donna (pseudonym), 56, 57
Double jeopardy, 192, 195
Doyal, L., 112
DREAM (Development, Relief and
  Education for Alien Minors) Act,
  236
Dreams, paid work as compensation for
  lost, 111–112
DTE (developmental theory of
  embodiment), 214–215, 225–226
Duncan, C., 162
Duncan, L. E., 74

E

Early adulthood, 36, 37, 41
Early retirement, 97, 141
Early socialization, countering, 221–222
Earner, value as, 139
Earnings, inequality in, 97. *See also*
  wage gap
East Asia, 228
Economic and Social Research Council
  (ESRC), 89

Economic conditions, in United States, 110–111
Economic (financial) need
    as factor in work-related choice, 153, 154
    of older workers, 143
    physical constraints on older workers with, 224–225
    as reason for working, 5–6. *See also* Secret poor study
    and work–life balance, 142–143
Economic security, 106, 128
Education level
    of Appalachian women, 196–197, 202
    of immigrant women, 233
    of secret poor, 111, 129
    and self-concept, 218
    and validation, 216–217
    and work-related choice, 51
EEOC. *See* U.S. Equal Employment Opportunity Commission
Ego development, theory of, 39–40
Ego integrity stage, 63
Eight stages of life, 35–36, 44
Ellingson, L., 88
Ellis, C., 88
El Salvador, 228
Emancipation Proclamation, 198
Embodied journeys, 88. *See also* Continued work–life missions
Emerging adulthood, discrimination in, 162
Emotionality, 166
Empathy, 40–41
Employment. *See also* Precarious employment
    bridge, 71, 142, 143
    for older adults, in the Netherlands and Canada, 140–141
    push and pull factors toward, 139, 145–146
    resources on, 259–262
    self-, 144, 155, 230
Empowerment
    from civic engagement, 245–247, 249
    from work, 63–64
Encore stage, 50, 72, 137
Engagement. *See also* Civic engagement
    community, 242, 246, 247
    disengaged, 44
    political, 242, 247
    productive, 243

    social, 143, 145, 243, 249–250
    work, 80–81, 143, 145, 156
English proficiency, of immigrant women, 233
Entry-level positions, 168–169
Environmental factors, in resiliency model, 21–25
Equal Pay Act, 70
Erikson, E., 7, 35–36, 44, 45, 50, 63, 74
Erikson, J., 35–36, 44, 45, 63
ESRC (Economic and Social Research Council), 89
Ethic of care, 40
Ethic of rights, 40
Ettlinger, N., 98
Europe, 228
Everingham, C., 73, 80
Existentialism, 62
Expectations
    about retirement, 157
    performance-based, in workplace, 163, 166–169
    social, and continued missions, 219–222
Extraversion, 23–24

F

Family
    conflict between paid work and, 136–137
    and continued life–work missions, 217
    role of Appalachian women in, 199–201, 205
    role of older women in, 105, 106
Family businesses, 155, 156
Family members. *See also* Children
    financial support for, by immigrants, 230, 231
    geographical constraints placed by, 223
    relationships with, 99
    social support from, 232–233
    work as shield from demands of, 128
Fatalism, 198
Fear, 127, 128, 231
Feelings About Life scale, 77
Female-dominated fields, 168, 183
Feminist perspective
    autobiographical writing from, 87
    on identity and meaning, 63–64
    on work identity, 98
Fideler, E. F., 145
Fideler, E. S., 50

Financial challenges, for older working women, 215–216
Financial contributions, of Appalachian women, 199
Financial factor, 51
Financial independence, 80
Financially-vulnerable individuals, identifying, 126–127
Financial need. *See* Economic need
Financial planning, 129
Financial safety net, 128
Financial support ratios, 242
Finland, 145
Fisher, G. G., 72
Flexibility, in work environment, 140, 143, 145–147
Fonseca, Jaime R. S., 10
Forced retirement, 73, 76, 77
   identity certainty and, 78, 79
   women who have to work after, 121–122
Formal channels, to protest discrimination, 179
Forti, R., 63
Fox News, 236
Framing effects, in media, 236–237
Frankl, Viktor, 64
Franklin, Aretha, 250
Franz, Carol, 35
Fraser, L., 112
Freedom, 154, 223–224
Freud, S., 35, 64
Friedan, Betty, 250
Frieze, I. H., 50, 154, 157
Full-time contract researchers, 99–100
Functional capability, social involvement and, 248
Funk, C., 162
Fuss, E., 51, 66

G

García, S. J., 233
Gardiner, J., 137, 138
Gateway model of retirement, 73
Gender
   and ageism, 184
   in sociohistorical context for retirement, 70
   in work–life balance studies, 134, 139
   and workplace expectations, 163, 166–169

Gender-based stressors, in resiliency model, 21, 23
Gendered model of workforce participation, 99
Gendered work, in Appalachia, 208
Gender-role congruity bias, 168
Gender stereotypes, 192, 199
Generational cohort, social involvement and, 248
Generativity, 7, 16
   ascendant, maintenance, and acceptant phases of, 36–38
   as factor in work-related choice, 51
   and integrity, 45–46
   and meaning of work, 47
   as reason for work, 50, 55–56, 63, 81
Geographical freedom, 223–224
Gergen, M., 154
Gerotranscendence stage, 44–45
Gilligan, Carol, 35, 40–41
Ginsburg, Ruth Bader, 250
Glass ceiling, 16
Global financial crisis (2008), 70
Global north, work–life balance in, 135
Goode, J., 91
Grace (pseudonym), 216, 218
Grandparenting
   by Appalachian women, 203–205
   custodial, 203–205
   for older working women, 116, 122
   in structure of life course theory, 43
   and work–life balance, 139, 145
Great Chicago Fire (1871), 200
Great Railroad Strike, 200
Greene, Sheila, 35
Greteman, B., 87
Grit, 191–193
Growing Old Disgracefully, 73
Guatemala, 228
Gwen (pseudonym), 216, 217, 219, 220, 223, 224

H

Hakim, C., 90
Hardiness, 231
Harper's Ferry, W.Va., 199
Hayes, A. F., 207
Haynes, C., 236
Head Start, 65
Health
   of Appalachian residents, 196–197
   of custodial grandparents, 205

and identity certainty, 80
and morale, 112
of older workers, 143, 144
of U.S. immigrants, 231–232
and work-related choice, 77, 112
Health care system, 129
Healthy aging, 21, 243
Healthy immigrant effect, 231–232
Heilman, M. E., 168
Helping behaviors, 172–173
Helson, R., 35, 77
Helton, L. R., 205
Helvetia, W.Va., 198
Henry, John, 199
Hinterlong, J., 242–243
Hiring process, discrimination in, 168
Hispanic women
  labor force participation by, 15
  poverty and wage gap for, 110, 111
Hobfoll, S. E., 232
Hobson, B., 138–139
Hogan, M., 243
Hollingshead, A., 76
Home, working from, 95–96
Homelessness, 120–121
Honduras, 228
Hostile discrimination, 170, 233
Household income, 77, 80
Housewife, ideal, 141, 145–146
Human-interest stories, about immigrants, 236
Husband
  as breadwinner, 111, 124–125
  death of, 113–114
  financial decisions by, 122–125
  illness of, 121–125
  living alone with, 42, 46
  medical expenses of, 121–122
Hutton, Elaine, 73

I

IBM, 145
Ideal housewife, 141, 145–146
Ideal woman, 138
Ideal worker, 138
Identity
  career, 15–16
  development of, 74
  influence of work on, 47
  in integrity stage, 44
  in maintenance phase, 37

national, 233–234
personal, 15–16
professional, 154, 222
as reason for work, 53, 57–58, 64
relationship of work and, 74–75
renegotiation of, at retirement,
  81–82
resiliency and affirmation of, 24
self-, 57–58, 106
third-age women's construction of,
  134
for women who need to work, 127
work, 74, 81, 83, 98
and work-related choice, 69–83
work-related choice and, 70–71
Identity and meaning study, 49–66
  authors' personal perspectives on
    careers, 64–66
  and career change/retirement, 66
  described, 51–53
  existential perspective on, 62
  feminist perspective on, 63–64
  identity-related motivators for work in,
    57–58
  legacy and generativity in, 55–56
  lifespan development perspective on,
    62–63
  love of work in, 56–57
  mission and meaning in life in, 53–55
  narrative prompts for, 51
  participant jobs and work settings, 52
  reasons older women continue to work,
    50–51, 53–61
  work relationships in, 59–61
Identity certainty, 71, 75–82
Identity Certainty scale, 77–78
Identity stage, 36
"Illegal" immigration, 236
Immigrant women, 227–237
  changing narrative about, 235–237
  continued work–life missions of, 218,
    220–222
  intersectionality for, 233–234
  Marta's experience as case example,
    229–232
  policy prescriptions for aging workers,
    234–235
  well-being, resilience, and control for,
    232–233
Immigration
  narrative about, 235–237
  in United States, 227–228

Income, household, 77, 80
Independence
 financial, 80
 gender-based stereotypes about, 166
 pride in, 113, 119
 as reason for working, 6, 50, 57–58
 of women who need to work, 111, 128
 and work–life balance, 145
 and work-related choice, 80
Independent contractor classification,
 235
India, 228
Individual factors, in resiliency model,
 21–25
Industry stage, 36
Informal economy, ageism in, 235
Initiative stage, 36
Institute for Women's Policy Research
 (IWPR), 202
Institutional factors
 in work–life balance, 140–141
 in work-related choice, 99
Institutional workplace discrimination,
 169, 182–183
Integrated stage, 40
Integrity stage, 7, 44–47
Intelligence, 166
Intergenerational learning, 245
Interiority, 63
Interrupted work histories, 215
Intersectional approach to work–life
 balance, 138, 148
Intersectionality
 for Appalachian women, 197–199
 for immigrant women, 229, 231,
 233–234
 for older women, 216
Intimacy stage, 36
Investment, in career, 139
Isolation, 232
IWPR (Institute for Women's Policy
 Research), 202

J

J-1 Exchange Visitor visa, 229
Janet (pseudonym), 54, 56
Jaslow, P., 112
Job lock (forced to continue working), 72,
 76, 77
 in family business, 155, 156
 identity certainty and, 78, 79

Johnston, D. K., 154
Jones, Mary Harris "Mother," 195,
 199–200, 205, 206, 208
Josselson, Ruthellen, 35
Julie (pseudonym), 124–125
Jung, C., 36

K

Kanter, Rosabeth Moss, 136
Karen (pseudonym), 55, 58, 61
Kathleen (pseudonym), 57, 58
Keller, S. M., 205
Kelliher, C., 137
Kenny, D. A., 207
King, Coretta Scott, 250
King, G. A., 21
Kooij, D. T. A. M., 21
Kroger, J., 74
Kumpfer, K. L., 21

L

Labor force participation
 by Appalachian women, 200–204
 by older adults in United States, 4
 by older women in the Netherlands and
 Canada, 142
 older women's reasons for, 4–5, 70–71, 76
 and participation in unpaid work, 99, 100
 preference theory of, 90
Labor organization, 198, 200
Labouvie-Vief, Gisela, 35
Late adulthood. *See also* Older adults
 age-based discrimination in, 162
 identity development in, 74
 midera correction in, 43–44
 revising life structure for, 43
 in structure of the life course theory,
 41–42
 well-being in, 229
Late mothers, retirement age of, 142
Late starters, flexible work for, 147
Latin America, 228, 231, 233–234
Latinos and Latinas
 aging of immigrant population, 228
 hostile discrimination against, 233
 sense of belonging for, 234
Leadership, 26, 137, 168
Leah (pseudonym), 125–126
Learning, 143, 245, 247
Lee, Robert E., 199

Legacy, 55–56
Legal immigration, 228, 233
Levinson, D. J., 41–44
Life-course approach
 sociohistorical context for retirement
  in, 69–70
 to women's work-related choice, 72–73,
  82
Life expectancy, 34, 111, 133, 191
Life history approach to embodied
 journeys, 214
Life purpose. *See* Purpose
Lifespan development theories, 7, 33–47
 development of care theory, 40–41
 ego development theory, 39–40
 Erikson's stages, 35–36
 generative stage of, 36–38
 gerotranscendence stage of, 44–45
 in identity and meaning study, 62–63
 integrity stage of, 44–46
 on resilience of Appalachian women, 206
 structure of life course theory, 41–44
 White privilege and sexism in, 34–35
Life structures, revising, 42–43
Likeability, 166
Lincoln, Abraham, 198
Linda (pseudonym), 55, 61, 115–116
Liptak, Mary Lou, 6
Lithuania, 145
Little League, 65
Live Longer, Work Longer (OECD), 141
"Living Comfortable" (pseudonym),
 117–118
Loe, M., 154
Loevinger, Jane, 35, 39–40
Loneliness, 144
Longevity revolution, 11
Longitudinal studies of women, 35
Lookism, 20
Loretto, W., 147, 162
Louise (pseudonym), 223–224
Love of work
 and identity/meaning, 56–57
 as reason to work, 53, 65
Luthar, S. S., 20
Lyness, K. S., 168

M

Macro factors, in multilevel models, 72
Madikizela-Mandela, Winnie, 250
Maintenance phase, 37–38

Male-dominated fields
 competency-based challenges in, 171
 managing workplace discrimination in,
  175, 176
 older women in, 183
 paternalistic behavior in, 173
 selection and hiring in, 168
 sexual harassment in, 168
Mandatory (compulsory) retirement, 70, 141
Mangione, L., 51, 63, 64
Manipulation, 180
Man's Search for Meaning (Frankl), 64
Marginalization, 24, 208
Marie (pseudonym), 222
Marital status
 and continued life–work missions, 217
 and economic conditions for women,
  111, 127
 and retirement age for women, 142
 and social involvement, 248
Marta (pseudonym), 229–233
Martha (pseudonym), 58
Master's of philosophy, 92n2
May (pseudonym), 221–222, 224
Mayor's Office on Women's Policy and
 Initiatives, 262
McCann, Lisa, 64
McGann, M., 162, 173
Mead, Margaret, 250
Meaningful relationships, 53
Meaningful work, 53, 225
Meaning in life
 and identity. *See* Identity and meaning
  study
 as reason to work, 53–55, 62
 for secret poor, 117–118, 127
 social activities that provide, 246–247
 and structure of life, 41
Meaning of work, for older women, 74–75
Media, framing effects in, 236–237
Medical expenses, as reason to work,
 121–122
Meir, Golda, 250
Men
 age and role in workplace for, 168
 competency challenges for, 170
 discrimination management by, 177–178
 paternalistic behavior directed toward,
  172–173
 prescriptive stereotypes for, 166, 167
 sexual harassment for, 174
 volunteering by, 241

Mensa, 218
Mentoring
    intergenerational, 245, 248
    resources on, 261
    for women, 181
Mexican American women, 233
Mexico, 228, 234
Michel, J., 106
Micro factors, in multilevel models, 72
Middle adulthood
    age-based discrimination in, 162
    in developmental theory of
        embodiment, 214
    in structure of the life course theory, 41
Middle age
    acceptant phase in, 38
    competency-based challenges in, 171
    ego structures in, 40
    interiority in, 63
    maintenance phase in, 37–38
    management of discrimination in, 176,
        180
    sexual harassment in, 175
    work–life balance in, 137
    workplace discrimination in, 162
Middle-class neighborhoods, secret poor
    in, 119
Midera corrections, 43–44
Mind–body connection, 243
Minority status, individuals with, 24–26,
    110, 181, 233
Minority stress, 24
Mission, 53–55
Mitchell, Valory, 35
Moane, G., 77
Moderation models, 206–207
Moen, P., 72
Monongah mining disaster, 200
Morale, 112
Mor-Barak, M. E., 51
Morgantown, W.Va., 202
Moustakas, C., 163
MSNBC, 236
Multigenerational workforce, 59–61
Multilevel models of work-related
    decisions, 72

N

Narrative study of identity and meaning.
    See Identity and meaning study
NAS (neonatal abstinence syndrome),
    204–205

National Collegiate Athletic Association
    (NCAA), 7
National identity, 233–234
National Institute on Retirement Security,
    215–216
National Labor Relations Act, 235
National Seniors Council, 141
Native American women, 110, 111
NCAA (National Collegiate Athletic
    Association), 7
Needing to work. See Economic need
Negative proscriptive stereotypes, 166,
    167
Neonatal abstinence syndrome (NAS),
    204–205
Netherlands, 9, 140–144, 148
Networking, 181–182
Neugarten, Bernice, 63
Nina (pseudonym), 219–220, 223, 224
Nonheterosexual women, poverty for, 110
Nonlinear career path, 90–98
Nonprofessional occupations, 77–80
Nurses, resiliency model for, 23

O

Oberhauser, A. M., 206
Objectification, of women's bodies,
    219–220
Occupational Safety and Health
    Administration, 235
Occupational stressors, 21
Oceania, 228
OECD (Organisation for Economic
    Co-operation and Development),
    140–142
Old age, in structure of the life course
    theory, 41
Older adults
    barriers to paid employment for, 112
    competency challenges for, 16–170
    economic conditions for, 110
    effects of stereotypes on, 197
    employment for, in the Netherlands and
        Canada, 140–141
    expectations of workplace performance
        for, 163, 166
    gender-based stereotypes for, 166
    immigrants as, 228
    labor force participation rate for, 4,
        201
    media portrayals of, 237

policy prescriptions for, 234–235
resilience for, 20–21
in U.S. population, 11
volunteering by, 241
work-related choice for, 51, 71–72
Older women
barriers to paid employment for, 112
cultural guidance on role of, 33–34
financial challenges for, 215–216
heterogeneity of, 137–138
individual-difference factors in
workforce participation for, 191–192
labor force participation by, 70, 142
life expectancy of, 191
in male-dominated fields, 183
management of workplace
discrimination by, 177–180
meaning of work and identity for, 74–75
personal and career identifies for, 15–16
poverty for, 129, 153, 215–216
reasons for labor force participation,
4–5, 50–51, 53–61, 106
as secret poor, 109–111
shifts in constrictive life systems for, 225
as social change agents, 248–249
social expectations and, 219–222
societal and workplace roles of,
105–107
work–life balance for, 137–138
Older Women's League, 242
Older Worker Program Finder, 260–261
Opioid addiction, 204–205
Organisation for Economic Co-operation
and Development (OECD), 140–142
Organizational support, resiliency and, 24
Organizations
fostering diversity within, 26–27
reducing workplace discrimination in,
180–183
Ortman, J. M., 191
Other-focused care, 220–221
Othering, 40
Outside pursuits, enhancing work with, 218

P

Paid work (remunerated work). *See also*
Work–life balance
conflict between family life and, 136–137
continued missions involving, 215
for custodial grandparents, 205
as respite from caregiving, 141

Paint Creek–Cabin Creek strike, 200
Parenting, 46, 58
Parker, K., 162
Partner, living alone with, 42, 46. *See also*
Husband
Part-time work
for Appalachian women, 201
in continued work–life mission, 215,
216
freedom with, 223–224
and work–life balance, 147
and work-related choice, 155
Passion
continued work–life mission in pursuit
of, 218–219
and work–life balance, 140
work missions as, 213–214
and work-related choice, 156–157
Paternalistic behavior, 172–173
Payne, S., 112
Pedigreed families, secret poor from,
114–115
Pensions
in Canada, 141
and financial strains for older women,
215, 216
and precarious work, 97, 98, 100
of women vs. men, 111
Personal-environmental resiliency process,
23–25
Personal goals, fulfillment of, 192
Personal identity, 15–16
Personal interests, 145
Personality, in maintenance phase, 37
Personal level
benefits of civic engagement on,
244–248
work–life balance on, 139, 143–144
work-related choice on, 51
Personal life stressors, 23
Personal reflection, 87–88
Person–job fit, 168
Pesce, C., 244
Pew Research Center, 162, 168, 174, 234
Phased retirement, 71
Phenomenological research, on ageism,
161–184
Philanthropic goals, working to attain,
80, 81
Physical activity, 243, 244
Physical care, for body, 224
Physical constraints, 222–224, 226

Physical disability, civic engagement and, 243
Physical domain, in DTE, 214, 226
Physically-demanding jobs, 173–174
Physical tasks, helping with, 172–173
Pink collar industries, 166–167, 170, 173
Pittsburgh, Pa., 200
Pleasure, for women who need to work, 128
"Polar Bear" events, 246
Political engagement, 242, 247
Poor older women. See Secret poor study
Positive aging, 15–16
Positive prescriptive stereotypes, 166–168
Positive role models, of aging, 247
Possible selves, integration of, 37
Poverty
    in Appalachia, 196
    for older women, 129, 153, 215–216
    for women of color, 110, 111
Power
    social, 214, 216–219, 225
    at work, 80
Precarious employment, 87–101, 135
    autoethnography as method, 87–88
    and career as part of women's lives, 98–100
    care work by women, 89
    and financial help for adult children, 140
    with nonlinear career path, 90–98
    work/career choice for women, 90
Preference theory of women's workforce participation, 90
Prescriptive stereotypes, 166–168
Presumed knowledge, age and, 170
Price, C. A., 74, 154
PROCESS macro, 207
Productive aging, 21
Productive engagement, 243
Professional identity, 154, 222
Professional occupations, 76–80
Promotion, gender-based barriers to, 168
Proscriptive stereotypes, 166, 167
Psychological well-being. See Well-being
Psychosocial adjustment, 16
Public policy
    for aging immigrant workers, 234–235
    effects of civic engagement on, 243
    encouraging civic engagement with, 244–245
    resources on, 262

Public sphere, freedom of movement in, 223–224
Pull factors
    in finding work–life balance, 135, 139–140, 143, 145
    in push/pull model of retirement, 72
Purpose
    from civic engagement, 249
    Jungian theory on, 36
    for older workers, 144
    as reason to work, 16, 53
    for women who need to work, 127
    and work–life balance, 146
Push factors, 72, 139–141, 143
Push/pull model of retirement, 72

Q

Qualitative studies
    of embodied journeys, 213–226
    of older women who need to work, 109–130
    of workplace discrimination, 161–184
    of work-related choice, 153–158
Quality of life
    civic engagement and, 245
    and roles of older women, 105–107, 192
Questioning, as response to discrimination, 179–180

R

Race
    in Appalachian culture, 198–199
    and gender-based wage gap, 202
    social involvement and, 248
Racism, 218
Radcliffe University, 75
Radtke, H. L., 135
Raging Grannies, 249
Rational choice theory, 90
Redlich, F., 76
Rednecks, 198
Reframing, of discrimination, 175, 176
Relationships
    meaningful, 53
    postretirement changes in, 154
    as reason to work, 52, 53, 59–61
    and work–life balance, 145, 146
    and work-related choice, 155, 157
Religious communities, 6

Religious organizations, involvement in, 242, 246
Remunerated work. *See* Paid work
Residence, geographical site of, 223
Resilience
    of Appalachian women, 206
    and health, 230–231
    of immigrant women, 232–233
    in later life, 20–21
Resilience at Work Scale, 25
Resilience model for older female workers, 19–27
    and ageism for older women in workforce, 19–20
    organizational resiliency, 26–27
    personal-environmental resiliency process, 23–25
    and resilience in later life, 20–21
    resiliency training for workers, 25–26
    stressors or challenges, 21, 23
Resiliency training, 25–26
Resource-extractive technology, in Appalachia, 195–196, 201, 208
Responsibility, 41
Rest, 139, 224
Retirement
    by choice, 76–79
    definitions of, 71
    early, 97, 141
    encore stage during, 50
    forced, 73, 76–79, 121–122
    gateway model of, 73
    in identity and meaning study, 66
    integrity without, 45
    life structure change with, 42–44
    mandatory, 70, 141
    preparation for, 153
    psychological and social consequences of, 153, 154
    push/pull model of, 72
    reasons for, 76
    societal expectations of, 157
    transformative model of, 73, 80
    transitional model of, 73
    work, health, morale, and, 112
Retirement age, 34, 70, 153
Richardson, L., 88
Roberta (pseudonym), 109, 118–119
Role models of aging, 247
Roosevelt, Eleanor, 33, 153, 250
Rothstein, M. G., 21
Rural communities, 196, 208
Ryff, Carol, 35

S

Safety net, financial, 128
Sarah (pseudonym), 213, 214, 216–217
Savings, lack of, 118–119
Scarcity hypothesis, 136
SCORE (Service Corps of Retired Executives), 259
Scripts, social. *See* Social scripts
Secret poor study, 109–130
    and economic conditions in United States, 110–111
    interview questions, 130
    lessons learned, 128–129
    literature review, 111–112
    sampling and interview methods, 112–113, 119–120
    synopses of interviews, 113–126
    themes, 127–128
Security, 106, 128
Seegert, L., 111
Segregation, in Appalachia, 197–198
Selection processes, discrimination in, 168
Selective optimization, 37
Self
    creation of, 62
    internalized beliefs about, 218–219
    sense of self, from work, 63–64
Self-awareness, 39, 244
Self-care, 41, 220, 221, 224
Self-concept, 218, 220
Self-efficacy, resiliency and, 23–24
Self-employment, 144, 155, 230
Self-esteem, 16, 50, 127
Self-fulfilling activities, 192
Self-identity, as reason to work, 57–58, 106
Self-regulation theory, 243–244
Self-schemas, 192
Senior Community Service Employment Program, 261
Senior Job Bank, 259–260
Sense of belonging, 234
Sense of control, 73, 80, 232–233
Sense of self, 63–64
Service Corps of Retired Executives (SCORE), 259
Service-learning activities, 245
Sexism
    benevolent, 170, 172–173
    in lifespan development theories, 34–35
    for older women, 20, 216
    in workplace, 161–162

Sexual harassment
  boundary setting in response to, 178, 179
  coping with, 176
  by customers, 174–175
  in male-dominated fields, 168
Sexualization of women
  in Appalachia, 199
  as workplace discrimination, 169,
    174–175
Sexual orientation, social involvement
  and, 248
Shapiro, J. L., 63
Sharma, D., 101
Sharon (pseudonym), 56, 58, 61
Sherry, A., 154
Shi, J., 71
Shyness, 166
Sisters of Mercy, 6
Skills, continuing mission to upgrade,
    216–217
Skills training, for older women, 4
Smith, Zadie, 227
Snowball sampling, 154
Social activities, for older women, 246–247
Social change
  grit required for, 192
  older women as agents of, 248–249
Social connection, as reason to work, 59
Social constructionism, 134
Social contact, 51, 143
Social discourses
  DTE domain, 214, 225
  internalization of, 219
Social engagement
  civic engagement for, 243, 249–250
  and work–life balance, 143, 145
Social exchange theory, 246
Social expectations
  about docility of women, 220–221
  about women's bodies, 219–220
Social isolation, 232
Social justice, 216–219, 225
Social learning theory, 247
Social level
  benefits of civic engagement on, 244–248
  work–life balance on, 139, 143
Social networks, resiliency and, 25
Social power
  continued work–life missions for,
    216–219, 225
  and DTE domains, 214, 225
Social resources, resiliency and, 24
Social schemas, 192

Social scripts
  about socioeconomic status, 222
  about submissiveness, 221–222
  age-related, 222
  in continued work–life missions,
    219–222, 225
Social Security, 70
  labor force participation and access to,
    201
  for older immigrants, 230
  and retirement age, 34
  for secret poor, 129
  for women vs. men, 111
Social status
  and civic engagement, 249
  and work–life balance, 139, 143
Social structure, from work, 80
Social support
  for Appalachian women, 205–207
  community engagement for, 242
  for immigrants, 231
  and resilience, 24, 232–233
  resources on, 245–246
Social support resource theory, 232–233
Society, older women's roles in, 105–107,
    192
Socioeconomic status, 222, 231, 233
Sociohistorical context, for transitions,
    69–70
Sonia (pseudonym), 220–221, 224
South America, 228, 233
SOWN (Supportive Older Women's
    Network), 261
Speed, youth and, 174
Stanford Center on Longevity, 11
Steedman, C., 87
Stereotype Content Model, 173
Stereotypes
  about aging workers, 234
  about Appalachian women, 197–199,
    208
  civic engagement to challenge, 249
  in continued work–life missions,
    219–222
  gender, 192, 199
  negative proscriptive, 166, 167
  positive prescriptive, 166–168
Stewart, A. J., 35, 71, 81
Stock-taking, in integrity stage, 46
Story circles, 163
Stowe, Harriet Beecher, 250
Stressors, 21, 23, 112
Structure of life course, theory of, 41–44

Submissiveness, 221–222
Successful aging, 21
Supervisors, discrimination management by, 179, 180
Superwoman schema, 105
Supportive Older Women's Network (SOWN), 261
Support seeking, 175, 176
Support system, networking to develop, 182
Susan (pseudonym), 5, 55, 61
Sweden, 145

T

Tanya (pseudonym), 5
Teachers' walkouts (2018, 2019), 200
Teixiera, Monica, 10
Theory of development of care, 40–41
Theory of ego development, 39–40
Theory of structure of life course, 41–44
Third age women, identity construction for, 134
Time
  commodification of, 137, 138
  movement of, 62
  perspective on, 38
  shifting of, for the long game, 72
  structure to, 146
Title VII, 235
Title IX, 7
Training, 16, 105
  career training resources, 260–261
  resiliency training, 25–26
  skills training for older women, 4
Transformative model of retirement, 73, 80
Transitional model of retirement, 73
Transitions, sociohistorical context for, 69–70
Transnational families, 230–231
Trust stage, 36
Tygstrup, F., 101

U

Unanticipated time shifting, 72
Undocumented immigrants, 228, 233, 236
United Kingdom, 147
United Mine Workers, 200
United States
  ageism in, 234–235
  aging of working women in, 15
  bridge employment in, 142
  economic conditions in, 110–111
  health of immigrants in, 231–232
  high school graduation rates in, 129
  immigration in, 227–228, 233–234
  life expectancy and retirement age in, 34
  longevity revolution in, 11
  older adult workers in, 4
  racial and ethnic diversity in, 191
  women-owned businesses in, 202–203
  work–life balance in, 145–146
University of Pennsylvania, 7
Unpaid work
  by Appalachian women, 203–204
  precarious employment and, 99, 100
Untaxed income, 125–126
Urban Institute, 260, 262
U.S. Bureau of Labor Statistics, 4, 241
U.S. Census Bureau, 11, 110, 205
U.S. Equal Employment Opportunity Commission (EEOC), 161–162, 181–182, 184
"Use it or lose it" principle, 242–244

V

Validation, in continued work–life missions, 213–214, 216–217
Value, as earner, 139
Van Mens-Verhulst, J., 135
Vickerstaff, S., 147
Vives, A., 105
Viviane (pseudonym), 216, 218–219
Voice, for older women, 247
Volunteering, 50
  and healthy aging, 243
  by older adults, 137, 241
  and work–life balance, 143

W

Wage gap
  for Appalachian women, 202
  and financial strain in retirement, 215, 216
  for secret poor, 111, 129
Walkerdine, V., 87
Wang, M., 71
Warmth, 172, 173
Weakness, 166
Wealth inequality, 110

Well-being
   and continued work–life mission, 225
   for immigrant women, 229, 232–233
   physical constraints on, 222–223
   as reason for working, 50
   and resilience, 21
   and work–life balance, 139
West Virginia, women in. *See* Appalachian
   women
Whiston, S. C., 73
White, Kathleen, 35
White privilege, 34–35
Williams, R., 96, 101
Wisdom, age and, 63
WISER (Women's Institute for a Secure
   Retirement), 261
WLPS (Women's Life Paths Study), 75
Woman, ideal, 138
Womanhood, caregiving as part of, 141
Women
   access to networking opportunities for,
     181–182
   age-based discrimination against, 162
   career as part of lives for, 98–100
   career choice for, 90
   care work by, 89
   expectations of workplace performance
     for, 163, 166
   identity development for, 74
   management of workplace
     discrimination by, 175–179
   paternalistic behavior directed toward,
     173
   prescriptive stereotypes for, 166
   sexual harassment for, 174
   sexualization and desexualization of,
     in workplace, 169, 174–175
   volunteering by, 241
   work beyond retirement age as issue
     for, 4
   work-related choice for, 72–73, 90
Women of color. *See also* Black women
   poverty and wage gap for, 110, 111
   workplace discrimination against, 20,
     162
Women-owned businesses, 202–203
Women's Business Development Center,
   260
Women's Institute for a Secure Retirement
   (WISER), 261
Women's Life Paths Study (WLPS), 75
Women's movement, 70, 74, 75

Womentoring, 248
Work and Family in the United States
   (Kanter), 136
Work engagement
   for older workers, 143, 145
   and work-related choice, 80–81, 156
Work environment, flexibility in, 140,
   143–147
Worker, ideal, 138
Work experience, outside pursuits to
   enhance, 218
Workforce involvement resources,
   259–260
Workforce participation. *See* Labor force
   participation
Work identity, 74, 81, 83, 98
Working-class women, 34
Working from home, 95–96
Work–life balance, 133–148
   in continued work–life mission, 224
   envisioning future of, 144–145
   and flexibility in work environment,
     146–147
   individualized meanings of, 138–139
   meanings of, 135–139
   for older women in the Netherlands vs.
     Canada, 140–144
   organizational support for, 26
   push and pull factors, 139–140
Work–life missions. *See* Continued
   work–life missions
Workplace
   age/gender and performance
     expectations in, 163, 166–169
   role of older women in, 105–107
Workplace bias, 16
Workplace discrimination
   institutional, 169, 182–183
   against middle-aged and older women,
     112, 162
   against women of color, 20, 162
Workplace discrimination study,
   161–184
   discrimination experiences, 169–175
   management of discrimination,
     175–180
   participants' demographic information,
     164–165
   practice applications, 180–183
   study method, 163
   workplace expectations by age and
     gender, 163, 166–169

Workplace Resiliency Inventory, 25
Work-related choice, 69–83
    factors in, 153–158
    and identity, 69–83
    identity certainty and, 75–82
    in later life, 71–72
    and lifespan developmental theories, 34
    and life structure, 41–42
    relationship of identity and work,
        74–75
    and social involvement, 248
    and societal role, 105
    for women, 72–73, 90
Work relationships, 52, 53, 59–61
Work satisfaction
    and relationships, 61
    and work–life balance, 139, 143–145
    in work-related choice, 154
World War II, women in workforce in, 50

Y

Yeakel, Lynn, 241
"You are what you do" discourse, 222
Young adulthood
    competency challenges in, 170, 171
    identity development in, 74
    managing discrimination in, 179–180
    volunteerism in, 241–242
Younger adults
    helping behavior by, 172–173
    mentoring of, 247, 248
    positive role models for, 247
Youth, preference for, 169, 173–174

Z

Zacher, H., 21
Zunzunegui, M. V., 246

About the Editors

Ellen Cole, PhD, is a professor of psychology at Russell Sage College. She teaches in the counseling and community psychology graduate program, helping to train students who are becoming licensed mental health counselors. She is a past president of the Alaska Psychological Association and the Society for the Psychology of Women of the American Psychological Association (APA Division 35) and former chair of APA's Committee on Women in Psychology and Division 35's Committee on Women and Aging. In 2016, she received Division 35's Florence L. Denmark Award for Contributions to Women and Aging. At age 70, 35 years after earning her PhD, she received a master of arts in positive psychology from the University of Pennsylvania. Since then, she has been working on several fronts to change the perception of aging and old age from one that is medically and negatively driven to one that focuses on quality of life and celebration. To that end, Dr. Mary Gergen and Dr. Cole have coedited *Retiring but Not Shy: Feminist Psychologists Create Their Post-Careers* and two double special issues of the journal *Women & Therapy* entitled *Positive Aging: What Feminist Therapists Need to Know.* She cohosts a blog with Jane Giddan at 70Candles. com and coauthored *70 Candles! Women Thriving in their 8th Decade.*

Lisa Hollis-Sawyer, PhD, is an associate professor in the Psychology Department and coordinator of the gerontology program at Northeastern Illinois University. She received her doctorate in industrial gerontology from The University of Akron and conducted her postdoctoral aging-related training at Boston University. Her research interests range from eldercare to aging workforce issues, with a focus on aging women's issues within these roles. She has authored or coauthored four textbooks and authored or coauthored

46 scholarly publications. In 2014, she received an APA Division 20 award on mentoring students in the field of gerontology. In 2017, she received the APA Division 35's Florence L. Denmark award for her research over 3 decades on older women's role transitions and quality-of-life outcomes. She is currently serving as cochair of the APA Division 35 Committee on Women and Aging.